Effective
Home-School
Relations

Effective

Home-School

Relations

JAMES L. HYMES, JR.

Professor of Elementary Education
George Peabody College for Teachers
Author of Understanding Your Child

Illustrated by
HAL DOREMUS

NEW YORK   PRENTICE-HALL   1953

PRENTICE-HALL EDUCATION SERIES

Harold Spears, Editor

Preface

Today, educators and conscientious parents are alarmed by community conflicts over public education. It is clear that there is not the oneness of thinking about children and about education that youngsters need. For years the growing complexity of our society has steadily pulled our homes and schools away from each other. Unfortunately, the distance has grown at the very time when our swiftly changing world has made new demands on education. This gap has widened, although the chance exists to capitalize on exciting new facts about children's growth, development, and learning.

Conflict is always distressing, but it can be useful. Recently, it has helped earnest citizen and devoted teacher to agree that home and school must rebuild their unity. The school should not develop a program in isolation. The teacher should not work with children alone. Home and school must supplement each other; they must make a consistent impact. The teacher should be a skilled team worker, in constant touch with his coeducators in the home.

Effective home-school relations can bridge the chasm created by the lack of understanding between parents and teachers. Effective home-school relations give parents peace of mind about their children's education and guarantee that today's knowledge will be used for the youngsters' well-being.

Home-school relations is a new field. Very little research and experimentation are available as direct guides, yet our knowledge is extensive in other fields which feed into and support this new area. This book taps these other fields. It explains certain principles that have emerged through the years of work with children and shows that teachers and parents have more adaptability in this new field than they give themselves credit for.

In home-school relations the teacher is the key, but he cannot work alone. To do his job he needs the backing of all his colleagues: special teachers, visiting teachers, psychologists, deans, counsellors, nurses, supervisors, and administrators. So, too, within the home all who are in touch with the children or who are a part of the family circle are involved in the educational process. Today, millions of these home "teachers" are working with schools. This book aims to make these working relationships even more satisfying and effective.

One debt of gratitude has often been expressed in private, but a public bow is overdue. In this writing, as in all else I have ever written, the dividing line between my contribution and that of my wife — critic, editor, and morale-booster *par excellence* — is a thin line indeed. Almost every idea was inspired in no small measure by Lucia Manley Hymes, M.A. in Child Development and Parent Education, "Room Mother, Den Mother, and mother of three."

JAMES L. HYMES, JR.

Table of Contents

1 HOME-SCHOOL RELATIONS: A MAN-MADE BRIDGE . 1

2 PARENTS AND THEIR CHILDREN 11

3 PARENTS AND SCHOOLS 35

4 TEACHERS' ATTITUDES AND APTITUDES 64

5 GROUP MEETINGS 90

6 FACE-TO-FACE RELATIONSHIPS 131

7 OBSERVATION AND PARTICIPATION 156

8 THE WRITTEN WORD 184

9 TWO OCCASIONS FOR VITAL RELATIONSHIPS . . . 202

10 EVALUATION 225

BIBLIOGRAPHY 233

INDEX 259

1. *Home-School Relations: A Man-Made Bridge*

In primitive tribes there was no need for parents and teachers to plan ways of working closely together. Home and school were one. The teachers were the mothers and fathers, the older children, uncles, aunts, and grandparents, all under the same roof. When other members of the community took a hand, as they often did, theirs was an extension of the hand of the family.

The curriculum was the life of the family and the life of the community. Manners and morals, skills and facts seeped in while work was done, food prepared, and thoughts exchanged. The youngster was immersed in this education as were his many teachers. No separation existed anywhere.

This same natural unity prevailed in the America of the frontier cabin and of the isolated valley farmhouse. But it is over and done with today. Our homes have been so changed by social forces that they are no longer equipped to be the sole centers of learning. These social forces create such demands for knowledge that the home alone could never impart all that man needs to know.

Additional centers of teaching have had to come into being. The school is now the primary supplement to the home.

Parents and teachers have had to create an instrument — we call it home-school relations — to link home and school together. This is our man-made bridge, a modern invention that tries, through various techniques which we think up, to achieve a unity that once came naturally. Modern living continually forces us to devise substitutes: finger paint to replace the mud youngsters no longer know, jungle-gyms to approximate the trees they can no longer climb.

What you do in any endeavor — how much of your self you put into it, how hard you work at it, and how much you think about it — depends on the value you put on it. If you appreciate what home-school relations substitute for — the natural unity through which the child historically learned the taboos of his tribe, the ways of his living, the modes of his work, the means of his survival — you will give this field the earnestness which is its due.

Some reading in anthropology will crystallize the contrast between modern living and a simpler way of life. There are many books to choose from. One you will enjoy is Children of the People *by Dorothea Leighton and Clyde Kluckhohn (Cambridge: Harvard University Press, 1948). This is the story of the Navajo in his childhood and youth. An interesting film, which also points up this same contrast, is* Karba's First Years, *dealing with child-rearing in Bali (twenty minutes) (New York University Film Library, 26 Washington Place, New York 3, N. Y.).*

HOME-SCHOOL RELATIONS IS NO WONDER DRUG

Some people think too highly of home-school relations. In their eyes it becomes a magical cure-all. They like to believe that as soon as they master the techniques all their problems will roll away.

Teachers will be free to teach as they please.

Salaries will be sky-high, and school buildings will be lovely to behold.

No one will ever be fired.

The children will turn into angels and will always do their homework. Drop-outs in high school will stop; discipline problems will never arise, truancy will be a thing of the past.

Even fathers will improve — they will come to every PTA meeting!

It is not effective thinking to regard home-school relations as a wonder drug. If you expect more of the field than it can do, you will be disappointed. Worse yet, you will be tempted to turn your back on the field when it could make an appropriate contribution to children's welfare.

NOT A SUBSTITUTE FOR GOOD PROGRAMS
FOR CHILDREN

Sometimes we educators put so much stock in home-school relations that we do not bother to examine our work with children. When the youngsters in our classroom are noisy and inattentive we leap to a solution: Get somebody to talk to the parents about teaching children obedience and respect. The real answer to this problem may lie in giving these active, bouncy youngsters more legitimate freedom in the classroom and more vital experiences.

Teachers may be irritated because the youngsters do not do their homework; they forget their books; they turn in sloppy papers. Our first thought is to have a meeting with parents at which someone will lay down the law on television, on children's need for proper working conditions at home, and the number of hours a child should sleep. Often we educators are the ones who are remiss. We ought to have more activities in our classroom and rely less on workbooks, textbooks, meaningless drill, and paper and pencil tasks.

We wish someone could induce parents to impress on their children the value of education. If the parents would only insist on schooling, we say, these adolescents would not be so boy-and-girl-crazy in class and would not drop out of school at the first opportunity. But the real answer may lie right under our noses. Our fare may not seem appetizing to independent adolescents. Maybe the curriculum is too bookish, too far removed from life and from young people's developmental concerns.

It is easy to think that the trouble is the other fellow's fault, easy to think that some quick trick will provide a remedy. But home-school relations cannot do everything. Although important, it is only one part of the total effort that a school makes for youngsters. When we treat it as a cure-all we are blind to other parts of the program that may need improving. When we fail to be self-critical, home-school activities boil down to "getting the parents on our side." They become a weapon against children and not one in their behalf. Parents and teachers form a protective alliance to maintain the *status quo*. Eyes are turned toward adult comfort; they do not go out to check on the children's well-being.

THE COMPLEXITIES OF FAMILY LIFE

Sometimes we have such high hopes for home-school relations that we forget the complexity of the lives we are dealing with. When we see a tired youngster coming to school, we want to grab the parent by the shoulder and make him read a good article on children's sleep. However, we have not seen the home with three children asleep in one bed, and father and mother in the same room. We do not have to live on a $29.75 salary check, or make it feed, clothe, and shelter five people.

We are indignant when we learn that Stephen has coffee and two jelly doughnuts for breakfast instead of orange juice, cooked cereal, bacon, eggs, and milk. We immediately plan a bang-up meeting on *health*. In our zeal we give no heed to the difficulty of changing food patterns. We forget that they stem from family habits, national customs, economic status, even the soil and the climate where parents grew up. We build ourselves up for a let-down because we think someone can say the magic word that will cut all these roots.

We are pleased when a speaker tells parents that children need active play out of school. We do not know about the father who works on swing shift and has to sleep during the day; about the trucks that rumble down the street; about the landlord who does not like children; and about the neighbors downstairs who always complain.

We count noses at our meetings and want everyone there. It is so good for them! But scrubbing the floor, darning a pile of socks, or going to the beauty parlor may be just as important for the mother's morale. Anything that lets her live more peacefully with her children is more important than hearing a speech.

If you do not become discouraged too soon, you can avoid the error of looking only at one side of the coin. You understand the complexities of raising children the more you visit homes. As you get closer to parents you become more realistic about the possibility of change.

You do not expect it overnight, as in your enthusiasm perhaps you once did. You do not despair of it, as perhaps your disappointment once made you do. You come to know that problems vary from the simple to the intricate and that you must measure progress accordingly.

PARENTS' ATTITUDES CHANGE SLOWLY

The past fifty years have taught us much about children and how they develop. Thoughtful people for centuries have puzzled over this mystery, but only in recent times has the child been made the object of scientific study. We have employed to good advantage controlled studies, longitudinal studies, and objective measurement techniques, as well as highly skilled clinical observations.

The new insights coming from these studies are one more reason for home-school relations. We know today that children are not Topsys who "just growed." They are helped or hindered by the way little events of their everyday lives are handled. Working with children is increasingly considered a job calling for some degree of expertness. Just *anyone* should not do the job (be he parent or teacher), operating on hunches and prejudices, and on old wives' tales about what is good and what isn't, what works and what doesn't.

We count on close home-school relations to spread as widely as possible our new knowledge about youngsters. We see close relations as a means whereby all children can grow up in homes and schools that are tuned to their nature and to their needs. We have high hopes, but again too high hopes build us up for a let-down. Disappointment sets in when we discover that fundamental changes in parent-child relationships can only come about slowly.

The new knowledge about children is deceptive. The facts sound simple as you put them: "Eight-year-olds are like this. . . . " "Children are wholes, in their physical-social-emotional-intellectual beings. . . ." "Each youngster is an individual. . . ." Almost anyone can memorize the principal child development generalizations. Much more than memory is needed to act on them.

Wise action comes only when the facts have been absorbed and integrated into a point of view about children — a way of feeling about the things that they do. Scientific facts are one basis for such a philosophy, but facts alone fall far short of bringing an easy flow of consistent treatment. A philosophy is built on facts in the head *and* on attitudes in the heart and on vision in the eyes.

Home-school relations can significantly share in building this philosophy among parents and teachers. At the very least, it can be one of the main approaches through which child development facts reach those who work with youngsters at home or at school. But even the best programs in home-school relations cannot quickly build a philosophy of living with children. A philosophy is not built at one parent-teacher meeting; it grows slowly, almost imperceptibly, through many experiences over the years.

If you keep in mind that much time is needed for an idea to take hold, you will be pleased with how your efforts in home-school relations contribute to the development of a philosophy. If you forget, you will look at those same efforts and be dissatisfied because they do not produce the speedy changes that you want.

TREATING HOME-SCHOOL RELATIONS
TOO CASUALLY

Some schools err by counting on home-school relations to do more than any one thing could do for the child. Other schools treat the field too lightly, never giving it the chance to make its contribution. They add it on, like a patch on the pants, to make a school look modern.

Working with parents has a very appealing sound. Making adjustments in order to gear a school to parents, as well as to

children, is not so pleasant. For example, look at the question
of seats. If parents are to participate in their child's education,
schools need comfortable adult-sized chairs in every classroom.
They also need a private conference room where a parent and
a teacher can talk and think together.

Or look at the small matter of smoking. Most schools still
allow smoking only in the furnace room! Grown men and
women planning together often like to smoke, and certainly in
a more attractive setting. Although parents do not want to
smoke while they are observing in a classroom, many a person
can hardly wait for a meeting to finish so that he can go outside
for a few puffs. Some ash trays will do more to make men
feel welcome in schools than all the pointed comments like:
"We are so glad to see some *fathers* here tonight." These are
little items, but they illustrate the broad generalization: If you
want the benefits that working closely with parents can bring,
your school must make some adjustments.

A school will be particularly reluctant to make changes if it
sees home-school relations only as a way to "sell the school" to
parents. These words, heard so often, imply a one-way street.
Home-school relations are regarded as the equivalent of parent
education. The parent is always the learner, always on the
receiving end. The school calls the tune.

Home-school relations must mean a two-way process. The
flow of ideas, energy, creativity, and leadership must be in
both directions at all times. Effective relationships demand a
free and easy give-and-take between the family and the school.
No one-way streets are allowed.

Schools and teachers are often uncomfortable when they are
involved in this kind of traffic. Life does not go on as usual.
Schools are led to changes in organization, curriculum, facilities, and treatment of children that they might not otherwise
have made. Changes come about more quickly than the
school's timetable calls for.

When you work with parents you pay a price. You adjust
to the other fellow's ideas, sometimes going faster and some-

times going at a slower pace than you desire. But there are rewards in working together that isolation can never bring.

THE GOALS OF HOME-SCHOOL RELATIONS

Teachers gain. Parents gain. But children are the real winners. The techniques of home-school relations exclusively involve adults, but children are the ones who benefit the most.

Home-school relations has two broad goals:

1. To bring about a better understanding, between teachers and parents, of what children are like;

2. To bring about a better understanding, between teachers and parents, of good education.

When these goals are achieved, parents and teachers work together as a united team, and youngsters gain in two ways:

1. They have a richer, fuller, more nourishing life, in school and out, than would otherwise be open to them;

2. They have more consistent guidance in school and out; they stand a better chance of living up to the peak of their powers.

These are our hopes for children. They are hopes with ceiling unlimited. No one can ever know for sure when the top has been reached. The task is to keep welding a tighter parent-teacher team and to keep that team in shape and on the job continuously. The more unity there is, the more the children will benefit.

Nothing we can attempt to do in home-school relations will ever bring back that degree of oneness children had automatically in primitive education. We may come close to that unity if we truly see the significance of our efforts. More certainly, we can balance whatever loss there may be if we do the most creative and critical thinking we are capable of. The children of the past never had the blessing of such thought.

THE ORGANIZATION OF THIS BOOK

This book suggests that you do in home-school relations exactly what you do every day in school with youngsters: Look at the humans you are working with, at their characteristics and needs, and see them in relation to the goals that you seek.

For example, one common goal in school is to teach reading. With that end in mind teachers look at children. They want to know: What are their characteristics? What experiences have they had? How long can they sit? What are their eye movements like? How much can they remember? What do they want to read about?

This book follows the same line of inquiry not about children but instead about *parents and teachers*. It sets forth two big goals of a better and a mutual understanding of what children are like and a better and a mutual understanding of good education. Then it reports, in relation to each of these goals, the characteristics of parents and teachers that have a significant bearing on work in the field of home-school relations.

With goals in mind, and with facts about grown-up human beings, the book then looks at the best practices that experimental public and private schools have developed so far. Some of the recommendations may be new steps for your school. Yet each and every recommendation is safely within the framework of usual education. They are the application *at the adult level* of the many principles about learning and teaching you already know from all the work you have done with children.

These principles have been tested with children and in teacher-training, in camping education, and in industry. Most of the practices with adults have been tested, too. You can use them and they will work. They will benefit children. Their widespread adoption can mean more peaceful homes and schools, with better teaching in both places. Abler, happier children will be the result.

2. Parents and Their Children

Good teachers continuously try to gear their work to the individual children in their classrooms. They try to work with the grain of the wood, not rip across it. This way of working with people is not only the humane and decent way; it is also the most efficient. If you work at a level where a child can succeed, feed into him satisfactions that he seeks, and steer clear of demands that are beyond him, real learning will take place.

Teachers must make exactly the same approach in home-school relations, but your guidepost is *not* what children are like. You need to know: What are *parents* like? What are *parents* eager for? What do they tend to reject? What pleases them and spurs them on? What irritates them? What can they do and are glad to do? What leaves them apathetic?

In home-school relations you are working with other adults. This is a new experience for most teachers. We can say a great many things with confidence about children: " 'Fours' find it very hard to wait and not to interrupt." " 'Sixes' need a lot of activity." "Eleven-year-olds think the sun rises and sets on

11

their gang." "Adolescents resent being treated like babies."
But what do you know about *parents?*

In light of their knowledge of children, teachers are forever
adjusting their ideas of what to do with them: "More committee
work is good at this age." "More first-hand experiences are
needed here." "Vocational information is vital at this age."
"Fairy stories fit in here." In the case of children we can be
guided by research and the accumulated experience of thou-
sands of teachers. But what must you be sure to do in working
with *parents?* What must you be wary of?

There are no age-level studies of parents. No longitudinal
studies that follow parents from the start of their family life to
its end. No controlled studies that contrast one group with
another. Yet we know from our work with children that education is hit-or-miss unless we do some thinking about the human
material in our classrooms. Goals can be wrong, methods can
be wrong, and timing can be wrong, unless these tie into what
children are like. Can you build some hypotheses about *parents?*

In working with children, research is the most reliable guide.
Each one of us, however, turns to at least two other sources for
general information about the nature of our youngsters. We
use our *memory.* We were each a child; we can recall to some
extent what children like and reject, what they can and cannot
do. We use our *eyes.* We see youngsters in our classrooms, on
buses, in department stores, on the street playing, and in the
movies. This daily observation gives us many valuable side-
lights about child nature.

Memory and general observation are subjective methods.
They lead us astray at times, but they are methods available
to each one of us in our study of parents. We can use them as
a start until more research about adults has been completed.
We see parents every day — many who teach are parents — and
each of us has had parents of his own. We have a vast personal
experience to draw on. We can learn enough about parents, at
least in a preliminary way, to insure that efforts in home-school
relations become more efficient.

PARENTS ARE IN LOVE WITH THEIR CHILDREN

One generalization about parents is supported by so much daily observation that it sounds almost trite when spelled out. Yet it is a basic generalization for home-school relations. Were it not true, work in this field would be almost impossible. Herculean efforts would be called for, and even these would hold little promise of success.

But the generalization is true. Because it is true, teachers can work in home-school relations with confidence. You can know that there are rich rewards here. You can justifiably feel that the cards are stacked in your favor in advance. A little effort will bring big results. A little concern will bring big responses. You have fertile ground here that you can work easily — not hard, baked, resistant, hostile soil.

The generalization? *Parents in America prize their children.* They work for them. They care for them. They want the best for them. A child in our country is treasured, not exploited. He is central, not incidental. Many a child has been described as "the apple of his parents' eye." This is true for all but an infinitesimal number of children in our country. The parents you deal with feel this way for they are in love with their children.

You have seen much evidence of this. Think of the crowds, in department stores at Christmas time, with tired feet, weary eyes, thinning pocketbook, but spurred on by: "What would he like for Christmas?" Family after family buys more than it should, works harder than it should, and plans more than it should, but it does it all for the children. A special, wonderful, and unique feeling of love is exemplified here that is full of meaning for home-school relations.

You have seen the same thing at birthday times. Nothing is too good. Nothing too expensive. Nothing too hard to find. This is the child's day and, in parents' eyes, that calls for supreme effort.

On any day watch at an airport or a railroad station when

a father comes home from a trip. The children rush to meet
him. The children are kissed first, then the mother. And on
father's face, and mother's too, a look of love and pride and
joy shines.

Do you know what a father does before he boards his train
or plane for home? His feet may hurt him from his work; he
may be pressed for time; he may still have business demands
upon him; but one purchase must be made before he sets out:
a present for the children! He may end up with something silly
like a souvenir ash tray, something small like a package of gum,
or a salt shaker from the airplane, but father always comes
home prepared for the question: "Did you bring anything for
me?" A father brings something, and he feels good about it.

A well-known advertisement warns: "Never underestimate
the power of a woman." Workers in home-school relations must
know that they should *never underestimate parents' love for
children*. One of the phenomena of the past quarter century
has been the flight of families from the cities to the suburbs.
Many reasons account for this suburban hegira, but one stands
out: *Children*. The suburbs mean play space, safety, a room
for each child. Fathers run for early morning trains, they buck
rush-hour traffic in their cars, and mothers drive to stores and
even mow lawns so that children can have a good life.

Business has long been aware of this fine feeling for children.
Read the advertisements, in magazines or the daily paper, for
children's musical records, encyclopedias, and children's books
of all kinds. The words say: "You want your child to have the
best," and Mr. and Mrs. America agree.

Think about the growth of summer camps and the widespread interest in private kindergartens and dancing schools.
Whatever seems to offer an advantage to children strikes a
responsive chord in America's parents.

The United States government knows this. Best-sellers of the
U.S. Government Printing Office through all the years have
been two publications for parents: *Infant Care* and *Your Child
from One to Six*. Other publishers have made the same discovery. Benjamin Spock's *Pocket Book of Infant and Child*

Care (New York: Pocket Books, Inc., 1946) has sold almost as many millions of copies as the ever-popular "whodunits" on drug store, cigar store, and railroad station counters. Almost every general magazine — *Better Homes and Gardens, The American Home, The Farm Journal, The Ladies' Home Journal,* to name just a few — regularly includes articles about child care. Americans are conscientious about their children.

America's great freedom may partially account for this love. In our country a child can rise. He may some day be President of the United States. Each youngster is worthwhile because he has within him a very special promise of unknown heights. America's unique democracy may be another part of the explanation. Children have rights, as do all other people. Our strong religious roots undoubtedly also nourish this feeling. Americans have accepted the Christian command to love little children.

Whatever the causes, the fact is there. An old song says: "Love me, love my dog." The truth for home-school relations is: *"Love my child, and I will love you."* A parent is ever ready to sacrifice his needs in behalf of his children's. This is the parent you work with in home-school relations — he carries a prized picture in his pocketbook, a lump in the heart, a warm love, and a great good wish for youngsters. Feel the same love, and that parent is your friend. Show your interest and your love, and that parent is on your side. Be casual, be off-hand, be cold toward children, and that parent can never work closely with you.

PARENTS AND CHILDREN ARE ONE

A second generalization about parents flows naturally from the first. Teachers focusing only on children are apt to miss it. You see the youngsters in the classroom alone. Within him, yet hidden from your eyes, are love, hope, wish, plan, possibility — his parents' feelings for him. The bond between parent and child is a physical bond, it is an emotional bond. To touch the child is to touch the parent. To praise the child is to praise the parent. To criticize the child is to hit at the parent. The two are two, but the two are also one.

You can never write out the full investment — in time, in energy, in worry, in effort — that every parent, even the most casual, puts into a child. Parents spend time on their children.

They spend money. They give up some of their own desires for their children's sake: jobs, fun, comforts, friends, more education for themselves. These are the obvious sacrifices, but you cannot always see what they sum up: The parent gives *himself*. He becomes one with his child.

A youngster is a name on a class book. This is the child the parent wheeled in the sunshine for hour after hour, the child who had colic and could not sleep at night, the child the parent carried upstairs and down for six solid months.

WE DIDN'T DO SO GOOD THIS MONTH, EH, POP?

A child comes to school for the first time. She is one of countless swarming faces. This is the child who was born right after an older sister had polio and died, the child who is not quite as smart as her parents wish, the one who has been made to take piano lessons since she was four. She is the girl who has few friends; her mother worries because she too was lonesome when she was a girl growing up.

You send a paper home with a red check mark on it. The child who wrote the paper was once so hard to toilet-train. She sucked her thumb and worried everyone about her teeth, and she cried inconsolably because she could not keep up with her older brother. She is the one who *always* put her fingers into everything, and would not stop.

You see the youngster, but you cannot see the special person each child is in the parent's eyes: satisfaction mixed with disappointment, dream mixed with resignation, a glow spotted with concern. The child never comes alone; the parent never comes alone. The tie that binds the two is a warm, tight, and firm bond.

The love each parent feels for his child makes him want the best for that child. But, in wanting this for the child, the parent is wanting the best for himself. The parent really comes to school with his child. The youngster's performance in school is like the trial run of a ship; the engineers are on hand with bated breath — this will tell them if they did their work right. It is like the first showing of a new car model; the designers are listening apprehensively to what the public says. It is like the opening of a Broadway show; the writer and producer are in the lobby, almost afraid to hear the comments of the crowd.

Parents' love for their children creates a latent eagerness to do the right thing and to cooperate with all who seek the child's well-being. But this same love must warn you: *Handle with care.* Everything you do in home-school relations touches on sacred soil — on the child *and* on the parent himself. In this field tread lightly. You are not talking about the weather, but about parents' children . . . and parents' efforts . . . and parents' hopes.

PARENTS WANT TO BE IN TOUCH
   WITH THEIR CHILDREN'S LIVES

Hand in hand parents go with their children to school, and, when school days are over, even down the church aisle at the wedding; into the classroom, and even to the desk on the first job (and on the twenty-first). The parent continually wants to know: How is he doing? Is he making good progress? This close bond between parent and child leads us to a third characteristic of parents: *They are eager to keep in touch with what is going on.*

Teachers are apt to take a child's attending school as a routine thing. All children do it; each September brings another crop. But there is nothing casual about school days from a parent's standpoint. The years from five or six to eighteen or twenty-two are a long stretch. It hurts parents if a curtain drops during these years, cutting them out from a significant part in their children's lives.

The youngsters go to school early in the morning. They come home in late afternoon. What goes on? What do they do? How do they act? How do they get along with others? The children tell a little; the parent guesses a little; and reports and materials brought home convey a little. But, if you have a child, if you love that child, there is a thrill in knowing fully. This is your youngster's life and you want a share in it. Parents accept the fact that a child must be away for a large chunk of time. They are deeply grateful, however, when they are not kept in the dark.

An excellent book dealing with parents and children in non-school activities, but rich in implications and suggestions and sound philosophy for home-school relations, is The Peckham Experiment *by Pearse and Crocker (New Haven: Yale University Press, 1946). Chapter X, "Schooldays," points up the significance of parents' being in on their children's lives: "The parental lack of knowledge of and participation in all that goes on at school is apt to be complete. Delivered up to the gate by its mother, the child goes to school for a prescribed number of hours each day. . . . In this process the parents have no place and play no part. Many of our members for example had never seen their children swim until they joined the (Peckham) Centre. . . . The pride and pleasure of the mother who first sees her child swim a length are the outward expression of a human need fulfilled. And who will deny that a father adds a cubit to his dignity — if not to his stature — when in company with his friends he sees his son do a good dive, play in the band. . . . This pride in the parents is . . . a natural stimulus to their own progressive development" (page 189).*

Also, a film can be rented, The Centre, *which pictures the same program (Communication Materials Center, 413 West 117 St., New York 27, N. Y.). In it you will see the Peckham people*

*working in the wisest way with whole families, not just the
child-part. As you watch the film keep asking yourself if
schools could do anything like this.*

A few nursery schools, particularly those in colleges and
research centers, have one-way vision screens. Parents can sit
in an adjoining booth and watch their children at work. The
youngsters cannot see the adults and do not know they are
being observed. The faces of parents, as they sit behind that
screen, are revealing. You see no inattentiveness. No lagging of
interest. Only a great and deep absorption.

As you watch these adults you are impressed with their pride
and thrill. You hear quiet chuckles. You have no doubts.
Parents cherish the opportunity to be in on their children's lives,
and they make the most of it.

PARENTS WANT TO PARTICIPATE

Parents want more than to know what their children are
doing. *They want an active share in the events.* They want to
do things for these children they love. They also want to participate *for their own adult sakes.*

We in schools are wary of imposing on people. We think we
must not ask others to do us "favors." We steer away from
requests for help. But this is a wrong psychology. Our hesitancy springs from wrong ideas about people, ideas we have
to revise. In truth, we do the adult a favor when we make it
possible for him to help.

*A basic book which states the foundation for this point of
view is* On Being Human *by Ashley Montagu (New York: Henry
Schuman, 1951). It is short (only 122 pages), readable, and
packed full of challenging ideas.*

The chance to be useful is a satisfaction that people need
more and more as they grow up. The adult wants to give to

others. He wants to be a part of a circle that is larger than himself. This is the unique stamp of a mature person. Three-year-olds feel some need to contribute; the thirteen-year-old is pulled a little more by it. In the adult years, however, this need takes on its full driving force.

Hearing people talk, you would never realize how much adults want to participate. It is not cricket to express this need too openly. People put on a hard shell and say: "I don't want to be the fall guy." "I always look for the easy way out." "Why do they pick on me for all the jobs!" Because we are not aware that certain satisfactions are peculiar to adulthood, we often accept the words at face value.

We know that each age of childhood is seeking to gratify particular needs. The infant seeks cuddling. Eleven-year-olds *have* to be in with a gang; their club of friends and their secrets buck them up and make them feel important. We know how much it matters to an adolescent to have a voice in his own affairs, to adventure, to make mistakes, and to be a person on his own.

We miscalculate adults. We think searching for particular satisfactions is "kid stuff"; that the adult is emotionally complete; that he has outgrown this business of needs. None of these is true.

Two recent reports carry the developmental needs of childhood into the adult years. Be sure to read the new edition of Robert J. Havighurst's Developmental Tasks and Education *(New York: Longmans, Green & Company, 1952), particularly Chapters 16, 17, and 18; and the* Fact Finding Report: A Digest *which came out of the Midcentury White House Conference on Children and Youth (Raleigh, N. C.: Health Publications Institute, 1950). Pages 6-56 give the heart of the matter.*

The growing period of childhood largely centers around self-discovery. The child — infant, preschooler, school age, and adolescent — is deeply concerned in finding himself. He needs enough security to be reasonably sure of himself and trusting of others. He needs enough independence to feel reasonably aware of himself and aware of how other people will accept him.

The adult does not have to be centered so exclusively on himself. He has found some answers by the time he has reached adulthood. Most grownups are free to apply themselves to a new concern: What can I do for others? How can I put myself to work? What can I give? In this new area satisfactions must come now, if the adult is not to stagnate.

The need to give is heightened by the way we live today. Not too long ago a man could more easily find this satisfaction in his work; a woman could more easily find it in her home. More chances were right at hand for the personal touch. Our machine world has taken away many opportunities. Today more and more people flip the switch, follow the pattern, play their small routine part . . . and go to bed. This is not enough to satisfy an adult. The mature person is basically unhappy unless he has something to care for.

The school can meet this requirement. Working for one's own child, working for children, working for the school that serves the community's children can give the adult this new and deep-down pleasure he is seeking.

Parents may need encouragement to reach out for the chance to contribute. Children do, in their search for satisfactions. Many youngsters need a gentle push into the next step of their growth. Even though they deeply want independence, some must be prodded to seek it. Even though they crave security, some wait for reassurance before they reach out for what they need.

Adults are the same. Their own growth, serenity, and deep pleasure demand that they contribute to a cause larger than themselves, yet adults do not always seek out the opportunity. You cannot force them, but you can guide people into ways of serving and they will be truly glad.

A excellent film to see is The Fight for Better Schools *(New
York University Film Library, 26 Washington Place, New York
3, N. Y.). As you watch it, note the energy and enthusiasm and
imagination that adults have, once the right vein is tapped.
One shot of a mother licking envelopes while holding her little
baby on her lap is a real symbol of this. The film also gives information about the National Citizens Commission for the
Public Schools (2 West 45 St., New York 19, N. Y.). This is an
organization of citizens who have rolled up their sleeves to
bring about the kind of education that children deserve.*

PARENTS HAVE MUCH TO GIVE

The questions that immediately arise are how can parents
help and what do they know about education. Observation of
parents — your own parents, those you know in your classroom
and in your neighborhood — ought to set your mind at ease.
Parents have much to give. Not only do they want to help, but
their life's experience also gives them a strong background for
making a significant contribution.

The parent is, of course, an amateur in education. He has had
no course training and has probably read no books that deal
with the technical business of school. The specific teaching
ways of the classroom are not his forte, but — *parents have lived
with children.* They have seen them grow. Even though their
only degree in child care is a *Mr.* or a *Mrs.*, parents are wise,
and schools need their wisdom.

Parents know their individual children. They know their
strengths, the budding interests, the beginning inclinations that
mark one child off from all others. They can recite the intimate
details of a child's past: his fears, illnesses, the exciting experiences, the good and the bad that made the child what he is
today.

Good schools are striving for an awareness of the individual.
Yet, instead of being delighted with this parent-knowledge and
seizing on it as a strong resource, some school people scoff at it.

They say: "All she cares about is her own youngster." "He thinks his offspring is a prize."

You know the old joke: "That child has a face only a mother could love." Some schools turn their backs on this subjectivity. They call it prejudice. They say it is emotional. The personal insights of parents may be all of these things but still be good. Education could make full use of them.

Schools are objective, parents are more personal. Schools see children in comparison with others, parents are inclined to see each child as himself. Schools see children in the present. This is the test score, like it or not. Parents see children as they might be. There is room for both approaches in the good education of children.

The emphasis in a teacher's professional training is on the group, on living with and guiding numbers of children. While working with groups, the teacher must somehow always see how things work out for each member. The parent often is bewildered by numbers of children and must bow to the teacher's skill in this area. But the parent may, on occasion, be the more sensitive of the two in putting the single child, the person, in his central place. A school suffers if it cuts itself off from this kind of special insight.

Parents, living closer to their children, see more vividly another basic concept, one that teachers frequently learn only through reading. Call it the continuity of growth — the emergence of a child's today out of yesterday, the slow development of the present out of a long past.

This concept of continuity has many implications for curriculum and teaching. As one illustration, only the person who is fully aware of it can afford patience and have confidence in children. Knowing that there was a yesterday and that there will be a tomorrow, he can tone down too-stiff pressures to achieve specific goals by the end of today.

Teachers are more apt to see children for spot periods of time: a class once every day for forty minutes; a term from September to January; a year from September to June. The parent is with the child through the whole sweep of his growth —from diapers to tuxedos, from rattle to baseball bat, from Pablum to fried shrimp. This continuous living together breeds perspective, a tolerant touch, a gentleness which would improve many a school.

Parents have still another insight into child development: *an awareness that children are whole.* It is hard for a parent to escape knowing this; it is hard for many a teacher to learn it.

Parents have their noses rubbed into their children's total lives. They know full well what it means when a youngster is sick or not his normal self. Every day some event reveals to them the tie between how their child gets along with his friends and his general attitude toward life. The intermeshing of a youngster's complete being is not theory to those who eat breakfast with children, who take them shopping, see them in the bathroom, watch them in the backyards and on the street playing.

Schools need sharp reminders of this wholeness of humans. Much of our practice still segments children: This is seventh grade; this is reading time; this group has the top ability. Closer relationships with parents could acquaint school people more intimately with the point of view that children are whole.

Parents usually are not aware of all they know. If you ask them face to face, they are the first to say: "You're the expert. I'm only a parent." Yet, in fundamental idea after fundamental idea it is startling to notice how the common sense of parents coincides with the learned sense of teachers.

PARENTS ARE NOT ANGELS

Parents are in love with their children.
Parents want to keep in touch with their children.
Parents want to participate.
Parents have much to give.
Thus far, parents sound like angels. Everything is on the

positive side. The reality of course is that parents, like children, are not all sweetness and light. Included in their number are show-offs, the power-mads, the mice, the lazy ones, and those who make you think they do not care.

The mere fact that a person is over twenty-one does not confer on honorary degree of good citizenship. The mere fact that a woman has given birth to a child does not wash away all her personal problems. Often, it intensifies them. Parents carry with them into their adulthood all the unresolved problems of their own childhood. Adult living brings additional difficulties to many people.

Teachers who have held meetings with parents know this only too well. They dream that the meeting will turn everyone into a paragon of perfection. A number of times, the meeting actually shows how difficult some people can be. Teachers discover that this little clique of parents wants to run everything. . . . Mrs. So-and-So wants to be in the limelight all the time. . . . A few are so competitive that they even try to outdo each other in making cookies and putting on the most attractive tea. The teacher assumes that *all* parents want to study about children. But no. Many of those attending have some personal need which prods them.

Teachers who have invited parents to observe or participate in their classrooms have encountered similar difficult and disturbing drives in some parents.

"Mrs. Jones came one day, and she talked to me all the time. She never got the point that I have a whole classroom of children."

"I thought I would go crazy when Mrs. Brown visited. She could not keep her mouth shut or her hands off things. She wanted to 'help' her youngster and all the others, and wouldn't let them do a thing on their own."

"Mrs. Franklin thought she had to be the disciplinarian for me. She stepped into two situations — I could have wrung her neck."

PARENTS ARE ALL INDIVIDUALS

You will not be dismayed by the discovery that parents are not angels if you keep in mind one truth that your work with children has taught you over and over: All youngsters are different. By the same token, *parents are all individuals.*

The first time you hold a room meeting with parents you will be struck by this fact. Fifteen mothers have come. Mrs. Brown over there is smart as a whip. She gets ideas before you finish saying them, and she often completes your sentences for you. Mrs. Jones is very pleasant, but you cannot always be sure that she understands what you mean. She nods and smiles as if she does, but you wonder.

Mrs. Howe looks so neat and fresh. Her only child is in your group; the family lives in a small apartment with a lot of gadgets. You are surprised that Mrs. Black could come. She has two children under six, a girl in the upper grades, another in high school, plus Tommy in your class. You wonder who is caring for the little ones while she comes to the meeting.

Mrs. Hill is talking, and that does not surprise you. She always has to argue. You sense how the group tightens up when she begins. The other parents do not realize it, but they are bothered by her haggling over every little point.

There is that Mrs. What's-her-child's-name? who never says a word. Mrs. Wright looks so nice; they have a lot of money. It is true, you discover, that the Smiths are having still another baby. Why do you suppose Mrs. Gray looks so thin and jittery? Maybe this second marriage isn't working out well, either.

Fifteen came, and twenty-five did not. Who stayed away? The ones who work during the day. Those who have infants at home or sick husbands or visiting in-laws. Some who cannot stand meetings: "It's just talk-talk-talk . . . the same old stuff." A few who think: "Oh, I don't count." There are some who are ill and some who just forgot.

The same question that schools face with children arises: What is real to each of these people? Some need facts. How

can they learn them best? How much and how fast? Others
need a chance to talk and time to figure things out for themselves. Still others think that children are their big problem but,
in reality, the satisfaction of their own adult needs is more
pressing.

We can and must build our generalizatfons about parents.
At the same time we must be sure to keep in mind that individual differences are as real with parents as they are with four-
and eight-year-olds and adolescents. The challenge is the same
as with children: You must accept the *real* person in front of
you. You must be prepared to work where each one is. You
have to adapt your goals to the extent of each one's absorption.

PARENTS' BEHAVIOR IS CAUSED

The varied needs of parents will not dismay you if you also
apply to adults the same insights into behavior that are your
standbys with children. We are learning, for example, not to
blame children, and call it a day. "He is lazy." "He is mean."
"He is spiteful." "He just wants attention." Name-calling is
not the answer. It even complicates the real work we have to
do: To find the cause, because there always is a cause; to treat
each particular cause in the special way that will remedy it.

Some teachers forget that adult behavior is also caused. They
tend to be intolerant of it. They are apt to take a superior
attitude: "She ought to know better than that. . . ." Or they
become very moral: "Wouldn't you think that an adult. . . ?"

Some educators set high standards that cannot be met. Then,
when the standards are not met, they become cynical and want
to wash their hands of the business of trying to work with
parents. "Mrs. Brown came to the meeting, but she still expects
too much of Billy. . . ." "Mrs. Stevens told me that she liked
the pamphlet I gave her very much, but I don't think she read a
word of it. She still nags that child every single minute. . . ."
"I almost think Susie's mother is two-faced. When we talked
she promised to give Susie more freedom, but she didn't mean

a word she said. She has that child tied to her more than ever
before. . . ."

Reacting in this way to surface symptoms, with adults or
with children, never helps. The need is to keep asking yourself:
Why? What makes a person act this way? What is the reason?
What do they get out of it? Only when you come down to
causes, and then do whatever your discovery of the cause leads
you to do, can you expect people to change. You have to be a
combination of detective and doctor at work.

*The point of view expressed here is an extension to parents
of a way of thinking about children which I have tried to develop more fully in the book,* Understanding Your Child *(New
York: Prentice-Hall, Inc., 1952). Read "The Fourth Idea: There
Is Some Reason Why," pages 99-180, and apply it to parents
whose behavior troubles you.*

Keep in mind that although some behavior is consciously controlled, not all of it is. Occasionally home-school relations will
seem to work wonders. The parent sees a promising practice,
hears an idea, or reads a book. He snaps up the suggestion and
puts it right to work; his behavior changes almost overnight.
If you look back on why the parent ever acted the old way in
the first place, you will probably come to this kind of cause:
He simply did not know any better.

When behavior stems from this reason it is usually easy to
change. A conference, a good leaflet, a meeting — any technique that makes the new idea clear — can perform the miracle.
This happens with youngsters too. They change quickly if the
cause is the simple one of not knowing, not understanding, not
seeing a better way to act.

The ability to improve quickly is true of all ages, but it is
not true of all behavior. Many times the child cannot control
what he does. All the talking in the world, the best lessons
imaginable, do not produce a quick improvement. The cause

of the behavior, the reason why, is somewhere deep down where words cannot reach it.

Adults cannot always manage all their own affairs, either. Not because they do not try. Not because they are weak-willed. Not because no one has ever told them how. It is because people, humans of all ages, get caught in a powerful web spun of two strong threads: the way they were treated in the past, and the way the present bears down on them.

Whether we like it or not, these threads have the power to make people act the way they do. These threads can go on making them act that way until some friendly hand helps them slowly to be free. Words — exhortations, pleas, instruction, advice — cannot do this job. Blame and threats only make the tangle worse.

UNDERSTANDING AND PATIENCE ARE NEEDED

Parents need understanding from schools even more than children do. The parents' advanced years, far from giving them control over all their acts, often put them more in the power of the past. A young child can regain his balance. Too many long years of bad living block some adults from being helped quickly.

Patterns of behaving — "She always has to be right" . . . "He gets so upset when he is crossed" . . . "He wavers so and never makes up his mind" . . . "She has such a chip on her shoulder" — have been practiced for so long, have been used in so many situations, and are so rooted in needs that no little pat on the back can shoo them away.

Unhappiness is buried so deep within some adults that it is not easily touched. A harsh father, a cold mother, a preferred brother . . . a fearful family, a demanding one, a worried house . . . playmates who bullied, harsh teachers — these are still real, and they influence the way people act today, even though they may have happened thirty years ago.

The present too is often hard on many parents. Basic social conditions determine the way some people must act. Some

families are under economic strain. Others feel tension because
they belong to a minority; the sound of their name, their skin
color, their religious beliefs, or their national background sets
them apart. All families are, to some extent, affected by the
highly competitive nature of our society. Some families are
particularly susceptible to this pressure; they are driven to
succeed, to be prominent, to rise to the top, and to drag their
children along with them.

In addition, each family has its own private personal story
which colors parents' efforts for their children, their relations
with adults, and their responses to school. Maybe a paralyzed
grandmother needs continuous care. Perhaps alimony to a
former wife drains the family's resources, or an alcoholic uncle
is a constant worry. An unstable business may make a father
edgy, or migraine may make a mother sharp-tempered.

Your work with children teaches you that youngsters with
real problems do change *if* they have continuous teacher-after-
teacher help. Only over the long haul can a united faculty,
agreed on the cause and the treatment, begin to see improvement in many a child.

You need the same patience when you work with adults.
You use every relationship to do what looks like the helpful
thing: your face-to-face talks, your group meetings, reading
materials, the parent's visits to school, everything. The next
teacher does the same, in the same consistent way. The school's
efforts may never be enough to effect a complete transformation
in some people. If the school does not get angry, does not
simply squelch troubled parents, and keeps operating on the
concept of treat-the-cause, home-school relations always will
have some impact and always will help.

One reminder: As you read and think about those few parents
who have more difficult problems than most, be sure to keep
your perspective. There are a *few* unhappy parents, just as in
each class of children a *few* youngsters are more troubled and
need your best thinking. Some teachers have their fingers
burned by these few adults, and carry over dismal generaliza-

tions to all parents. This is not sound practice with adults, any more than it would be with youngsters.

MANY PARENTS ARE UNSURE

You will do well to realize that parents have been hard hit in recent years. If you are realistic you will not be let down. You will not expect miracles, neither will you get angry with mothers and fathers and give up in dispair.

Mothers and fathers today are like workmen in a factory trying to turn out their product by kerosene lamps, like carpenters trying to cut with a dull saw, like farmers trying to plow with only a balky mule.

Modern life has taken away many of the tools parents need to do their job of child rearing. Space is gone for many families. Real jobs that children can handle, necessary chores that are a part of family life, are almost nonexistent. Animals that youngsters can care for are missing. Materials children can work with — water, sand, mud, boards, leaves, trees, dirt, streams — are no longer right at hand. Even the whole silent structure of *This is right* and *This is wrong* is crumbling. In its place are alternatives and choices; these are much less supporting for parents.

Probably never before have parents been so earnest about children and so full of good will. Probably no time in history has ever given parents so many problems to face, so many decisions to make, and so few tools to work with. All parents are caught. They do what they can, although often that is far less than they know how to or want to do.

The family job has been further complicated because the rules have kept changing. Parents have heard first one thing and then another.

"Let him cry. It's good for his lungs." *"If he's crying there must be something wrong. Pick him up."*

"Don't pick him up. You will spoil him." *"Hold him and play with him. Don't you know that babies need love?"*

"Feed him every four hours on the dot." *"Feed him when he is hungry. He will make his own schedule as he goes along."*

"Take his thumb out of his mouth. Do you want to spoil his teeth?" *"Thumb-sucking is normal. It comforts the baby, and it won't hurt his teeth."*

Many mothers and fathers today are badgered from all sides. Grandparents have said one thing ("You aren't going to let him say *that* to you, are you? . . . If he were my child. . . . These children today!"), and some "experts" have said another. Conflicting advice is complicating enough. To worsen matters, other "experts" have come along and disagreed with the first.

See the film Family Circles *(thirty minutes, sound) (Communication Materials Center, 413 West 117 St., New York 27, N. Y.). Watch at the start of the film for the many different ways in which family life today differs from that of earlier times. The latter part of the picture is concerned with various home-school activities, which will also interest you.*

It is not unusual at PTA meetings or other gatherings for a mother to stand up and say: "Of course, I'm just a parent, but. . . ." The poor parent who does not know a thing!

It is not unusual for parents to say to someone who looks like an expert: "You probably wouldn't approve at all of what I am doing with my child, but. . . ." The poor parent who is always making mistakes!

Parents have had not only an avalanche of advice, much of it conflicting; they have also been blamed for everything under the sun. Juvenile delinquency, the low state of our country's morals, speeding on the highways, carelessness about the value of a dollar, the drop in church attendance — these evils all go back to parents. At least, that is what the headline writers and speech-makers seem to imply. Many parents have believed them.

It is not unusual for parents to say (and for many more to feel): "I've probably done all the wrong things with my child. . . ." They have finally been beaten down.

It is worth your time to look up the May, 1947 issue of The Child, *the monthly magazine of the U. S. Children's Bureau. Read the article, "Stop Sniping at Parents," by Samuel Whitman. In just a few pages it states a point of view that can be fundamental to your thinking.*

The magazines today are full of articles about children. Almost every newspaper has a column or two telling parents how to raise their children. Books on child care have been best-sellers. Pamphlets, particularly those with the word "discipline" in the title, go like wildfire.

Much of the printed advice and information is sound. It is a very promising development to have facts about child growth, and tips and suggestions for parents, available at every newsstand. Historians may later consider this stride in adult education one of the more significant advances in the twentieth century.

In another sense, this gush of information may be an indication of sickness. Child care columns would not invade the "slick" magazines nor would books about children break into the "whodunit" market were there not a real hunger for advice and counsel. It is hard to tell how much of this eagerness to read about children is a normal, intelligent, and comfortable approach to wise parenthood, and how much of it means: "I don't know what to do, but I certainly hope the other fellow does."

Many parents today need reassurance much more than they need blame; they need praise for what they have done well rather than advice on what they might do; they need an awareness of their own good ideas rather than the other fellow's answers to their questions.

The Pocket Book of Baby and Child Care, by Benjamin Spock, M.D. (New York: Pocket Books, 1946) is probably on the right track when it says to parents at the very start: "Trust yourself." This book and many others do their best to persuade parents that they know more than they think they do. But this is hard for many mothers and fathers to believe today.

3. Parents and Schools

In America, education has an A-1 rating. Our free society does not peg children at some one historical job or income or location. No one can tell what a youngster may become. Each child carries his family's burning hopes — for more fame, more friends; more security, more income, more comfort; more responsibility, more respect. Each family recognizes that education is an important rung on the ladder into this dream heaven.

This generalized faith in education is evidenced by the fact that our school system never stops growing. We began with a concept of free public elementary education. That in itself was a revolutionary idea, one that only a people committed to education could have developed. Then we saw that a free secondary education was necessary to give every child his right.

We have almost achieved these goals, but our plans continue. At the lower end of our age levels there are many free public kindergartens. Where the five-year-old group has become established as a part of the public schools, the people's faith in education is leading them to create free four-year-old groups. Today there is talk of the nursery school as the next step in public education.

At the upper age levels the free junior college is accepted more and more as a part of the educational structure. Many communities are maintaining their own local colleges so their young people can have four years of education beyond high school. Only a country committed to education could consider federal scholarships for bright college students. Only a country dedicated to education could develop as many city colleges and four-year community colleges as America has. Only a Congress persuaded that education is good could pass a G.I. Bill of Rights.

This favorable disposition toward more schools is the appropriate outcome of the widespread love which parents feel for their children. Love of children on the one hand and belief in education on the other are two bulwarks to the field of home-school relations. Either one alone could say: This field is worth every effort teachers put into it — parents are ready to do whatever is needed. But the two go together in mutually supporting each other and creating an immense reservoir of good will for education.

MILLIONS OF PARENTS ARE WORKING WITH TODAY'S SCHOOLS

At this writing, membership in the National Congress of Parents and Teachers is 7,219,165. In 1897, before the first national convention of this organization was held, one of the founders, Alice Birney, said: "If only fifty mothers come I shall be satisfied. Yes, even if only twenty-five are there." [1] No organization could grow to this astounding membership, or

---

[1] Harry and Bonaro Overstreet, *Where Children Come First*. Chicago: National Congress of Parents and Teachers, 1949, p. 10.

grow as rapidly as the National Congress, or grow as steadily
without the foundation of Americans' great interest in children
and in education.

Membership figures alone make it apparent that millions of
parents are having satisfying relationships with schools and
teachers under the auspices of the National Congress of Parents
and Teachers. Further proof of the excellent job the National
Congress is doing is its official magazine, *National Parent-
Teacher.* This sound journal for parents is published monthly,
September through June, at the amazingly low price of $1.25
a year. No better bargain exists for parents, and parents know
it. The low cost, the skilled editing, and the magazine's sensitivity to parents' problems are further tributes to the strength
and importance of the National Congress and to the satisfactions
the Congress brings to its members.

Further proof — the most convincing kind — comes through
the countless stories of the good work that individual PTAs are
doing in local schools to bring about a better life for children.
That well-named book, *Where Children Come First,*[2] tells many
of these stories in a way that leaves no doubt: Many, many
parents are finding fun, deeper satisfactions, and a real sense of
usefulness through working with schools.

Recent years have also seen the development of the National
Citizens' Commission for the Public Schools, an organization
which has its headquarters at 2 West 45 St., New York 19, N.Y.
Leaders in all fields of public endeavor are on the Commission.
The willingness of nationally-known men and women to give
their time to the cause of better public education and the cooperation of all agencies of mass communication — press, magazines, billboards, radio, and television — in promoting this cause
further reveal the public's readiness to pitch in for schools.

The Commission tries to spur local and regional groups of
citizens to know their schools. Its efforts have led to the formation of many community councils, several excellent surveys,

[2] *Op. cit.*

and the publication of many pamphlets. The success of this new group — particularly its achievement in involving so many influential citizens in studying their local schools — is remarkable proof that education has a top-notch credit rating.

> *The Commission maintains six regional offices: A southern office at 902 Realty Bldg., Louisville 2, Ky.; a western office at 1014 Eighth St., Sacramento 8, Calif.; a New England office at 41 Mount Vernon St., Boston 8, Mass.; a Rocky Mountain office at 1100 Fourteenth St., Denver, Colorado; a southwestern office at 1104 Main St., Dallas, Texas; and a midwestern office at 643 Midland Bank Bldg., Minneapolis 1, Minn. National headquarters, and each regional office, maintain a clearing house of reprints and reports: case histories of parents' and citizens' efforts to improve their local schools. Write or visit the office nearest you for a full list of the materials available.*

MANY PARENTS HAVE UNPLEASANT
MEMORIES OF SCHOOL

The reservoir of good will for education is full, yet it has chinks in it. These can easily become larger, if they are not identified and if too much pressure is put on them. Teachers should recognize all the strengths, but we must also face directly the potential breaks in the dam and take them into account.

Despite the friendly feeling for education in the abstract, many parents have unpleasant memories of their childhood schools — memories which weaken their enthusiasm to work with teachers today.

In yesterday's school many of today's parents were slapped on the back of the hand with a ruler. At one time or another a considerable number had to sit in a corner with dunce caps on their heads. Many had to stand in the cloakroom because they were *bad*. As many as 25 per cent failed in first grade, and others became repeaters in later grades.

Teachers mistakenly assume that everyone feels friendly toward school. We had a good time when we were pupils. We at least liked it will enough to decide: I want to be a teacher, too.

For us and a few other children, school — 1920, 1930, 1935 — was fun. We learned things, and that was exciting. We won spelling bees and got gold stars. What could be nicer? The teacher praised us and we liked that. We were *good*.

Many other children were afraid most of the time. They were shamed and publicly embarrassed. They had to do homework, keep their hands folded neatly on the desk, tip-toe in line. Of course, this was yesterday's school, the school the *parent* went to when he was a child. All of this was years ago. Today the parent's *child* probably goes to a different building, almost certainly has a different teacher, and is surely treated in a kinder way. But impressions and feelings and attitudes are not easy to shrug off.

Even nowadays, come June, the educator who tries hard to create in children a liking for school is greeted by a rash of cartoons depicting the youngsters deliriously singing such ditties as: "No more pencils, no more books; no more teacher's nasty looks." Every fall there is a similar discouraging crop of magazine covers and jokes that portray children as being sad and blue because school is beginning.

The people who draw the cartoons are of parents' age. All of this humor may be pleasant, good-natured teasing that none of us really means. Or it may be a reflection of the feeling many adults still have about teachers and schools.

Every teacher at some time or other has telephoned to a parent and met a very quick and worried response: "What has Johnny done now?" There are homes where a call from teacher is worse than hearing from the rent collector. The idea somehow persists that schools always mean trouble.

We have all heard of mothers, fathers, and grandparents

sending a young one off for his first day at school with: "You better be good. They will make you behave in school." The concept of the teacher as a Gestapo-like agent has firm roots.

The teacher who unexpectedly visits a child's home often senses embarrassment in the air. The mother is apt to give excuses and apologies for everything not looking shipshape, even when it does. The teacher is the snooper.

It is no simple matter to arrange a love-match between teachers and people who feel this way about school. The teacher who has Johnny in her classroom this year may be a wonderful woman — the soul of sympathy, appreciation, and kindliness. She may deserve none of the feelings that some parents hold toward her. She gets them anyhow.

It is not always fair or reasonable, but humans do carry over feelings from one situation to another, from one time to another, and from one person to another. You can pass a law against it, but the chances are that you cannot change it.

Of course, many parents look back on their school days with warm feelings. They can still remember individual teachers who were key people in their lives. Schools have to realize, however, that not everyone feels kindly toward them. In every community some people do not.

You cannot judge by words alone. Parents do not say: "I hate teachers." But feelings can exist even if no words are given to them. Feelings can exist even if the people who harbor them are not aware of them. You have this one certainty: Every parent you work with was once a pupil. You have to think about the question of how each parent feels about his pupil-hood.

Does your school start with an even chance? Is it free to make whatever impression it can on the people it deals with today? Do you get the brunt of any angry left-overs from yesterday's education? Are you ahead of the game with some parents because they loved school when they were kids and they now come, full of good feeling, prepared to work with you?

> *To verify what went on in your community, check your school's records for 1925-1935. How many children failed first grade, for example, during that period?*
>
> *It is revealing, also, to ask parents: "Can you remember any time when a teacher punished you?" This question some-times brings out affirmative replies that are a monument to teachers' ingenuity in devising unusual punishments and to people's capacity to remember vividly occasions that were painful to them.*

MANY PARENTS HAVE BEEN "BURNED" BY TODAY'S SCHOOL

There is another side to the picture of PTA memberships. Included in the millions of members are too many parents who are responding only to a sense of duty. When a child is old enough to start to school, his mother (if she is a "good" mother) joins the PTA. Both parents are supposed to go to the meetings. Mother is expected to *serve* in some way. It is "the thing to do."

Their sense of duty is not strong enough to keep many from seeking a way out of doing their share. The woman elected

Room Mother may at first feel imposed upon. She soon learns from her friends: "It's better to get it over with early. If you do it now, they won't ask you again." That is certainly not a commendable attitude to start relations with!

Another mother is asked to be on the Telephone Committee. (The job is to nag all the other mothers into nagging their husbands to come to the meetings.) She drags up every excuse that she can think of for evading the job, but the desperate tone of the Room Mother or the teacher — "We've asked everyone else, and they all say 'No,' too" — finally persuades her. After a while her reluctance changes into the rationalization: "It could be worse. At least, they won't ask me to do anything else."

Sometimes this forced relationship with the PTA serves, although very indirectly, one good purpose. It makes mothers appreciate their younger children at home. The little ones are the perfect excuse. "I'd really love to help, but I have Billy at home you know, and so I just can't."

A magazine writer recently expressed himself this way: "From the time your child enters kindergarten until he finishes high school, you are fair prey for the PTA. There is no way out. Child psychologists hammer at you that you must back up your child, give him security, and identify yourself with a group of people that you have never even heard about. . . . " [3]

True, not everyone feels this way, but schools should not build this feeling into *anyone* — this negative, resistant, always-wishing-for-an-out attitude. It is not comfortable for adults. They do not like themselves for feeling the way they do, and they don't like the teachers and the school for making them feel that way.

Included in the millions are too many parents doing jobs they are asked to do, without knowing why they are performing them. The teacher calls a parent who owns a big car: "The class is going on a trip," and that is that. Where are they going? The teacher (or the Room Mother) does not say. Why are

---

[3] James Holt McGavran, "Don't Believe What They Say About Grandma!" *Saturday Evening Post*, September 22, 1951, p. 148.

they going? That isn't made clear either. What has led up to their going? No one says a word about that. What will they accomplish? The school just wants the parent and her car on Wednesday at nine.

Humans like to help but they like it best when their part is put in a setting. If they know what is going on and how they will contribute to it, they get a pleasing sense of tying in to something larger than themselves. But if they are one cog in the wheel and feel unrelated to a whole, then they sense that someone is taking advantage of them.

Included in the millions are too many parents doing little jobs that do not carry them ahead in their understanding of children or education. Often the jobs are superficial, like arranging parties or bringing food for special occasions. Often they are "calendar pad" jobs — calling and writing to notify everyone of the dates and times of meetings.

Included in the millions are too many parents dutifully attending PTA, standing up to be counted so that their child's class can win the attendance prize, but actually wishing they were at home with their television.

BAD MEETINGS DISCOURAGE MANY PARENTS

Teachers are experts at group meetings. Meetings are their bread and butter, the kind of thing they do with children every day of their school life. Yet teachers hold back this knowledge and let parents flounder, trying to conduct the PTA. Inexperienced and in their bewilderment, parents lean heavily on Robert's Rules of Order. The meeting is wooden. Rigid rules stifle group thinking; the meeting creaks and groans as it bobbles along.

Inexperienced and on their own, parents fall into other traps that make PTA meetings less satisfying than they could be. One prevalent practice is to plan the program for the whole year ahead. Advance planning, in fact, has become the hallmark of a well-managed PTA. A published program, a booklet, or a mimeographed sheet tells in April exactly who will speak in September, October, and on up to the next April. This is efficiency that kills.

Some advance planning can identify the dates of the major meetings in advance; it can outline the broad goals and general paths that a year's program will follow. But the specifics must be determined by the burning issues of the moment. Flexibility in program planning often means last-minute adjustments. But it has this virtue: Meetings are timely. They catch people with live bait. Parents come, and they care.

The school that specifies too far ahead the topics of its parent meetings will almost certainly be caught in a cut-and-dried routine. Conscientious people attend, but their nagging sense of duty is a far cry from the eager interest that adults can show. The applause at the end of the meeting is only a faint promise that any of the ideas will be acted on.

Many people stay at home. The faithful smugly say: "What a shame that the people who need it most are not here!" They imply that the absentees are lazy or indifferent. Their absence is taken as one more proof of how much the stay-at-homes need "it." Does anyone stop to wonder: What do these parents really need?

A very practical reason for the prevalent practice of planning far in advance is the anxiety to get good speakers. It is perfectly true that "famous" speakers do get quickly dated. If the PTA has its heart set on having a well-known person, it has to make the arrangements a year ahead.

But who is a *good* speaker? Is it the well-known author who has written a book, the teacher from the nearby college, or the "expert" from the neighboring community? Or is a good speaker the person — famed or obscure, golden-tongued or stammering — who can stimulate thinking on this particular problem that these people right here and now are puzzled about?

Too many program committees apply only one standard: "I hear *So-and-so* is a wonderful talker" — but about what? Can he help with this problem that the group is facing right now? "They tell me that *So-and-so* makes a marvelous speech" — but is it within the scope of problems that are bothering this parent body? "They had *So-and-so* at the Glendale PTA last year, and he was just wonderful" — but that is Glendale.

Program planning usually means getting "personalities" — names to fill a spot. Each month a hole must be plugged. Filling the gap is the important thing, and it does not matter with what. Invitations to speakers convey this desire to get a name. So often PTAs say: "Choose your own topic. Anything you want to talk about will be all right. Whatever you say will be fine!" The crux of the invitation ought to be a firm insistence: "This audience is concerned about . . . ," but such definiteness is often missing entirely.

PTAs get lost in abstractions. "There is a wonderful film. They used it last year at Lincoln. . . ." "She puts on a demonstration, and they say it is very good. . . ." "He is so sincere, don't you think?" These are good words but they are general and off in the wild blue yonder.

People will stay at home despite the most famous names. Or they will sit, look, listen — and forget. The real lure for a meeting should not be some glitter that shines brightly in an announcement. Primarily, people want the chance to solve problems that matter to them.

Despite the millions who belong, not all parents see the PTA as a problem-solving organization. One school in September knew that its parents were bothered about discipline. The parents were anxious to discuss the practices followed in various homes and to define reasonable standards. Mothers and fathers were keenly aware of a number of specific problems: How many movies a week should be allowed? How late should high school youngsters stay out? How often should the car be used? *Discipline* was chosen as the theme for the year. Several members of the program committee suggested different kinds of meetings.

Tradition was the first damper. "Our Christmas program

must come in December. It was so lovely last year. . . ." "One
meeting ought to be on Founders' Day; we always do that. . . ."
"Shouldn't the last meeting be some kind of picnic or party?
We usually have one. . . ." "Everyone will be so busy in February and March with our Carnival that we can't have any
real meetings then."

So the group had one meeting on its year's theme, in January, on "The Family and Its Children Today." *Reverend
Smathers* was the speaker — "Everyone says he is so inspira-
tional" — and it was just one more meeting like all the rest. The
idea of "do-what-we-always-do" knocked out every chance to
get today's questions answered.

Paying too much attention to program suggestions which
have been developed for widespread use can also throw cold
water on a particular group's interest. "This year in our state
we are studying. . . ." and some state guide sets the pace. Or:
"We're following the national magazine and the study course
for February is. . . ." Or: "Our meeting is on the theme of
American Education Week. . . ." The approach is not: What
questions right here need solving? It is rather: What do those
people over there — in Chicago, Washington, the state capitol
— want us to do?

Schools have long been trying to throw off the control of
regent's examinations and of the state-wide syllabus. We have
been fighting for the right to look at the youngsters who face
us today in our classrooms, not at a course of study written in
the state capital, to tell us what to teach. Parents and teachers
have to fight, too, for the same freedom with our adult programs — the right to look at our own concerns and not at those
of the other fellow.

The fight is largely with ourselves. State guides and national
study outlines are always prepared simply as suggestions. No
central headquarters wants its guides followed slavishly, at the
expense of a real local concern. Many a state department of
education has found that schools persist in following for years
a state syllabus for children after the state department has

withdrawn it. Evidently, we are all inclined to read *require-ment* when the intent is merely *suggestion*.

The result of all these disheartening experiences with today's school is that underneath the seeming strength that millions of PTA members indicate, there are weaknesses in people's attitudes towards school. General good will is there. Basic interest is there. A latent urge to work and to help. But many a parent will need time and persuasion and many positive experiences before he is convinced that working with the school is worthwhile.

SOME PARENTS SUSPECT THE MODERN SCHOOL

There is still another chink in the reservoir of general good will toward education. Many parents today look with a suspicious eye at what the modern school is doing. A great many changes have taken place in education, so many that when parents do visit school their first reaction is: "It wasn't like this when I was a child!" Some mean that they are pleased. Others use the same words to imply: "I'm not so sure I like what I see."

Doubt and difference of opinion about education are matters of serious import. If there is a split between parents and teachers, youngsters are caught in the middle; they are pulled in two directions by home and by school. Schools are harassed; they do not get the support they need. Homes are robbed of a comfort they deserve — the certainty that the school, responsible for so much of children's time, is doing the right thing.

It is essential that parents and teachers agree on *good* education. Only when such unity exists will children experience the consistency of treatment they need for their full development. Only when mutual trust and understanding exist will homes and schools find their creative energies, unplagued by doubts and arguments and suspicion, released to work for children.

Changes in education go back at least to the early 1900's, if

you consider John Dewey and his work in Chicago as the
beginning of experimentation. For a whole half-century change
has been creeping in. At first new words were more evident
than new deeds, but words can be almost as upsetting as
practice.

Schools in the 1920's remained about the same as they had
always been, but much talk of "progressive education" was
prevalent. Parents began to hear phrases like "the whole child,"
"the activity program," "units of work," "a child-centered
school," and "creative expression." Classroom work went on
very much as usual, but education had a different sound.

Today the vocabulary is still expanding. Parents are becom-
ing acquainted with new terms like "core curriculum," "workshops," "the social studies," "in-service training," "integration,"
"readiness," and "homogeneous grouping." Schools are gen-
ally far behind the shining new vocabulary. In the past twenty
years, however, the weight of all the talking has begun to touch
what actually goes on.

Teachers on the job may not be aware of how much change
has taken place in schools. New teachers, learning only the
new vocabulary in their training, may have even less idea. But
many a parent, coming back to school for the first time with
his own child, feels like a stranger.

The parent wants to know: "Why don't they teach the alphabet in first grade? They did when I was in school" — just
twenty years ago.

"Why don't they put more stress on phonics? They did when
I was in school" — just twenty years ago.

Teachers tend to take the changes for granted. We are
aware of the gap between what we know how to do for children and what we are doing in our classrooms. We are insensi-
tive to the wide chasm between what we are doing (inadequate
as it may be) and the schools of a generation ago.

*A few good books and pamphlets interpret to parents what
modern schools are doing. You will find a list of these in the*

last chapter. All of them however are about the new education in general. By all means know these materials and make them available to parents, but don't fool yourself about what they can do. Parents are somewhat interested in schools and education, modern and any other style. Their paramount desire however is for knowledge about the particular school their child goes to, the education in the specific grade he is in right now.

School after school has had a rude awakening. Some that had won great professional respect have been suddenly overturned with community dissension. A formula with a predictable outcome can almost be written: Add one superintendent with leadership ability; throw in good supervision; stir in some teachers who have studied recently — and you get a first-class explosion.

We speak of the straw that broke the camel's back. Schools today are nearer to this breaking point than we realize. Superficially they look strong. But strain and stress, almost to the snapping point, is underneath some.

Teachers are not aware of how close many schools are to this danger point. Nor do we realize how much in the future schools will be crowded to the edge.

For one thing, schools will feel continuing pressure to change. Our high schools have been relatively untouched by the experimentation and research of the past years. At the very point when the impact of new facts was about to land on the secondary school, World War II intervened.

A little experimentation had sprouted: cooperative work programs, summer work programs, the core curriculum, and so forth. These are cropping up again because they did not stem from whim or fancy. They are rooted in an accumulation of knowledge about adolescence. Stronger than ever today, the pressure for change is still on the high school.

The pressure comes from psychology. It comes with just as great a force from the practicalities of everyday life. Our high schools are now fully folk schools. Everybody goes, not only the college-bound. Inside of schools the talk is on: "These students don't need geometry. They need to know how to figure their income tax and how to buy insurance." "They don't need English literature nearly as much as they need child care, consumer education, and family life education." "They don't need an advanced course in science; they ought to be learning how to fix a vacuum cleaner and an oil burner." "They don't need to know so much European history but they do need some pertinent facts about Asia and Latin America." Talk comes first; the changes are sure to follow. But will they put teachers even more out on a limb?

It is not only the high school which must continue to improve. Our most recent insights into people put great stress on the early years of life. The elementary school, to keep up with what is now known, has to move downward to reach children when they are five and four and three.

We know much more today about children's emotional development. To keep up with this knowledge, the elementary school almost certainly has to provide even more chances for play, for the arts, for the expression of feelings.

Our brand-new world interdependence insists that schools do something different with history, with literature, with languages, with geography through all the grades as well as in the high school. Our bright and shiny new creation for ending the world with atomic explosions; our "born-yesterday" advances in communication; our one-after-the-other discoveries in all fields of science — each of these is demanding of educators: You must keep children up with us.

Schools cannot simply plunge into new programs. They can be sure that parents want the best for their children, but not all parents are as eager for change in education as they are for new cooking stoves. The first step for schools is to know realistically that many parents are already out of touch with school practices, they feel left behind, and they are suspicious.

Many local branches of the Association for Childhood Education International invite parents to attend their meetings.

*This idea ought to be expanded to include all of our profes-
sional gatherings. If parents could be in on the start of ideas
at faculty meetings, district teachers' meetings and others,
they would not be so taken by surprise when changes do come
into being.*

SOME DIFFICULTIES IN MAKING CHANGES

If teachers had their wish parents would simply accept any
changes in schools. We get angry when they do not.

Why on earth, we ask, will people rush to buy a new brand
of coffee that is "super-aromatized," but still cling to the old
kind of school?

Why do they trade in their car every year for the newest
model, but still hang on to old ways of teaching?

No one wants to cook on an old-fashioned wood-burning
kitchen stove, yet sometimes a real estate agent tells a prospect:
"You don't have to worry about the school. It isn't one of those
modern ones. They believe in the good old-fashioned ways
there."

We often look with envy at doctors. The medical man goes
to his professional convention or reads the latest copy of his
professional journal. He learns that the authorities now recommend *Optiomycin* instead of *Pessiomycin.* That is all he needs
to know. He is free to act on his knowledge. No one questions
his prescriptions. People flock to the doctor who is up-to-date.
The teacher who tries out a new idea is fired — "He went too
fast for his community."

We overlook the fact that the doctor has great advantages
over the teacher. Changes in medical practice usually stem
from clear-cut objective laboratory research. The new drug
and the new surgical technique are not recommended until
someone has proved in very definite fashion that they work.

Modern education has much sound research to back up what
it is doing. We probably fail to make this research widely
enough known and understood. On the other hand much of

school practice is not grounded on completely provable fact. Classroom activities stem from assumptions about human nature, from values and ideals, from judgments, and from good guesses based on experience. The doctor is on firm ground because research is his backing. Because of the nature of schooling, everyone has some right to speak up where education is concerned.

In education we always have to ask parents to buy a new model sight unseen. We get impatient. We wish that parents would defer to our professional training and accept our word that the new ways are a good buy.

Further, the doctor gets a quick check when he makes a mistake. The patient either improves or he takes a turn for the worse. In education we can never be quite this sure. The youngster has to live out his whole life, and even then the answer is never clear: Maybe another way would have been better. In our field there is much more room for differences of opinion.

> *We owe it to parents to let them become familiar with the evidence about modern education. You ought to have on hand such reports as* Appraisal of Newer Elementary School Practices *by J. Wayne Wrightstone (New York: Teachers College Bureau of Publications, 1938);* New Methods vs. Old In American Education *by G. Derwood Baker et al (New York: Teachers College Bureau of Publications, 1941);* Story of the Eight-Year Study *by Wilfred M. Aikin (New York: Harper and Bros., 1942). The comparative data generally favors modern education; this will comfort some parents. As you use this data keep in mind that, no matter how good the evidence is in general, parents most of all want facts about their local school and their own particular child.*

The teacher is in a unique position when differences of opinion must be settled. You are a professional worker. At the same time you are the hired hand of a whole community of lay people. Our schools are not a private laboratory for

educators. Democracy rightly makes them the people's schools.
They exist to promote the common welfare as the people see
that welfare. Our history says that these schools can never
rise above the wishes of the people.

One complication is that all of these people once were pupils.
Many of them think they know all about how schools should
be run.

These people had primers — once. They learned their multi-
plication tables in a certain grade. They made maps in another
grade that showed every state's capital; they had to paste a
puff of cotton on the map to indicate the state's main crop.
They had to practice their penmanship. School is no mystery;
many people think they know what it is all about.

In the absence of convincing evidence you cannot blame
adults for falling back on their own experience. You hear people say: "What was wrong with yesterday's school? Look at
me. I went through it and I'm all right." The willingness to
take a chance on an unknown that might be even better is not
very widespread where children are involved. The stronger
urge is to play it safe.

Communities do have the final say about education. We keep
wishing that, if parents have to be our bosses, they would at
least be easygoing and give us great freedom. It may be hard,
however, for adults to be this kind of boss, considering how
the world treats many people today. Parents are out in the
hard, cold world. They have to make quotas if they are sales-
men; they have to watch the weather if they are farmers; they
are at the mercy of those bureaucrats if they run a business;
they must keep their eye on the fellow down the street if they
own a delicatessen.

In comparison, teachers seem to have a soft life: nine to
three, weekends off, a long summer vacation. In the world
outside, the machines are demanding; competitors are tricky;
the government does not know where it is going, but. . . .
Just let those educators dare to change the schools! The public holds the reins.

Once the teacher was a learned person. Everyone looked up to him. He had a special authoritative position. Today, with universal education, teachers are a dime a dozen. The public insists on staying in the driver's seat and has to be convinced of teachers' competence.

Yesterday the schoolmaster lived in parents' houses; he ate at their table; he worshipped in their church. You could find him sitting on the porch or shopping at the store or riding in the buggy.

In more and more towns today, nobody knows anybody. Teachers usually must live in the community where they teach, but "living" can mean a back bedroom in a rooming house or a bed at the YWCA. An anonymity pervades life. The woman in the super-market may be the teacher. She may be the new woman who has moved in down the street — "in the Guffey house where the Franklins used to live." Or she may be someone who has motored over from the other end of town to pick up a bargain in soapflakes.

Working out the proper roles of the professional educator and the citizen under these new conditions is not easy. Schools that are sensitive to parents' side of the problem will at least know enough to wonder: How *do* parents feel? Are they pulled backward? Are they free to consider changes on their merit?

SOCIAL CONDITIONS AFFECTING
   PUBLIC ATTITUDES

In trying to analyze parents' probable reactions to schools it is important to consider the temper of our times. These are confused times for parents. Many uncertainties color people's responses.

Internationally, we do not know whether we are coming or going. Each day brings no solutions, only more pin-pricks. We have been jabbed by the Berlin blockade and the harassing situations in Indo-China, Korea, Iran, and Egypt. . . . Only a daily reading of the headlines tells whether the world is still at what-passes-for-peace. No one can count on it.

Internally, the same now-we-are-down, now-we-are-up goes on. We worry about a postwar depression and then about inflation. People are working hard at their jobs and are playing hard at their fun but in the midst of a bombardment of scares, threats of spies, disturbing tales of immorality and bribery and scandal, fears of fantastic weapons.

In such unsettled and dizzying times, trouble flares up easily. When tension mounts, pity the poor fellow who is different. When life is easy going the majority can take him or leave him alone. In stiff times the one who differs becomes a target for hostility. He may get it in the neck for doing nothing more troublesome than simply minding his own business. And schools, already out of focus and different from many parents' stereotype, are actively irritating.

Today schools have to ask continually for more of the taxpayer's money. They must charge more because school costs have increased. Books, paper, desks, maps, floor wax, chalk, light bulbs, footballs — at every turn the bills are higher than they used to be. This annoys people who are increasingly price-conscious, tax-conscious, cost-conscious. Although teachers' salaries have barely kept up with the increase in the cost of living, the taxpayer is aware that yesterday they used to be $1,400 and today they are $2,400.

Schools must also charge more because they are doing a tremendously bigger job than ever before. More children have been born. These children have had better health — they are alive and in school, learning. We all ought to cheer about this, but more children mean more teachers . . . more buildings . . . more supplies. Those darn schools are always asking for something!

This is a bad time to pass the hat. Adults today dig down deeper into their pockets for all the things they want: coffee, cigarettes, clothing, cars. Everything costs more. Life is complicated because the citizen has to stretch what is left after he has given to the government for taxes a larger share of his money than ever before.

Full employment plus salary increases have given many people the money both to pay the taxes and to buy much of what they want, but there is real hardship on some and much squealing from others.

Schools have been forced into nagging the public. A building is constructed, but by next year it is too small. More money must be raised, and an extension added on. By the next year the building is again too small. It is cruel to kill a dog by cutting off his tail an inch at a time. Some taxpayers feel that schools have been treating them that way.

In the process, today's children have not been getting a fair deal. Their class size has been much too large, particularly in the lower elementary school. Not enough trained teachers are available. Half-day sessions have increased. Parents know that the quality of the program, particularly the amount of individual attention, has declined.

Schools are not responsible. Teachers are not. The trouble goes back to the war, to the cost of maintaining an armed-to-the-teeth peace, to shortages of materials, to people moving around after the war. . . . but the taxpayer cannot blame the whole wide world. He *can* blame schools and teachers. We become that much more vulnerable.

DISAGREEMENT AND AGITATION

Much that is explosive in all of these pressures is still dormant. If schools and teachers can see the spot they are in; if they can have faith in the basic good will and wisdom of parents; if they can find effective ways to talk with parents — teaching them and learning from them — a faculty can keep the spark from being touched off.

In too many communities the explosion has already come. In some cases honest disagreement over goals or methods has upset the school. In some, honest concern about immorality or delinquency or other evils focused on the school as the scapegoat. In some communities, doubtlessly the school deserved the trouble it got by not doing its job well. Probably in most situations no one cause has operated singly. Each plays its part, and in each torn community there is a mixture of reasons.

One new note must be recognized however: Today there are organized groups, critical of public education as a movement, which stand ready to capitalize on any public school trouble. Whether or not the Edgewood School is a good school is unimportant; whether the Frankie Howes in that school have received a good education is immaterial; whether the questions at issue are simple or subtle makes no difference. A public school is in trouble and today a small minority — organized, with funds, offices, means of communication — is ready to exploit that trouble.

The September, 1951 News Exchange of the Association for Supervision and Curriculum Development (1201 Sixteenth St., N.W., Washington, D. C.) lists forty articles, pamphlets, and books on the recent wave of attacks on public education. This is an excellent source list. Perhaps the most discussed materials (ones you might begin with if the facts on the attacks are not clear to you) are: This Happened in Pasadena *by David Hulburd (New York: Macmillan, 1951);* American Education Under Fire, *a pamphlet by Ernest O. Melby (New York: Anti-*

Defamation League of B'nai B'rith, 1951); and "Who's Trying to Ruin Our Schools?" by Arthur D. Morse, an article in McCall's, *September, 1951.*

To remind yourself that attacks are not a totally new thing you should also read That Men May Understand *by Harold Rugg (New York: Doubleday, Doran Inc., 1941).*

It is always too bad when differences come to a head, when issues become confused with personalities, when opinions can be expressed only violently. In a democracy, even at this serious stage in disagreement, the processes of discussion, of interpretation, of concession can usually iron out trouble. Today an active few are on hand with kerosene, however. They are ready to keep the coals hot and to fan the flames. They want a fire; they do not want the heat to die down.

When troublemakers are about, everyone has to give a great deal of thought to security. Counting on the usual methods of protection is not safe. Fights do not flare up and then go away; they are egged on. Sores do not open and then heal over; they are infected and reinfected. Schools are in this spot today. These are not usual times. The enemies of public education have a blowtorch in their hands.

Each school needs rumor-proofing for its own well-being, and to protect parents. The time has come to knock the wind out of some of the big lies.

The parent counts on the school to do a very important job. He counts on the school to prepare his child for work, for college, for citizenship, for family life. These are not academic goals. Mothers and fathers translate them into promotions, cash in the bank, health, happiness, success, their child's survival. The parent who feels that his school is falling down on the job has every right to be upset. In fact, if ever parents are not angry at a real failure of the school you have a sure sign that schools no longer matter.

But disquiet is unfair to parents, hard on them, if it is injected needlessly and wrongly. When homes lose confidence unnecessarily in something so basic as the school, they suffer terrible insecurity. They should not have to bear this cross.

Parents ought to know about several "tests" designed to help them measure how good their school is. One that received the widest circulation appeared in Life, *October 16, 1950. The most recent is* Good Schools for Children, Southern Association's Cooperative Study in Elementary Education *(316 Peachtree St., N.E., Atlanta, Ga. Fifteen cents.). To balance this at the secondary level there is* Good Schools Don't Just Happen, *a publication of Science Research Associates (228 Wabash Ave., Chicago 4, Ill.). The National Citizens Commission for the Public Schools (2 West 45 St., N. Y.) has* What Do We Know About Our Schools? *Chapter 15 in Wilbur Yauch's excellent book,* How Good Is Your School? *(New York: Harper and Bros., 1951) suggests one hundred items for parents to look for in their school.* Promising Practices in Elementary Schools *(Atlanta: Southern Association of Colleges and Secondary Schools, 1952) is an attractive picture book parents can use as a set of standards. None of these is infallible as a "test" in the usual sense of the word, but every one of them would make a good basis for discussion with parents.*

PARENTS AND TEACHERS CAN GET TOGETHER

Our task is clear-cut: We must get together with parents and agree on good education. This ought not to be a hard job. School advances have not been thought up out of the blue. The modern school story makes sense. Teachers can be proud of it, and parents will feel good about it, if they know the truth.

These last twenty years, and the thirty which preceded them and laid a foundation for them, have brought outstanding increases in our knowledge of children. The basic research, with its outpouring of new facts and insights, has been almost as fruitful as in technical fields. The thinking about the impact of our changing world conditions on children today and tomorrow has been keen. There have been great improvements in the tools for learning: better books, much improved school furniture, more science apparatus, better lighting, tremendous advances in audio-visual aids. More conscious attention has been given to teaching as a profession, through greatly improved professional associations, longer periods of teacher training, more supervision on the job. This half century is stamped with constructive emphasis on the child and his schooling.

One fact goes even deeper: *No fundamental conflict exists between the wishes of parents and those of teachers.* Language gets in the way of understanding. Look for example at "progressive education." Talk about it in those words and you have a fight on your hands. People get emotional, and wild charges fly. Yet the parent will be the first to say: "Experience is the best teacher." And there you have it — different words, but a good definition of what progressive education stands for.

The parent, out of his life's experience, will argue: "Seeing is believing." There you have it again — different words but they add up to full support for the trips, the movies, the visitors that progressive schools utilize.

The parent firmly believes in the adage, *Make hay while the sun shines.* He does not know it, but here is the wisdom that is responsible for the modern school's great concern with readiness.

The parent says: "I'm from Missouri. You have to show me." What better case could be made for the projects and activities that are central in today's school program?

The parent is convinced: "You can lead a horse to water but you can't make him drink." Isn't this the reason why schools work so hard to achieve a rich classroom, offering a wide variety of activities all going on at once?

The parent knows: "You catch more flies with sugar than with vinegar." Doesn't this buttress the friendly atmosphere that good teachers strive for in their classrooms today?

Nor does support exist only for the school's way of working. The modern school's goals come, in a large part, from an analysis of the world outside the classroom. Parents work and live in that world. They are the ones who know.

The salesman who has faced the strain of bitter competition senses deeper than most of us why schools must give children some inner security. Security is no academic word for him; his life makes him long for it.

The foreman knows at firsthand how much cooperation really matters today. The engineer feels keenly the need for an education which gives experience in problem solving. The housewife can make the best case for schooling in the wise use of leisure time. The insurance agent is very aware of the need for lessons in healthful living. The employer knows that people have to learn to get along together.

There are here great reserves of understanding to be tapped. They do not always come bubbling up to the surface. Sometimes when parents do speak up at school meetings they say the very opposite of what you want to hear. One person accuses educators of having their heads in the clouds: "You ought to meet a payroll. Then you would know what life is like. You would not treat these youngsters with kid gloves. You would get them ready for life."

A businessman wants more competition in school; he blames us for stressing cooperation too much. A workingman wants more discipline with rigid rules and harsher punishments: "It's a tough life, and these kids have to learn to take it."

These lone voices are jarring notes. The key they hit is so antagonistic. School people occasionally draw back. We feel afraid that the commonsense practicality of the street will be in conflict with the art and science of child development.

Such harsher notes win out only when there is no real chance for free discussion. Sometimes they stem from zealots who ride one point on every occasion. Sometimes they are honest convictions but held by only a few people who happen to be more outspoken. Often others say them as an off-the-cuff stock solution which they really reject when they think about their own experiences more carefully.

The answer is not to provide fewer opportunities for the *practical man* to speak, but to provide more. When the chances are limited, only the fanatic talks. When the chances are wide-open, everyone can speak. When the chances are few, quick remedies pop out. When the chances are many, thoughtful solutions are reached.

With all people contributing, out of the experience of farm and home and shop and factory, of the worker and the supervisor and the employer, the man on his own and the man on the team, a balanced point of view will emerge. Goals really related to life as it *is* lived and to life as it *might be* lived will become more clearly defined to school people and to parents.

PARENTS ARE ADULTS

The parents you deal with in home-school relations are adults, and adults can take a fact. They can make a comparison. They can reason. Your big job as you work with them in building a better understanding of children and a better understanding of good education is to give them enough to think with.

That man sitting across the desk from you or seated in the audience may do a good or a poor job of raising his children. He may have been an honor student when he was in school, or he may have given up after eight years because long division

was too hard for him. But, today he drives a car. He buys
furniture on the installment plan. He talks the policeman out
of giving him a summons for speeding. He knows when to
laugh at the boss's jokes. He watches for bargains, pays an
income tax, holds a job. The chances are he fought for his
country and solved problems, thinking on his feet, as they
came at him with lightning speed.

That woman in your room meeting or in the PTA may be
full of questions about the school's practices, or she may have
only one or two. But she runs a house, and that is a complicated
job. She is on a church committee and carries responsibility.
She entertains. She manages a family budget. She solves a
hundred problems in human relations every day of the week.

Don't undersell these people. Don't underfeed them. Give
mothers and fathers the chance to hear, the chance to see, the
chance to think, the chance to speak that an *adult* deserves.

4. Teachers' Attitudes and Aptitudes

Just as all parents once were pupils, so too all teachers once had parents.

The real people we deal with today — the Mr. and Mrs. Cheathams and the Dr. and Mrs. Lowes who come to the meetings — may be very decent people. They may be friendly and quite willing to work along with us. But, just as we sometimes get the brunt of what a teacher once did to parents years ago, so today *we* may express feelings that really should have been directed against our own mothers and fathers.

This sounds roundabout. Yet it is hard, otherwise, to explain the coldness that parents sometimes meet. Some schools shut them out completely. One, for example, sent a notice home: "Do not come to school except in an emergency. The principal's office will let you know when there is an emergency."

Other schools seem to take a sly delight in pricking the parent on a sore point: "John is doing satisfactory work. Of course, I have to help him a lot." "Nancy is a very average girl, but I think she will make out." "I just don't have the time to help every Tom, Dick, or Harry who doesn't get his lessons."

School after school dotes on telling parents what to do: Get the children to school on time; make sure they have their lunch money; get a notebook that is just like this one; make sure they have this exact kind of blanket for resting. Is this bossiness an echo of school people's own childhood?

Even more harshness comes to the surface when some teachers talk about parents, although not to their faces: "I'm not going to have her butting into my classroom and telling me what to do." "She thinks her child is the only one in the class; did you ever see anything so pushy?" "I treat them all alike in my class and I tell parents that; they don't have to come and talk my ear off about their darlings." It is a great sin to do what some teachers scornfully call "catering to parents."

But wht parents are we so opposed to — today's or yesterday's?

Most of us loved our own parents, yet mixed in with real love can be some anger and resentment. This is not surprising. Our mothers and fathers did wonderful things for us, yet they were also the people who said *No*. We had good times together, yet they were the people who spanked us. Along with all the good things they gave us, they were the people who sometimes made us wait or who occasionally forgot. Most of the time they boosted us up, but there were also times when they let us down.

Every child growing up knows many moments when he wants to hurt his parents or get even with them or get back at them. He loves them, to be sure. But at the moment when they will not listen or when they insist or when they hold out, real fury is in with that love.

Young children show us this anger best. They are not old enough yet to cover up their feelings. You see the two-year-old clench his fist and hit his mother, the three-year-old kick out and really try to hurt. These angry feelings occur in the

later years, too, but older children have acquired the power
to keep them inside.

We forget these angry times. When we are children we
get over them quickly. Then too we are all told: "Love thy
father and thy mother," and we do. But the nice words and
dimming memories must not blind us to some of the ingredients
of that love.

Our own parents were Authority. They were Disapproval
at times. They were Punishment and Disappointment. We
found it hard to get even when we were growing up. We were
small then and impotent. Besides, it never is nice to "get back
at" your own parents. But here are more parents, different
parents: We can hit them where it will hurt! [1]

Certainly a few teachers, without knowing that they are
doing it, pay back the wrong parents — they are getting even
for what once happened to them. Certainly also, none of us
faces today's parents with a completely clean slate of feelings.
We may have our hostility under better control than the few;
we may have less to be angry about and have a blacklog of
strong positive memories. But we all need to know that dealing with parents is not a new experience for any teacher. Every
one of us worked with parents once before in our lives, when
we were children growing up.

Each one of us has to think through: Just what do we bring
with us on this second turn at bat?

*If you are teaching now, try writing out a short statement
about "The Parent Who Makes Me Angriest." After you get
it all down on paper think out for yourself: Why should this
make me so angry? Why can I take other kinds of behavior
but be so upset by what this parent does? What is it that*

---

[1] *The Saturday Evening Post* of October 13, 1951 reports on page 92 "The
Perfect Squelch" that probably delights many a teacher. A mother is being
shown through a private school and asks a great many questions of the Headmistress. After poking into every classroom and prying into every detail the
mother asks: "What kind of children do you prefer to have in your school?"
The Headmistress replies: "Orphans!"

*really makes me blow my top? As you puzzle about it you
may come to realize: It isn't what this parent does; it is something else that someone else once did.*

I LIKE "THE LITTLE ONES"

This business of self-understanding is very important. The
question comes up in still another area: How do you feel
about working with *adults?* Your day-by-day work is with
little people. Can you shift gears easily to work with grownups,
or is shifting a major operation?

Some people are drawn into teaching because they feel at
home only with dependent, immature people. You hear them
say: "Oh, I like 'the little ones,'" and they gravitate toward
kindergarten or first grade. They steer away from those big
strapping hulks in fourth grade who are all of nine years of age.

But some pull toward dependent people exists whether you
work with the first grade or with the senior year in high school.
The teacher is hardly ever on the same plane with students.
Good teachers have a fine relationship with their youngsters.
On occasions during the day no line is drawn between student
and teacher; both are simply people and get along together
that way. But these are incidents: a passing comment about
the weather, a reaction to the school dance last night, a joke,
a reference to the football team or to how the major leagues
are shaping up.

For the most part, even with the best of relationships,
teachers and students are never equal. The teacher *fails* or
passes; the teacher *grades*; the teacher *tells*; the teacher *super-
vises*; the teacher *approves* or *disapproves*; the teacher *advises*;
the teacher *punishes*; the teacher *checks* on attendance and
performance and behavior and dress.

The teacher, even the friendliest in the world, is *Authority*.
Sometimes the Policeman, sometimes the Guide, or the Instructor, or the Paymaster giving out the rewards. The teacher is
always in a superior position — except for a few fleeting moments that pass quickly in the day.

Some people use this power in a controlling way. They like the change in tone that comes over a classroom or auditorium when they step in. They are pleased by the meekness of students. They get a satisfaction in pointing out mistakes, in using the whistle or the red pencil or the chord on the piano.

More decent folk also enjoy the relationship, in a kindlier way. They like the eager look when kindergarten children wait for the teacher to continue the story. They are pleased when the high school graduate comes to see them up on his first return from college. They are thrilled when a sixth grader picks up a passing remark they have made and brings in a picture the next day that illustrates the point.

This latter type of relationship may be nicer, but the flow is in the same direction. A younger person thinks teachers are wonderful. A younger person listens and tries to do what will please.

Being on a pedestal is not the best preparation in the world for working with equals. When you teach children, it is easy to confuse yourself with God. The children are so small. You know so much. The children lean on you. You have to tell them what to do and what not to do.

It is easy to learn to like being agreed with, having your way, being the final authority. But with equals you are just one. Whatever weight you carry comes from the rightness of your ideas or the adequacy of your presentation. No crown is thrust upon you. You are not God; you are just one in a whole group of angels.

A few individuals have chosen teaching because they thrive on a higher-up position. Maybe all of us, however, have learned some ways of acting like a king---a nice, friendly, kindly soul, or a bossy little monarch. But neither role is of much use when peers, parents and teachers, have to work together.

THE TEMPTATION TO TELL ALL THE ANSWERS

The role that teachers play with children can handicap you in still another way in home-school relations. When you are with children all the time you "tell them." It is easy to go overboard in this direction with parents, too.

So many of the facts and skills that you have to transmit to youngsters are *tellable*: "Carry the one over to the next column." "This is called 'the remainder.'" "Hold the needle this way." "Always start in the right-hand column." "Make an 'n' like this." "You must water the plants or else they will die." Telling, telling, telling is poor practice for working with adults, yet you do it so much with youngsters the pattern may be hard to shrug off.

The questions children ask in school are apt to have a clear-cut answer: "What is the date of the founding of St. Augustine?" "What does an alderman do?" "What do you mean by a major chord?" You can tell them or a book can; then they will know the answer.

Teachers use this same directness in dealing with children's social behavior: "You shouldn't shout that way." "It isn't nice to interrupt." "You have to wait your turn." "You mustn't take things that don't belong to you." "You have to be kind to new people when they come to our school." "Boys are supposed to let the girls go first."

If you don't tell them, you can get a good book that will. The class without texts hardly exists. You turn to a basic reader to teach first-graders to read and, for the eighth-graders, to a text on the growth of American democracy; you turn to a text for science, for arithmetic, for spelling, even for health.

It is not surprising that teachers should be such wordy people or that we should lean so much on the written word. We have probably heard more lectures in our lives than any other group of humans. We have probably read more books — textbooks and course books — than most other humans. The idea gets under our skin that this is how to clear things up: Know the answer and tell it, or else have people look it up in a book.

Books are essential tools in all education; lectures are a valued instrument for teaching. Schools can lean too exclusively on these methods in working with parents, however. Do we

tend to think, for example, that every parent would do an excellent job of raising his children if he would just read a book
about it? Do we tend to think that one good speech at the PTA
will straighten everyone out?

Some learnings are subtle. They relate to how you feel more
than to what you know. They are relative to the people involved and to the specific situation. No one can *tell* the other
fellow; he has to think it out for himself. He needs facts, guidance, and the experience of others; but he must arrive at a
decision that is his. A good book or a good talk or a good
demonstration can play some part; but the person finds the
only answer he can act on inside of himself. He cannot get it
wholesale from anyone else.

> *See the film,* Palmour Street *(thirty minutes, sound) (New
> York University Film Library, 26 Washington Place, New
> York 3, N. Y.). Ask yourself: What makes this the wonderful
> family that it is? When you have your answers, puzzle over
> the next question: Could you get over to other people these
> essentials of family living in one lecture? This is an excellent
> film to help you see that people are good mothers and fathers,
> not on the basis of a few learned techniques, but because of
> their feelings and attitudes.*

Parents will not push us into changing our telling ways.
They are apt to go right along with us and say: "We don't
know anything. We need someone who has had experience to
tell us what to do."

Their schooling taught them that. The youngsters of 1930
(the parents of today) sat in a group in school but only as an
assembly of individuals. The teacher up front knew all the
answers. If a child wanted to talk he raised his hand. Working together was called "cheating"; each person was supposed
to keep his eye on his own desk. Thinking together was called
"whispering"; that was a major crime. Small wonder today that

people come to a meeting to listen and wait for the leader to show the way.

People were taught this blotter kind of education. The other fellow's ideas were supposed to seep in, preferably through the seat of the pants. Unfortunately many problems about children, family life, schooling, which concern parents today cannot be solved this way. Even though we teachers may also be steeped in the lecture approach and persuaded that reading a good book will save the world, we have to take the lead in involving parents in a better kind of education.

This improved education must be one which will give reassurance about their children to those who need it; give facts about child growth to those who are ready for facts; give the chance to talk to those who need discussion to clarify their thinking; give a good human relationship to all.

TEACHERS IN RETREAT

With children and with parents many teachers are trying today to swing away from a know-it-all relationship. Occasionally the swing goes too far. The teacher in effect abdicates. Autocracy is abandoned but in its place comes a do-nothing *laissez-faire*.

With children this means that since the teacher is not the boss the children *are*, and anything they feel like doing is O.K. Not many classrooms are like this, but a large amount of *laissez-faire* exists in teachers' relationships with *parents*. Schools call it "democratic" when the parents run the whole PTA, for example. Teachers are content to sit in the back row and skip out just as soon as the meeting is over. Anything the mothers work out is all right . . . "but I certainly hope the meeting doesn't last all afternoon."

Teachers hold membership in the PTA, but they are passive. In one school the organization puts on a very elaborate Spring Festival that upsets the curriculum and the children for weeks, *but the parents like it*. Another school was given heavy velour curtains for its stage. The school needed curtains as much as it needed the mumps, *but the parents wanted to give them.* In many schools attendance is taken by grades at each PTA meeting. Teachers see that this puts a very unfortunate pressure on individual children whose mothers cannot possibly attend, *but it is the parents' idea.* Often the PTA expects children in the younger grades to put on a performance at the start of each meeting. Teachers are aware that these shows are a strain on the children and very artificial, *but the parents expect them.*

The parents are responsible in each of these instances — the parents alone, unaided, working in the dark. Full of good will. Wanting to do what is right. Trying to be helpful. They are thrown on their own limited backgrounds with no check on whether their ideas are the best that could be developed. The teachers are in retreat.

It is hard to find a middle ground wherein the teacher is a contributor, a person with a very special background of training and experience, but still only one contributor. The role in which you are the boss is simple to play. And it is simple to wash your hands of the whole thing. These are the two extremes. True democracy is the third alternative.

In a democracy the experts must have a solid place, even though ultimately the people decide. Wisdom and experience and knowledge must be heard, even though in the final decision one fellow's vote is as good as the next one's. It is not good democratic action when any resource is wasted, any more than when one point of view rides herd.

There is a challenge to teachers here to find their legitimate place, not automatically in the lead as they are with children, nor resignedly in the rear as they tend to be with parents. Contributing your ideas and experience without throwing your weight around is not easy. You must let others learn by their experience while still making *your* experience available. The PTA — as an organized group or as a term to symbolize many different home-school activities — means *Parent-Teacher* participation.

A *film worth seeing in this connection is* Experimental
Studies in the Social Climate of Groups *(University of Iowa
Extension Service, Iowa City, Iowa). This does not deal with
parents and teachers, but with teachers and children. Putting
the camera right on three groups of youngsters it shows
vividly three kinds of relationships: Autocracy, Democracy,
and* Laissez-faire. *As you watch this third, hands-off approach ask yourself to what extent teachers are like this in
many parent activities.*

TEACHERS ARE OUT OF TOUCH
WITH FAMILY LIFE

One obstacle that stands in the way of close home-school
relations is the fact that not enough teachers are in touch
with the complexities of family life. Despite the common bond
of the child, the paths of the school and the home are different. Each can go along, losing sight of the other.

Today more and more teachers are married. That helps.
More and more colleges give their students some experiences
in homes, and that is all to the good. But the teacher on the
job, even the teacher who is herself a mother, becomes so engrossed in school work that she comes to believe the whole
world revolves around it.

Teachers, for example, seldom have any feeling for what the
start of a day is like in a family:

The husband who must get off to work, who is irritable
until he has his coffee, whose thoughts are all on the order
he hopes to land at 10 this morning;

The shirts that came back from the laundry with the collars
too starched;

The suit that everyone forgot to pick up at the cleaners;

The bread for toast that got moldy in the bread box;

The older girl who *hates* the one dress that is pressed and
ready for her to wear;

The boy who suddenly discovers that all of his socks have
holes in them;

The little girl whose shoes are still wet from the puddles she stepped in yesterday;

The phone that rings;

The man at the front door who wants to be paid for the newspapers;

The pencil, that should be by the telephone, which the children always take and never put back.

Schools see only the child who, hair combed and books in hand, walks into the classroom. The bell rings and the day is started . . . the *school day*, and the youngster must not be late. To the teacher's ears that bell begins the morning; actually the morning has already been long under way. In the teacher's eyes promptness is the one virtue and tardiness the one vice; actually the morning has already been full of both heaven and hell.

Teachers may be equally untouched by what the rest of the day is like. In many homes both mother and father go to work and spend their full time lost in the tasks their jobs present. While they work, all the home and family chores mount up, the endless *must-be-dones* that other mothers are giving their full time to. The shoes that must be bought for Billy — he has completely worn through the ones he is wearing;

the uniform that he needs for the Cub Scouts; a new toothbrush and a light bulb for the bathroom; taking Sally back for her cold shots — she missed the last date because she was sick.

The odds and ends that are a family range from the seemingly superficial ("I must get Betty's hair cut. Her grandmother is coming to visit us and she looks so shaggy.") to the seemingly fundamental ("At last I have a date for John at the dentist. I should have done it earlier; he says his tooth is hurting him now."). But you can rate the jobs only on paper. They all have to be done.

The range of family activities is enormous. Mothers and fathers are forever on the go — to see the photographer early in October so pictures of the children can be sent to their grandparents for Christmas; to shop in November so the overseas packages get in the mail on time; to patch those favorite blue jeans; to buy a birthday present for Jimmy (his party is on Saturday); to complain to the electric company about that last bill, and to find a carpenter who will do that little job of putting the shelves in Georgie's closet; to plan three meals a day and to buy sheets when they are cheap; to check the oil in the car and order coal for the furnace. . . .

The school sees the child from 8:30 A.M. to 3:00 P.M. He is sitting right at his desk. If you want him you just have to call his name. He is there and available. You do not see the time, the energy, the money spent, the problems solved, trips made, and the people talked to — the background that lets the child be there, sitting and available.

To get the feel of all that goes on in a family you have to spend time in a home. Don't go as a visitor, sitting on the sidelines. Take over the mother's job for a weekend! You cannot expect to see family life by baby-sitting when the children are all asleep and your main job is only to make sure that the house does not burn down.

A secondhand way of seeing a family in action is through that excelelnt film Palmour Street. *(See page 70.)* *(See page 70.)* *Keep your eye on the mother and make a note of all the different jobs she does in addition to straight "mothering."*

SCHOOL PRACTICES THAT IRRITATE

Blind to the problems of family life, schools are apt to pile on demands and requests — the special something that is a simple "one-thing" to the school but a disturbing "one-*more-thing*" to the home.

The white dress that has to be made — "All the girls in the chorus must wear them."

The song book — "You can buy them at Schlaffens" — a trip downtown.

Lunch money — "Be sure to bring it every Monday morning" — but who has just the right change, and who can remember that this is Monday?

Add any one of these to the new baby at home, the sick grandparent who must be visited, the dinner party for the husband's boss tonight, the drain that is stopped up, and the vacuum cleaner cord that is broken. The school's little "one-thing" gets magnified many times its size.

You need somehow to develop keen feelers that let you know how school action will strike the other fellow, how it will fit into all the demands upon him, whether it really is a small matter or an aggravation. No list can guide you. Each community has its own pressure points. With each school practice you have to ask yourself: Does this work out well for families, or is it good only for the school?

What about the starting hour: Is it so early that everyone gets ulcers? Or does it fit smoothly into the way these families live?

Or homework: Is the whole family getting gray hairs trying to get it all done? Or is it the right amount, considering all the demands on these youngsters?

Or expense — for books, dues, parties, dances, yearbooks, presents for teachers, room fees, special equipment, class rings, gym outfits, laboratory charges: Do these add up to what parents feel "free" public education should cost? Or do they cost more than homes can stand?

Knowing that there are two sides, the family's and the school's, can often give you the answer. Simply to raise the question makes you sensitive to it. But you often need more than your own judgment; you have to know for sure how the other fellow feels about it.

Teachers need to sit down with parents to explore what irritates them, what parents would change at school if they could, and what rubs them the wrong way.

Principals can do this through an "open office hour" — well-publicized, at the same fixed time every week — when coffee and doughnuts are served. Anyone can drop in just to chat and to say what is on his mind. Teachers can keep their ear to the ground by being available for conversations before and after group meetings, and after school.

Don't wait passively for someone to voice a grievance. Go out to ask people for their opinions. Your willingness to examine practices constantly — the little, everyday business of schooling, as well as the big major policies — is the way to make sure that paths do not drift apart.

SERVICES TO PARENTS

Sensitivity to family life is more than keeping down the irritants. You have to take positive steps too, rendering services that families need.

War-time child care centers discovered this. Working with busy mothers on whom all jobs were pressing hard — home life, wife life, mother life, work life — some of these centers went beyond the education of children. They developed services aimed at making all of family life go more smoothly.

Some services were very simple. One teacher took photographs of children at play and ordered prints for the mothers who wanted to buy them. This kindly little gesture enabled the war-working mother, who did not have the time herself, to send a photo of the children to their father overseas.

One center kept on hand a supply of toothbrushes, combs, shoelaces — the little articles that youngsters lose or break and cause an annoying, time-consuming trip to the store.

Another center sold what it called Home Service Food. Its kitchen prepared the main dish for the family's supper and sold it, all packaged, to mothers when they picked up their children. The mother, busy on a war job, was saved time in menu planning, food shopping, food preparation, cooking, and clean-up.

Many centers had Toy and Clothing Exchanges. Parents brought outgrown articles and swapped them for the discards from other families. Families were saved money and valuable shopping time.

The practices these centers developed fitted the people they served. Their ideas may be a far cry from what Glendale School needs today, or Lincoln, or East High. You and your parents will have to work out your own specifics. Your families may appreciate a photographer who takes not staged, stiff pictures, but shots of children at work and play; or a barber who comes right to the school; or a provision whereby music lessons can be fitted into school time; or a more generous attitude about letting a youngster miss some school for important shopping or needed trips to the doctor.

More essential than detailing the specifics is your understanding of the basic approach: Serve families, and they stay with you as friends. If you forget that children come from families, bonds are always weak. Remember that children have two lives, one at home and one at school. Remember that parents have many lives, as mothers and fathers and as citizens, wives, husbands, workers, neighbors. Be sensitive to all the human relationships and learn to see more than your classroom alone.

In this way you feel along with parents and think along with them; they are your allies.

YOUR TEACHING EXPERIENCE AS A RESOURCE

Each of us has to analyze his own background to become aware of the blind spots, the complicating feelings, the lacks that he brings to this new field of home-school relations. However the score adds up, every teacher can feel confident and good about one thing: *Work with parents draws on exactly the same principles as does work with children.* Probably every one of us is better prepared to be helpful to parents than we give ourselves credit for.

Home-school relations is a new field, but it is not a separate field, different and apart. It has its roots in the education that each of us knows well. It puts to work between adult and adult a conscious philosophy, a sound psychology, and a keen sense of curriculum. You use all of these every day in your work with youngsters. To make a contribution in home-school relations you have to carry these over from children, where you have learned them well, to the problem of adults working together, parents and teachers.

The one big job is to square every approach to parents with the principles that have proved effective in work with children. We have not always applied this rigorous test to our activities in home-school relations. Tradition, external pressures, mechanical considerations have been the determinants, more than sound experience on how people learn.

CURRICULUM VERSUS COURSE OF STUDY

With youngsters, for example, all of us who teach are clear on one thing: There is a distinction between the *course of study* and the *curriculum.* The former is the more narrow book or unit or syllabus that the children follow. We still regard the course of study as important, but we know that it is not the whole of education.

Today we are much more concerned about the curriculum — the broader term covering everything that happens to a youngster in school. His experiences in the lunchroom are included; what happens in the auditorium and on the playground, in the classroom every minute of the day and before school officially starts and after it officially ends; the tone of what people say, the emphases they place.

We know that children are learning all the time. We know that they are determining their behavior by the books we give them to study, *plus* every incident, every little event — every nuance. We have learned, with youngsters, that we teach through our lectures and our lessons and our assignments. *We know too that we teach through everything we do.*

We must carry this principle on up to the parent-level. It is even more important that we apply this idea to adults. With them the lessons are new, and difficult, and we have fewer relationships than we have with children. Only the consistent, steady, everything-saying-it way can build the necessary understandings. Home-school relations must be a continuous demonstration to parents of what good living and good education are. What we do to parents, what they do for themselves, must be consistent with what they have to learn.

This basic idea is a part of our know-how. Yet we are casual about it with parents. We are thoughtless about what we let them experience. We do not put our basic idea to work, with the result that too many bad lessons sneak in.

Look at the roll cal land attendance-taking at PTAs. We are struggling to make clear to parents a new concept of education in which youngsters learn because they want to. We are trying to show that children will study, if they are working on ideas they care about, and that their motivation can be inherent in what they do. We are trying to do away with all those stars and checks and prizes that we once thought we had to rely on to get youngsters to work. Once we believed we had to *make* them; today we feel that we can *let* them.

Yet we go on teaching parents the old idea. We let PTAs convey the assumption: Nobody in his right mind would want to come. . . . Nothing worthwhile is going to happen. . . . The only way you can get anyone here is to threaten to count noses (that will frighten some into coming) and to give a prize to the class with the most parents present (that will lure others).

Small wonder that many parents do not yet have a "feel" for the modern school. Small wonder too that when parents get together questions about spanking are so common. The books say, "Don't do it," but our nose-counting and prize-giving are

a kind of spanking; we punish the "bad" ones who stay away. Small wonder that parents are so confused about rewards. The lecturer talks against them, but PTAs use them to get attendance. We need to bring our left hand and our right hand together.

Our written communications to parents are another illustration. Parents hear beautiful speeches about the value of creative expression, the need for creative materials, creative teachers, and creative work by children. But when the school sends out a notice it is badly mimeographed, unattractively spaced, ordinary and unimaginative. It conveys the facts, a skeletal background, the minimum essentials — if it does not land in the wastepaper basket first. But the school demonstrates no flair, no zip. A unique, artistic notice would carry the implication: There is a thrill in creating.

We want parents to know the values of committee work for children, yet we let the grownups sit in the big auditorium and listen.

We want parents to know how important it is for children to work with others and to get along together, but we let the grownups huddle in the back row and wonder who that lady is over there in the red hat.

We want parents to get a picture of a live, problem-solving, working-at-full-steam classroom, so we let parent meetings start with the sleep-inducing routines of "the minutes of the last meeting . . . the treasurer's report . . . the report of committees . . . Bzzz."

We want parents to appreciate how a good school individualizes its work for children and how it uses many approaches to learning, yet we use over and over with grownups just one approach: the lecture.

We want parents to see teaching as a sensitive job demanding trained skill, but we let older children or anyone who is available "keep an eye" on the group of preschoolers whose mothers are in a meeting.

THE IMPORTANCE OF INTEREST

Another basic idea is today a standard part of our work with children. In the classroom we are convinced that we must begin at the point where the children's interest is. Then youngsters "eat up" their learning. They want to work hard. They raise questions and volunteer information. They search for what they want to know, digging it up on their own and bringing it all together.

Day after day we have learned: Interest is the best indicator of readiness. If you approach children on the basis of their interests they learn quickly, eagerly, and what they learn "sticks to their ribs." It stays with them and becomes a part of them, something they can use.

You know what happens, too, if a youngster is not ready: He is left cold. If you bring sufficient pressure — a big reward or a stiff punishment — he may work hard enough. But for all his willingness, the learning comes slowly. And sometimes willingness is not enough; the learning cannot be mastered now. If the problem is not real to a child you have a struggle on your hands — a losing, wasteful, fruitless struggle.

Infants have taught us this best. You can work and slave, you can bribe and threaten, but the baby who is not ready does not learn toilet-training. You see this clearly even with six-year-olds. You can have the best books, you can give endless time to them, but if the child has not grown enough so that reading is important in his life, he does not learn.

Young children show us this principle best, but the principle holds true of all people. Babies help us to see it, but what we see is a basic idea that applies as much to eighty-year-olds as it does to eight-year-olds and infants. You have to begin where people are.

Adults differ from children in one way. The short time the child has lived, his physical immaturity, means that he cannot possibly apply himself to certain learnings. The younger the child the more the problem *must* be one the youngster feels and accepts as his own.

Adults' greater physical maturity means that *biologically* they are able to work on more and more problems. Because of their maturity adults can also more easily accept verbal reasons and can see more into the future to find reasons. Physiologically, adults are in a better position to give of themselves even if they do not feel a keen concern.

This sounds as though you do not have to begin where adults are troubled, as though you can talk them into any idea. Adults "are old enough and they *ought* to be interested," even if they are not.

The same maturity of the adult, however, results in another condition which completely wipes out any leeway you might have. When you deal with children you deal with a captive audience. The law says the child has to come and stay and suffer through. The adult never "has to." He is a free agent.

In his daily life he chooses his own brand of cigarettes. He decides for himself whether to buy a 17-inch or a 21-inch television screen. He has his own favorite newspaper. He skips the editorials if he thinks they are dull and he can turn to the comics and sports page. He picks one make of automobile as the best, and he snaps off the radio when the commercials get too long.

In home-school relations you deal with this free individual. He can come or go. He can listen or doze or stay home on his sofa. Nobody can give him a *C*. It boils down to one answer: With adults (perhaps even more than with children) you must strike where the person's interest is.

This need not mean that the parent scratches his head and wonders out loud. It need not necessarily mean that he has thought out his problem and can write it on a slip of paper: "I want to know. . . ."

But it always means: *The person has to care.* The problem has to matter. It must make some difference to him. He has to feel it is important in his living. Operate on this principle, and you will uncover in adults — as in children — a combination of enthusiasm and willingness and ability to learn that will surprise you. And what people learn will affect how they act.

No doubt most of us are a little frightened at the thought of meeting adult questions head-on. In a room meeting, if someone says in an angry tone: "Well! I don't see why you allow . . ." we almost drop through the floor. We ought to throw our hats in the air. Someone is angry. He is disturbed. He is bothered enough to speak up. But our impulse is to protect ourselves and to turn off the fire. We give some vague answer, or we lapse into pedagogy. We make our reply sound good, but we shut off the person.

Some teachers are experts at winning arguments . . . and withering interest. In the safety of the after-meeting they gloat: "I put an end to that all right," and they go on to dream of other ways they might have squelched the hecklers.

Parent puzzlement is the very thing we need, but we slip away from it. We do not need the anger, but that does not have to bother us. We do need the interest, the fire, the concern. When people feel keenly, they will work. They will study. They will talk and react and respond. When there is no fire they may look more peaceful, but they are asleep intellectually.

Some change must go on inside of us before we can be truly glad when people react. Maybe we can come to see that this is our chance. This is the time to say: "That's a good question. Let's look into it . . . read about it . . . see what other schools do and how other people feel . . . watch how it works out . . . thrash through the pros and cons."

ACTIVE LEARNERS

At this point, another principle of good education is very applicable. In teaching children we are so familiar with it that we toss it off lightly in a pat phrase: *Learn by doing.* Don't be misled about its fundamental importance by the easy way you can say it.

A teacher's job, with parents no less than with children, is to involve people in activity that relates to their problem. The more the learner (adult or child) does about his question — from very active thinking up or down to physical exertion — the more he makes the learning his own.

A significant movement you ought to know about is called Education for Responsible Parenthood. From the Health Publications Institute (216 N. Dawson St., Raleigh, N. C.)

you can get a booklet, Education for Responsible Parenthood, which describes the program. The basic idea is to "help parents help themselves" — a grass-roots approach which is almost a guarantee of good learning. The booklet, incidentally, also includes many suggestions on group leadership.

In your classroom, because you recognize this principle so well, you use many techniques to involve children in the search for their own answers. Your youngsters dig up facts they need in the library. They organize into committees and subdivide the research to be done. They write to sources for information. They go off on field trips to see for themselves. They bring authorities into the room and ply them with questions. They conduct experiments to gather their own evidence. They paint murals, dramatize, and in other creative ways use the facts they have gathered, making them more their own. Even the lower elementary school employs panels, discussions and committee reports in which the children, not the teacher, are the active ones.

There is no dearth of technique. Every teacher has many tricks up his sleeve for involving children in significant learnings. As you move into work with adults in home-school relations, remember: Nothing about any of these techniques stamps them *for children only*. Every one of them is usable with parents. Every one of them is an idea that you feel at home with and can use to help parents learn more effectively about children and about good education.

STAY WITH THE PROBLEM

Your work with children will also remind you: *Good teaching necessitates continuity*. You stay with a problem over a period of time. The same need exists in home-school relations.

Child or adult, the learnings that matter take time. Each experience makes a dent; each added experience makes the knowledge go a little deeper. Significant learnings are never a one-shot affair. They are the slow accumulation of a deeper and deeper grasp.

We strive for continuity with children. Maybe we think adults are brighter. We skip all around Robin Hood's barn with them: a lecture on child care this month, a cooking demonstration the next; discussion of the school's guidance program in January, and a picnic in April. The little dent that was made smooths itself out. It never is re-enforced. Each time, like the first time, is a wasteful beginning anew.

Many reasons explain why this hop-skip-and-jump with adults is so common. The heavy reliance on outside experts is one major cause. It is almost impossible to build a program with continuity if you are willing to take whatever a speaker is willing to say, and whenever he is willing to say it. Traditional meetings — "Our Christmas program . . . the Thanksgiving theme . . . American Education Week . . . the regular Spring Meeting" — are a second cause.

A misconception about fathers also plays some part. There is a prevalent belief that men like to hear a man; we therefore fish around until we find someone in pants, regardless of whether his specialty fits into our continuous study. It would be fairer to assume that men, like women and children and all other humans, are willing to listen to anybody who has something to say about vital issues.

Men are also popularly supposed to be all stomach and no brain. Or all pocketbook and no ideas. Or all business and no soul. The meeting once a year to lure the men is therefore often a complete tangent, skillfully designed to "keep the boys happy."

Perhaps our biggest problem is a time perspective. Education and child rearing are new fields of study for parents. We forget that it takes four steady years of training to begin to make a teacher. We forget that when we were learning these same ideas we heard lecture after lecture and read book after book. Our tendency is to say these hard-to-get ideas *once* to parents, and then we are irritated when they do not understand. Our own experiences in learning, as well as our daily work with children, ought to tell us better. Ideas have to come at parents slowly, over a long period of time, and in many different ways.

THE NEED FOR VARIETY

Every day in the classroom you realize: No one problem excites all children equally; no one approach reaches everybody. You have seen this so often with youngsters that you keep many activities going on, all at the same time, so that each child can find something worthwhile to do. This basic idea must also be applied to adults.

Not enough schools are carrying over this idea intelligently into their work with parents. Present practice is like a vaudeville show. Schools, trying not to leave anyone out, turn the year's program into a variety performance: a movie one month, a social time the next; a good talk one time and a play by the children another. But the program just skips along the surface. It puts the need to meet individual differences in conflict with the need for continuity. Many interests are touched lightly, but none is stirred.

To meet effectively the wide range of individual differences we must see how big a job of communication we have. Every device through which humans can talk and work is needed, and all must be operating full tilt all of the time.

There are some times when parents need facts. The outside expert can give them, but so too can a reading panel, a committee report, a survey, a symposium, observation, participation, an Open House. Some of the facts must reach everyone. The all-school meeting is one possible technique, but so too is the *written word*: a letter, a note, a poster, a booklet, a mimeographed report, an exhibit. Some facts do not concern everyone. The Room Meeting may be one answer, or some such grouping as an Early Childhood or Upper Elementary School parent-teacher meeting. Or the facts may best be conveyed face-to-face or to small groups or through a selective mailing of printed materials.

There are times when parents need discussion and the chance to question. These mean more to them than piling on additional information. The panel may be your solution, but so too may buzz sessions or an open discussion, study groups or a personal conference.

Some questions may have easy answers that need be said only once. Other problems may be more sticky and call for parents and teachers coming together week after week. Some people may feel long-time concerns that will have to be tackled again and again in the course of a year. Others may be pressed by something urgent; the problem demands that you meet night after night to work it out.

Only as all techniques are explored can sufficient room be found for individual differences. Only as we adapt what we do to each person's readiness will true understanding be built.

5. Group Meetings

The most common means of communication between parents and teachers is the group meeting. You ought to be clear about the general purposes group meetings serve, to be aware of the variety of types of meetings, and to have some know-how in conducting meetings. With this background you can feel confident about holding meetings of your own parents in your classroom.

Room meetings are the most natural grouping. The children are the same age. They are having similar experiences in your classroom, on the street, in clubs. They are presenting similar problems at breakfast, at bed time, in play, with brothers and sisters. United by these bonds, parents have much to talk over and to think through together. If you are informed about group meetings, you can enable these parents to work together effectively.

The experience you provide through meetings of your parents in your classroom can also carry over to the larger PTA. Parents can learn in your room what a good meeting is like. They can bring an educated taste *and* experience in participation to their larger all-school gatherings.

SOME BROADER PURPOSES OF MEETINGS

Teachers spend so much time at the receiving end of meetings that we come to think of them as a natural part of life, like breathing and eating and the leaves on the trees. But meetings are only a technique. They are a means. They are man-made. They do not have to be.

Meetings are useful only when they serve a distinctive purpose. Unless the purpose is one that you and your parents are seeking, you do better to skip group meetings entirely and to turn to another avenue of communication.

Group meetings can do three things. The first purpose is self-evident: to give out information. This is valid, but you need to remember that meetings are not the only way of achieving this purpose. The written word, easily available to teachers, is another means to the same end.

The second purpose is to pool the ideas and experiences of many people. This is a unique need in our society because democracy is based on the idea that wisdom comes from the sharing of thinking. We are dubious about too much reliance on any one wise man — king or dictator, "Great White Father" or "expert."

No technique leads to this important goal as well as the group meeting, but — not all kinds of group meetings achieve this end. The simple physical presence of people does not insure it. People must participate.

The third purpose, like the second, can be achieved better through group meetings than through almost any other means: to foster a sense of groupness. People feel strength when they leave their isolated shells and merge into a oneness with a whole. The football player on a smooth-running team knows this feeling. The violinist in the symphony orchestra has it. We all get this satisfaction at times through group singing. Square dancing can give it to us; rowing in a shell; even cheering with others at a game conveys some of the feeling.

This goal is intangible. People do not often speak of it. Even so, this is no casual concern. It is one of the drives that pushes people into marriage. It is, in another sphere, one basis for religion — the wish, as old as mankind itself, to find a bigger *whole* in which the human can both lose himself and find himself (stronger) again.

Certain kinds of group meetings bring this satisfaction to people and, in turn, evoke from them a deeply appreciative response. But, like the second purpose, groupness is not achieved simply by physical presence at meetings. The feeling grows as people share, as they think together and participate, as they respond to what others say. Open give-and-take must go on or this great goal is missed.

SOME SPECIFIC OBJECTIVES
OF PARENT MEETINGS

These broad objectives must be seen in conjunction with the more specific, more down-to-earth, objectives in bringing parents together. These too help you determine whether you need a meeting or some other technique and, if a meeting, what kind.

Each group has its own unique problems. Usually, however, parent concerns fall under four big headings:

1. Parents want to understand their children's growth and development better.

2. They have questions about the school's program — areas of doubt to be clarified, ideas and suggestions to present, misunderstandings to be ironed out.

3. Parents want an opportunity to work out agreements affecting all the children who play and work together — the amount of spending money, for example, or hours of television viewing, movies, bedtimes, and so forth.

4. Parents are concerned with the wider community which touches the child, the school, and family living.. One group, for example, worked out a poison ivy eradication campaign. Another group was anxious to discuss what they could do in order that their children would grow up in a peaceful world.

Knowing this variety of concerns lets you check on yourself. Sometimes teachers are so anxious for children's behavior in class to improve that they throw all their weight behind meetings on child development; they are impatient to call in the expert who will set these parents straight on children's emotional needs. Parents may share this interest, but it is not necessarily uppermost in their minds at any one time.

You need a check on certain parents, too. One outspoken member may sway a group. He speaks up first and talks so definitely. He has the plan all worked out in his mind, and the group goes along without any mature consideration. In all democratic proceedings you must beware of the vocal minority. One safeguard is your ability to throw other ideas into the ring before a final decision is made.

There is no perfect way to determine a group's interests. You face this same challenge with your children. Sometimes you hit the nail right on the head. Other times an idea that looks perfect falls flat on its face; the youngsters' interest peters out. In the final analysis your basic protection is your readiness to change whenever you see that interest is flagging. Flexibility is worth a dozen techniques.

Adult groups often delegate program planning to a committee. Frequently such a committee uses a questionnaire to get a more definite expression of opinion than their own informal dealings with other parents can give. Very often — just as with children — some question comes up, perhaps at your first meeting, and everyone's facial expression, buzz of comment, nodding of heads almost shouts: I'm IT. Start with me.

The classroom group ought to be free to look right at itself, to decide what is important to it, and to decide whether it needs any meetings, or dozens of them. Too often some fixed concept prevails about the number of times the group *ought* to meet. The teacher announces that once a month would be about right, or tradition sets the number, or parents assume it. If no real problems exist, the group should never meet. If the problems are tough ones, perhaps people ought to meet every day for a week.

The question of "How often?" should not be decided first, nor decided independently, nor should it ever stem from anything outside. The problems alone determine frequency. The answer flows naturally from: "What are we faced with? What do we want to do? What are our objectives?"

The same test applies to the kind of group meeting. No one method of meeting is better or worse than another. No one method is good in general or bad in general. That one is right which flows sensibly and logically out of the nature of the problem. It is good if it is attuned to bringing a solution to the problem. It is the one to use if it takes you and your group to the general objectives and to the specific objectives desired.

FACT MEETINGS

Certainly the most widely used meetings are those that "tell them." This one type is employed so everlastingly and so inappropriately that you can easily feel it ought to be banished forever. Actually many times a straightforward, across-the-board, here-are-the-facts presentation is exactly what is called for.

People are stuck in their thinking and in their action. They need something to go ahead on. Someone who knows must stand up and say: "Here is the story. . . ." When you feel that people need facts, don't hesitate to have a lecture-type meeting. Imparting information is its legitimate function.

To protect yourself against the too easy assumption that a lecture is always just what the doctor ordered, keep in mind two basic criteria for this kind of meeting:

1. A lecture must grow out of something.
2. It must lead into something.

The proper and most useful time for the lecture is when people who have had some experience say: "We have gone this far, but now we are blocked." Their own examination of the problem, or the living they have done thus far, has brought them to the point where they are ready to lap up new information.

And then they go ahead on their own again.

That, ideally, is what the lecture approach should do. It

should come at exactly the time when people are baffled. Their appetite for facts is whetted. This kind of meeting satisfies them and enables them to move on in their own search for a solution. The lecture is not the stopping point, but more nearly the *mid-way* —the fresh pouring in of ideas that leads to further thinking.

Seen in this light, in its unique and special setting, the lecture is only one of many techniques for meetings. It is by no means the cure-all. Its uses are valuable, but they are definite and limited. Coming at the right time, a lecture can do a skillful job of moving people forward. Coming at the wrong time, it can stop thinking.

AT THE START OF THE SCHOOL YEAR

One right time is at the start of each school year. That is a good time for every teacher to stand up in front of the parents in his room and say: "Here are the plans for this grade. . . ."

Of course you cannot say: "This year we are going to . . ." and be letter-perfect about it. You will build a large part of your program after you live with your children. You will take many leads from these particular youngsters — what they say

and see and do. But you can say: "These are my general goals.
. . . This is how I plan to start. . . . This is the material we will
use at the beginning. . . ." *And* "This is *the why* that underlies
the program." Give an honest, frank, direct picture which
recognizes that parents are adults, that they can take a straight
story, that they appreciate getting the facts.

Some teachers hesitate to have such a meeting. They are
afraid it is not democratic. They feel guilty about pouring out
information: "I don't want to do all the talking." They try to
short-cut their story, to skip over parts of it, to hurry along, to
change the subject as soon as they can. But a straight story
right from the shoulder, spelled out in all of its detail, is exactly
what people want and need. Teachers have the vice of talking
at people too much. Your vice can be a virtue at this time!

Other teachers love this opportunity. But they want this
first room meeting for their comfort, not for the parents'. This
is the teacher's time to tell the parents: *Send* the children on
time. . . . *Don't* get them here before eight o'clock. . . . *Be sure*
they have the proper lunch money. . . . *Give* them a good breakfast before you send them. . . . *Mark* all of their clothes prop-
erly. . . . For the parents the meeting is like school all over
again: They sit and listen to what the *boss* thinks is important.

Some schools prefer to use the first PTA meeting to give
parents information about the year's work. The principal intro-
duces the new teachers, and it is pleasant in a lukewarm way
for the parents of the first-graders to crane their necks to catch
a glimpse of the new seventh grade teacher before he slumps
back in his seat again. The principal makes a speech. The
audience is so big he has to use general words like *citizenship*
and *personality* and *curriculum*. Even he says that it is hard to
reach everybody, but the words are good words, and they
have a lulling sound. Only later, when some crisis comes up,
do parents realize: Yes, but we do not really know what the
children *do*.

At the beginning of a year a parent wants to know specifically: What is going to happen to my child in this class . . . and

why? We in the school business are supposed to be good at teaching. Here is a real test of whether we know our trade. Can we do a teaching job with adults? Can we bring parents through, not vague and wondering, but with the certainty: Now I know. . . . Now I understand. . . . Now I can see the reason why. . . .

Almost surely, words alone will not do it. You have to tell your story, but that need not mean a lecture from start to finish. If you are using a new textbook this year, have enough copies on hand so that people can look through the book and see for themselves. Have copies of last year's text so they can make a comparison.

If people are puzzled about reading charts, bring out the work that last year's class did. Your group this year will differ, but at least parents have the real stuff to look at, instead of just description and words and hollowness.

If you are trying to help adults see the place of drill in a modern school, show the drill sheets you created for individual children in last year's group. Pass the sheets around. Let the parents see with their own eyes that drill ties right in with youngsters' work, that it is adjusted to that fine point where each child needs practice, and that each youngster gets drill as he needs it.

Perhaps you dramatize a comparison: "This was done at the start of school last year, and this is the same child's work at the end."

Perhaps you pinpoint a difference: "Look at page 12 of the old book and at page 16 of the new."

Perhaps you use a display to help people get under their skin some of the big ideas in good education: "These were both done by children of the same age and the same intelligence, but do you see? This youngster has matured more quickly. The other fellow will catch up, but we have to treat him as he is right now."

Teachers would do well to visit a modern museum. Once a museum was as dead as its exhibits. Visitors looked into the musty cases and said, "Uh-huh." But today museums are show places. Their directors are showmen. They have thought a lot about how to catch a person's eye and keep it, and about how to make him think while he stares.

For this first meeting, and for all the meetings that follow, you need to be imaginative in the same way. How can you turn your blank walls and your windows and the desk tops and the bookshelves — everything — into a living exhibit of education? All of this, plus what you say, lets people get their feet down on the ground. Parents like that solid sense: Now I understand.

Not that one meeting makes education clear once and for all. Many teachers have even found it wise to limit the first meeting to one phase of the grade's program: This is what I do with reading, or This is what I plan for social studies, or This is the arithmetic your child will have this year. And then they follow up the first meeting with more to come. Not necessarily one a month — that is the old formula. Such a time schedule can be too slow if people feel genuine interest. One meeting a week may not be too much if the interest is sharp.

ALTERNATIVES TO THE LECTURE

The start of the school year is only one time when fact meetings are helpful. At many other times parents will want and need a straightforward story. Even to achieve this special purpose, however, there are alternatives to the lecture. You ought to be familiar with them. Your room meetings can consider them as possibilities, and you and your parents can suggest them when the total school PTA is planning its program.

One very useful fact-giving device is called the *reading panel*. Members of the parent group go to books to get information. They read, select, edit, and then report back to the total group by reading quotations from the books they have read.

This device has many advantages. The most obvious is that it ends the deadening reliance on an outside speaker. The next meeting does not have to be geared to *Who can we get?* and *When can he come?* Meetings can stay problem-focused because people right on the spot are responsible for digging up the facts.

Another great advantage is that the members of a reading panel put some effort into finding facts. The result is that they get learning in return. This is very different from sitting back comfortably and listening to a speaker. The speaker's facts remain primarily his. He organizes them, he selects them, he says them. The audience has life too easy. The reading panel avoids this passive way.

As the reading panel is ordinarily used, every effort is made to keep it a simple and comfortable technique. The assignment does not fall on one person who is faced with a time-consuming and difficult search. A panel, composed perhaps of three or four people, looks for answers. The task is divided into as many bits as busy people can handle: "You look up Gesell. You see what Baruch has to say. You check in Jersild's book; and Mrs. Thompson, why don't you read the section in Olson to get his ideas?"

And the panel, when it reports, does not have to make speeches. Speech-making frightens many people. They are not accustomed to talking in front of groups. They worry so much that all the fun is lost and the job becomes a burden. The reading panel gives you a meeting at which famous specialists are the "speakers" with their words coming by courtesy of Mrs. Brown, Mrs. Jones, Mrs. Gary, and Mrs. Thompson. Most parents feel they can manage this task.

Another alternative to the lecture is the *symposium*. Again people right at hand can be used. Their presentations are brief, perhaps five minutes or so for each. No one has the task of filling a whole long meeting. The persons chosen — they may be parents, teachers, doctors, anybody — usually have the facts that are needed either from their training or their experience. They may turn to books, however.

The symposium differs in two ways from the reading panel. In the symposium people speak for themselves; they usually are not reporting only the thinking of others. And, most commonly, the speakers talk in their own words rather than relaying the words of others.

If local people are the participants, the symposium and the reading panel have the same advantages: The group is freed from all the bonds that leaning on an outsider imposes. The emphasis remains on the problem to be solved and on the facts needed for the solution, not on a glittering name.

A third alternative is the *committee report*. This is so familiar to teachers of children that it is worth mentioning only because we need many reminders to rid ourselves of the persistent assumption that facts for adults come only through someone labeled *Expert* who must live one hundred miles away.

Just how a committee functions depends, of course, on the problem it is tackling. One grade was concerned with its outdoor play program. A committee of parents visited all the other third grades in town to see how many minutes of play they provided, what equipment they had, whether the time was used for free or organized play, and who supervised the period. Then they reported to the next meeting of the parent group what they had seen.

Mothers in another meeting were concerned about the way arithmetic was being taught. One parent visited the state teachers college fifty miles away and talked with a professor there; another parent interviewed an instructor at the state university, seventy-five miles in the opposite direction. The Committee of Two reported to the other parents what it had learned.

Committees often look up information in books, just as a reading panel does, but they also use the questionnaire and the interview and the opinion survey. They often turn to specialists, but they also turn to other parents and to businessmen, farmers, and workers. The final answer to how they work always stems from: What does the group want to know and who can give them the facts?

Whether the technique is the reading panel, the symposium, or the committee report, the consistent element is that the group, or members of it, dig up the facts themselves. This is good education, and it ties in almost automatically the two criteria for "tell-them" presentations (such meetings should grow out of something, and they must lead into something). When a group has invested its time and energy in fact-gathering, you have a guarantee that something will be done with the facts.

THE QUESTION PERIOD

Very frequently a fact meeting is combined with some opportunity for audience participation. Following a speech, there often is a question period. The opportunity provided varies from a little chink to a wide open door.

So many people say: "This group isn't accustomed to talking in public. I really don't think they will have any questions, but you can try." Such an attitude underestimates people. Unless the presentation has been far afield from their concerns, adults will always have reactions of some kind. Even though they have had little group experience, people will speak up — if they are interested.

When you admit defeat in advance, however, you are sure to lose. The chairman says "Are there any questions?" in a timid uncertain voice that implies: *Oh dear, there probably are none.* And then, before anyone can catch his breath and organize his thoughts, the opportunity is cut off with a quick and relieved: "Well, I guess there are no questions. Thank you, Dr. Gulch, for speaking to us." And that ends that.

Sometimes the chairman limits the opportunity for reaction

in still another way. He asks: "Are there any questions?" and then he relaxes. He knows full well there will be. He has planted them in the audience.

Using stooges is rationalized by the excuse that if someone will start the ball rolling, others will feel free to talk. Aunt Tilly and the principal sit up the night before thinking of something to ask. Then at question time they brightly speak up, as though they really want to know. This is a dirty and a self-defeating trick.

Planting questions in the audience is like father running his youngster's electric trains. It is like mother touching up her daughter's painting to make it look pretty. Or like parents doing their child's homework so that the youngster can get a good mark. You are used to this back-seat driving with children. You do not like it because you want the child to have the chance to do the learning and the growing. Carry this good ideal over to parents.

You say about a youngster's poem: "It is not perfect, but he wrote it himself." You look at a five-year-old's boat; it is not a world-beater, but it is his own work. The scenery for the school play would be more artistic if the art teacher had done the painting, but you are proud of the fact that "The children did this." Keep the same standard in your meetings with parents.

You can get a "perfect" meeting where a great many questions are asked by people who do not really want to know the answers. Or you can have a meeting where the questions may not be as well worded or as quick in coming, but they come from the heart. The first is the show; the second way is learning.

A third way that limits the opportunity for participation is to ask the audience to write out questions on slips of paper. Perhaps this device has some merit. It does provide a start for those who are really inexperienced in meeting together. Some few groups may need the protection of not having to think on their feet and to speak in public.

But this approach should be recognized for what it is: a beginning way. Such a description does not disparage it. It simply makes clear that you only use this technique early in the game.

You do not want to keep a person (or a group) at the beginning stage a moment longer than he wants to stay there himself. When you have a youngster who can read well, you do not make him stay with pre-primers even though he is in first grade. When you have a child who can swim well, you do not make him stay in the shallow water even if he is young. The teaching art lies in moving along with people as they are ready to go, keeping them always up to the peak of their abilities. Don't underestimate people's readiness to raise questions.

Hesitancy about question-asking is related not only to inexperience; it stems even more from not-caring. If a presentation is simply academic, if no one is bothered about the problem, even a Demosthenes will clam up. If the topic is an exciting one, the filling-station man and the farmer, the little storekeeper as well as the lawyer will react.

Keep check both on how ready your parents are to speak out, and on the challenge you are presenting to them. More than an intellectual gain — the clarification of ideas, the addition of more facts — is at stake. The individual who goes through the process of organizing his thoughts, formulating them into a question, and speaking up to a group does something for himself as a human. The process lets him see himself in a new and stronger light. Don't deny anyone this opportunity.

DISCUSSION MEETINGS

The whole constellation of fact meetings aim to tell a story. But unless this story is heavily interlarded with the chance for discussion, it is never digested. The ideas stay in some top part of the brain for a while, and then are sloughed off. The individual needs the opportunity to make his own personal interpretation, to put his own importance on a fact, to give it his own slant, to set the fact down in the place that seems proper to him. Once the person responds and replies and reacts, the idea seeps deeper into him. There is more chance that the knowledge will affect his behavior.

Room meetings lend themselves to such discussion. The group is small and people feel free to speak up. The parents know each other well, and that loosens their tongues, too. Usually the whole setting is comfortable and familiar and informal.

The one ingredient that must be added to stimulate discussion is some common experience which the group can use as a springboard. Observation in the school can provide this base. Sometimes the previous meeting — the lecture, the reading panel, the symposium, the committee report — can be the jumping-off place. Usually it is wise to provide some new experience, related to what has gone before, as a common ground to spur group thinking.

FILMS

One of the most popular ways of starting a discussion is to show a film. Some of the reasons why this technique is so popular are questionable, however. A few program planners think about films the same way they do about speakers: "I hear they showed a movie at Riverview School last month. Couldn't we get it, too?" "I read about a new film the other day. Maybe we could show it in January." The film is sometimes chosen, whether or not it has anything pertinent to say to the group. Such a film is a weak basis for discussion.

Some committees hope that, even if the discussion falls flat, at least the film will be good. This negative attitude gets over to audiences; they sense where values lie. Yet this feeling is very prevalent. It may be a carry-over from our misuse of films with children in school. There are schools that show films every Friday to every grade whether or not they fit into the classroom program. The show keeps the children quiet, anyway. The feeling may be the product of our movie-going habits. We usually go to the movies simply to sit back and be entertained. If you start to react, the person in back of you says "Shush!"

Because these feelings are so common, be cautious in your use of films. The number of good films is increasing, but those available at this time are still so few that only rarely can a group get the film that is exactly right for its needs. The available film may be beautiful in general. Your question has to be: Is it "beautiful" for this particular group at this particular point in their thinking?

There are three useful annotated lists of films: 1) the 1949 revision of Films Interpreting Children and Youth, *by Hampel, Dale, and Quick (available for fifty cents from the Association for Childhood Education or the Association for Supervision and Curriculum Development or the Association for Student Teaching); 2)* Using Mental Hygiene Films, *a complete listing as well as a discussion guide (Lansing: Michigan Department of Mental Health, 1951);* Motion Pictures on Child Life, *compiled by Inez D. Lohr and published by the U.S. Children's Bureau, Washington, D. C.*

Instead of showing a film about children in general — whatever picture happens to be available from the film library — having parents observe on the playground and then meet to discuss what they have seen might be a thousand times more pointed. Instead of showing a film about education in general, having parents observe in the classroom and use their observation as the basis for discussion might be much wiser. Instead of showing a film about mental hygiene in general, it might be much more productive for you to present the story of some child you have worked with and to ask the question: "What would you do to help a youngster like this?"

Films have a very moving impact. They make a "good" program. But they are at their best when they tie in to what has gone before and lead into what must come after. Like so

many activities, they are never right in general. Films have
a technical excellence, and our movie-going and television
habits are so set that people enjoy almost anything that flickers
before their eyes. Yet you have to keep in mind why you want
a film: You are seeking a brief and common experience for
people to use as a springboard for discussion. The film is not
the finale to a program, but the overture; not the final gun, but
the opening whistle.

DRAMA FOR A TAKE-OFF

Because so few films are available, some groups are beginning to use a very ingenious substitute: the play, put on by
live actors.

The American Theatre Wing Community Plays has produced, and the National Association for Mental Health dis-
tributes, a set of plays that are brief, rooted right in the
problems parents feel, and adapted to discussion.

> *The scripts for three plays for parents are available:* Scat-
> tered Showers, *primarily for parents of young children;* Fresh
> Variable Winds, *for parents of pre-adolescents;* High Pressure
> Area, *for parents of adolescents. A fourth play,* The Ins and
> Outs, *written for teen-agers, can also be used with parents.*
> *Excellent discussion guide can be bought for each play.*
> *Write to the National Association for Mental Health (1790*
> *Broadway, New York 19, N. Y.)*

Promising as this technique is, only a handful of professionally written scripts is available at this time. You can get very
excited about using them in a school or room meeting: "I hear
they are wonderful" — and they are. "I hear the people at
Lincoln loved it" — and they did. But be sure that this play
and the discussion it promotes fit into what your group has
been studying. Use this technique as it is intended — as a basis
for discussion, not simply as entertainment.

These plays have one great advantage: You can put them

on when you are ready for them. You are not at the mercy of
the booking schedule of the film library. You can own the
scripts at little cost and use them when the time is right for you.

Some schools have persuaded local little theatre groups to
learn the lines and to put on the performance. Other schools
have used a college or high school drama club as the actors.
But even this much technical preparation is not necessary. It is
perfectly possible for anyone (parents included) to read the
lines from the script, to perform without benefit of scenery or
costumes, just to stand up in front of the group, script in hand,
and be the cast.

The plays are not magic, but when groups are really involved
in the human problems the plays deal with, the response is
rewarding. The audience forgets that they are not seeing a
polished performance. Their thinking goes to what is being
said, not how it is being said. Their ideas revolve around:
What would I do? and not How are they doing?

The plays have even stimulated some teachers who like
to write to produce their own playlets, geared to situations
their parents are puzzled about. The great skill these teachers
draw on is not their genius at the typewriter but their sure
feel for family life in their communities. Try it some time!

One other advantage of these plays, of all drama, and of films,
must be mentioned. Plays usually have an especial appeal to
parents with little formal schooling. So often meetings are
geared to a high intellectual level. The verbalizations and
generalities call for more experience with books and with
words than many parents have had. The dramatic approach
seems to ring a bell with everyone, however. The appeal of the
true-to-life content is a great bridge that overcomes many of
the barriers that the lack of schooling presents.

SPONTANEOUS DRAMA

A few groups have very successfully pushed this technique
a significant step further. They have turned to what is often

called *role playing*. Members of the audience, right on the
spot, are asked to make up and act out briefly some situation
that the whole group is interested in. The American Theatre
Wing Community Plays are limited in number, but the ideas
that can be dramatized are numberless. They are as many as
the problems that people have.

One group, for example, had been thinking a lot about
adolescent development: how independent that age is, the
difficulty parents face in setting limits that the young people
will accept. The chairman set the stage for the drama this
way: "Let's have someone play the part of a mother. Now
another person to play the part of a father. We also need a
third person to be their high school age daughter. The daughter comes in and announces to her parents that she is going to
hitchhike to the football game in a neighboring town. You
three people act it out for us, and then we shall all talk about
the problem."

Note that the people are playing a *part*. They are not necessarily doing what they would do in real life. They are not
demonstrating the right thing to do. They are not showing
other people what they ought to do. Theirs is a *role*. They
can't go wrong, no matter what they say. Because their only
purpose is to set the stage for discussion, the lines they make
up as they go along are bound to be useful. The actors are not
playing themselves; they are a *mother*, a *father*, a *daughter*.

People hesitate to stand up and say: "This is what I would
do." They do not like to be that publicly on the spot. But once
you assure them enough — "Just pretend. Do whatever you
think this father would do" — then some always will enter into
the spirit of the play. Role playing is like a parlor game. It is
like charades. It is acting just for the fun of it.

*You can use an identical technique to demonstrate "the
right thing to do." Occasionally such demonstrations have a
place in a meeting. One group, after much discussion, agreed*

*that it was wise to suggest substitute activities to children
instead of flatly saying No. To make this agreement more
vivid in their minds, they then held practice sessions. Some
parents played the role of the child making the difficult re-
quest; other parents played themselves, coming through on the
spur of the moment with safe and acceptable substitutes. If
this idea interests you, see* Reality Practice As Educational
Method, *by Hendry, Lippitt, and Zander (New York: Beacon
House, 1947). This is a very stimulating, idea-packed
pamphlet.*

Role playing has an element of surprise in it. The actors do
not know what they are going to say or how their character
will develop. They take their leads from what their partners
do. They may start out to be soft or stern, democratic or bossy,
but the play changes as it moves along. And it cannot go wrong.
Whatever is done is grist for discussion.

One group was troubled about how to get children to take
responsibility. They acted out a typical situation the parents
had faced time and time again in their homes: a ten-year-old
boy, and the mess in his room.

Another group was bothered about quarrels between their
children. Again they drew on material that every one of them
knew at firsthand. Members took the roles of father, mother,
school-age child, and preschool youngster.

The material comes right out of people's living. It is on tap
all of the time. The simple trick of acting situations out gives
both a focus to the discussion and a reality that sets brains
working overtime.

*Think up various problem situations which you know con-
front and puzzle families at home. See how many you can jot
down. Having a wide variety of "plots" up your sleeve will
stand you in good stead as you work with parents.*

PUPPETS

Playing a role should be fun. No good is served if people feel forced into spontaneous drama or shamed into it or dragged into it by a feeling of obligation. At first you must be prepared for some hesitancy. Some groups have experimented with hand puppets to overcome their resistance. Puppets make it even more clear that the show does not focus on how Mrs. Brown handles Grace when she is "fresh," or what Mrs. Jones does with Billy when he is jealous. The *puppet* talks, not the person. The puppet is like makeup; it hides the actor. It is even better than makeup — it takes no time and no skill to slip the puppet on your hand.

Groups using puppets have been amazed to see how appealing the true-to-life material of spontaneous drama is. Time and time again the actors start by holding the puppet up and making him act. But as they become engrossed in the play, the actors more and more forget to make the puppet wiggle. They throw themselves into the role and drop the camouflage that the puppet provides.

Of course, some people say: "Oh, I don't know how to operate a puppet. I wouldn't be any good." Usually only a little reassurance is needed: "You don't need to be a puppeteer. Just hold it on your hand and make him move every now and then. We're not expecting a perfect show. All we want is some behavior to talk about."

Jean Shick Grossman, the author of one of the most sensitive and reassuring books for parents, Life with Family *(New York: Appleton-Century-Crofts, 1948), has been the leader in experimenting with puppets in discussion groups with parents. She has put her ideas into a useful, sixty-cent pamphlet,* How to Use Puppets in Parent Discussion *(New York: Play Schools Association).*

THE FUNNY SHEETS

We have not begun to explore all the ways in which we can capitalize on resources right at hand to start a group talking. One new development is the use of funny sheets and magazine cartoons. In late years much humorous material has poked fun at this business of living with children. One recent cartoon, for example, shows a very bedraggled husband and wife limping out of a house where they have been paying a call. Very obviously the children in the house have given them a rugged time. The husband says to the wife as they go down the walk: "Today they call it self-expression. When I was a kid we called them brats."

When a group is concerned about discipline you can flash a picture like this on the wall with an opaque projector or simply pass it around from hand to hand. Parents see it, laugh — then the buzz of conversation and discussion begins. You have an easy opening into the questions that parents fret over: How far should you let them go? Aren't there some limits? What should you do when. . . . ? The start came from a cartoon in a magazine or newspaper that you would buy, anyhow.

Many cartoons poke fun at school. One, for example, shows a kindergarten child about to beat another youngster over the head with a hammer. The teacher is standing by, watching and wondering: "Oh dear! If I stop him I may give him a complex of some kind." This is school stuff, but parents wonder about it at home too. Seeing it, laughing at it, they begin talking easily about the time in their house . . . about how they heard that in school . . . about the boy they saw who. . . .

If you want to try out this technique on yourself, look up the June 23, 1951 issue of The Saturday Evening Post. *You will find two pages of cartoons by Ted Key entitled "A Few Wry Looks at the Parent-Teacher Associations." You can use these pictures as the basis for a discussion of what is right and*

what is wrong with our present ways of working together.
Keep your eye open for cartoons like these — about children,
parents, teachers, schools. Clip them out and start a collection.

FICTION

In a more serious vein, some groups have used fiction as their
springboard. Countless short stories in popular magazines and
in anthologies, and sections of novels deal with problems in
human relationships. These were written primarily to enter-
tain. They have all the holding power that good writers can
bring to them. You do not have to hit a parent over the head
to get him to read this kind of material.

Yet the stories deal with true-to-life situations: about children, mothers and fathers, parents and in-laws, modern living,
about all the conflicts and the "puzzlers" that people meet.
Sometimes the author's solution becomes the jumping-off point.
Sometimes the author simply sets the stage and makes the
problem vivid to the reader. Each person, and the group, is
left to wrestle with it and come out with his own ideas.

The dramatic quality of the stories, their readability, the
fact that these are stories about the other fellow, the accessi-
bility of the stories — many factors recommend fiction as a base
for discussion. This technique deserves more use than schools
give it.

The Study Guide, Children Are Our Teachers *(Washington,*
D. C.: Superintendent of Documents, 1949), contains many
references to fiction and autobiography relating to the years
of 6 to 12.

YOU DON'T NEED TO KNOW ALL THE ANSWERS

These right-at-hand discussion starters — the spontaneous
play, puppets, comics, fiction, and other ideas you can think

up — are a rich mine for teachers. Yet many a teacher steers away from them and even from films. We doubt our ability, not as discussion leaders — that is another problem — but as experts in child development. "I wouldn't know what to say if they got into a discussion of jealousy. I'm no expert." "I'd be on the spot if they talked about discipline. How do I know that what I do is right?" We do not want to get out on a limb where we may say the wrong thing or, worse yet, have nothing to say.

To work with parents you must have a good knowledge of child development, but you need not be a know-it-all, any more than you need to know the answer to every question your children raise in class. You would be a walking encyclopedia if you knew all that. And you would need to be a super-specialist if at every point in a discussion with parents you could say: "This is right. . . . This is wrong. . . . This is what you do."

You may get some comfort out of having one of the following bibliographies of books about children and family life by your side: A Reading Guide for Parents *(Chicago: National Congress of Parents and Teachers, 1951);* Readings on the Psychological Development of Infants and Children, *prepared by Charlotte Del Solar and Milton J. E. Senn (Washington: U.S. Children's Bureau, 1950);* The Child, the Family, the Community — A Classified Booklist *(New York: Child Study Association of America, 1947).*

Don't worry too much about your expertness. Remember that parents do not want only answers. To the world in general they may say What would you do? They may even turn right to you and ask: "What would *you* do?" The sound as though they are very determined to get a right answer from someone. Don't be fooled by this.

Parents get a lot of comfort from hearing that some other family has faced the same problem. The mother sitting next to them says "That's our home to a 'T'," or "You would think that was our Johnny in the film." Learning that someone else has the same problems is every bit as important as finding the perfect solution. The parent gets consolation and peace of mind from discovering that he is not the only one. He gets reassurance and new confidence and a fresh breath. Often these are all a person needs to go back to his problems and work out some solution that seems right to him.

Teachers frequently think that a good meeting is one which gives all the answers. Actually, the key to success is often the relief from worry that frees the parent to find an answer. Your "expertness" is not as crucial as providing a chance for people to compare notes and talk together.

Don't be dismayed even when a group really needs a fact or an answer or authoritative experience. If you do have a solution of your own, probably you should bite your tongue and not say it. If you were to tell them, that would be that. The discussion would be ended. Over. People would have your answer, skin-deep, and then everyone could go home and forget it.

With children you have no hesitancy in saying: "I don't know for sure." You say: "How can we find out? Where can we look it up? To whom can we talk? What can we do?" And the next steps in your program emerge. The absence of an immediate answer is not a sign of failure; it is a good sign of wise teaching.

Do the same thing with parents. When a group gets to that point in its thinking where it needs definite facts to go on, turn to a different kind of meeting for your next get-together. Out of this background the reading panel, the committee report, and the symposium or possibly the lecture can make its real contribution.

You will feel more confidence in this whole area if you are familiar with the various discussion guides that are available.

*The New York State Society for Mental Health (105 East 22
St., New York 10, N. Y.) has published* A Discussion Guide for
Parents *(thirty-five cents) which is designed to go along with
the following pamphlets: the* Pierre, the Pelican *series;* Enjoy
Your Child: Ages 1, 2, 3; Understand Your Child from 6 to 12;
and Some Special Problems of Children Aged 2 to 5. *The U.S.
Government Printing Office (Washington 25, D. C.) sells*
Children Are Our Teachers, *a study guide to accompany the
pamphlet* Your Child from Six to Twelve *(fifteen cents) and*
Discussion Aid for "A Healthy Personality for Your Child"
(ten cents).

BUZZ SESSIONS

One device, recently developed, is a great aid in securing
wide participation. It is a good technique to use after a film,
a play, puppets, after any springboard technique. It is even
valuable in a large auditorium following a speech. The device
goes by many names. The term *buzz session* is as good as any
because it sounds the way the method works.

In a buzz session small groups of people bring their chairs
together and talk to each other for a few minutes. Each group
is formed from the people who happen to be sitting near each
other. No rules says how many people shall be in a group. Six
is probably a good maximum, since the aim is to provide a small
circle where people will feel free to talk.

This technique has several advantages. For one thing, it is
easy to operate. To form groups you do not have to count
people off or get bogged down in machinery. The usual procedure is for the chairman simply to suggest: "Talk it over with
your neighbor and the people right around you for a few
minutes. Turn your chair around so you form a small circle."
If only three get together, that is all right. If four face each
other, fine. If it turns out that six are in a group, well and good.
Don't strain to make each group the same size. Work for
groupings that come about naturally.

A second advantage is that everyone participates. Following the buzz sessions only a few people may stand up and speak to the whole group, but now there is a buzz. The groups are small. People feel the intimacy. Each person has the chance to talk.

Each member gets the other fellow's slant too. Usually about five minutes or so is allowed for buzzing, but in this time each member of the circle hears many ideas. A modification of opinion is bound to take place. A train of thought is certain to start.

When the buzz sessions are over, the audience re-forms. Now the ideas or questions or reactions that came out in the small groups are pooled in the whole. The buzz sessions do not take time to elect a chairman or to appoint a secretary, but there is some natural selection. One person speaks up for his group. Ideas that would stay hidden in many people's breasts have a spokesman.

The spokesman tells more than his own reactions: "In our group there was a feeling. . . ." "One member said that he thought. . . ." People find confidence in reporting someone else's ideas when their tongues might be tied in expressing their own.

Buzz sessions are the freest approach to participation. If you are chairman of the meeting, they are most confidence-inspiring. The five-minute buzz gives you a chance to catch your breath and to organize your own reactions. And when you hear the buzz that goes over the group you have never a doubt about the many ideas that will flow.

You know that people have been thinking. You are sure that there are ideas galore. You can relax because you will not have to beg or cajole or pray for participation. Responses are sure to come; all the talking tells you so.

You have one other great source of joy: You have already had a good meeting! The total group discussion is bound to be good — but like the dessert after a meal. By enabling people to get together in buzz sessions, by setting the stage so that they feel free to respond, you have already done a big job. By freeing everyone's tongue you have let loose as many ideas and opinions and thought-provoking experiences as you ever could in a meeting as a whole.

Buzz sessions really give you two meetings in one. In themselves they serve fine ends, *and* they give you the basis for still more discussion. When you know you cannot go wrong, you feel safe.

THE PANEL

One widely used discussion technique is the *panel*. This brings together people who have differing points of view on a question that suggests ample room for discussion. You cannot have a bona fide panel when everyone thinks the same or when there is only one side to the question. The panel is well suited to splits which should be brought out in the open so that all can see and study them.

The panel is not a debate. The participants do not have speeches written out to read when it is their turn. On a panel, people speak off the cuff. This is an informal process. They say what they feel as the discussion moves along. The meeting gains tremendously from this simplicity and honesty and directness. Discussion is unrehearsed and spontaneous — not a staged performance.

Panels can be overused. They seem like such a good way to let a number of people participate that many panels are overloaded. So many people are invited to take part that each has trouble getting a word in edgewise. Embarrassed about keeping quiet, participants finally speak up, not out of conviction but because they think they "ought to." No law governs the number to be on a panel, but there are advantages in keeping it small. Ten or twelve people can be unwieldy, whereas any number under six can usually be easily managed.

Often the participants are chosen for their fame or social standing or because they represent some organization. The human give-and-take that the panel excels in is deadened by considerations such as: "We ought to have her." "They will feel hurt if we omit them." Don't lose the live differences of point of view in a cloud of protocol.

Sometimes, too, the panel is used as a kind of Hollywoodish super-galaxy of stupendous stars. Instead of having one famous speaker, the panel is an excuse for four or five or six "experts," all primed with their pet talk. If you want speeches, call it a symposium. This is a valid and useful technique for meetings, but it serves a totally different purpose from the panel.

When a question is a hot one, when there are differing sides, when these ought to be brought out in the open, when the problem is so real that it should be handled in the most human way — it is a shame to let a panel slip over into a speech-making marathon.

Sometimes we misuse the panel; we err, too, by not using it enough. The panel is the ideal technique for the burning issue, but many times we feel more comfortable keeping differences of opinion under cover. We like to steer clear of them. We act on the theory that if we don't recognize problems, maybe they will go away.

Our work with children ought to tell us differently. Every day we see that real needs do not vanish because they are not met. Far from evaporating, they get stronger if ignored; they take on an importance all out of balance. Yet when we face up to a youngster's need, it settles down into some appropriate place. We can handle it, once it comes out in the open. Squelched, the need festers and ferments.

Adults' strong concerns operate the same way. Some parents may be angry because they think the school has no discipline; some may be upset because they like the old ways of teaching better; some may be seething because the report cards do not satisfy them. You can pretend not to see, but the upset feelings do not disappear.

This is the time to use a panel. Bring the objections out in the open. When complaints are bottled up, everyone is at dagger's points. Once the ideas come out, you often find more agreement than you realized.

Some issues remain unresolved but the panel makes them clear-cut. You can see what the next steps have to be. Perhaps some points of disagreement go to a committee for study; the committee report is the program for the next meeting. Perhaps one calls for more research; you urge people to come to school

to see for themselves, and what they see will be another meeting. And perhaps another point calls for some special facts; that may be when a lecture will help.

THE ROLE OF THE CHAIRMAN

We are wary of panels because we do not like problems. Panels worry us, too, because the chairman's job seems difficult. The panel is in fact a distillation down to four or five or six out of a large group. The worries that plague us when we think about any discussion rise to nag us here.

A number of pamphlets and short books have been written to help discussion leaders. One good reference — specific, readable, and inexpensive — is Decision Through Discussion: A Manual for Group Leaders *by William E. Utterback (New York: Rinehart and Company, 1950).*

Any opinion meeting is unpredictable. If you have a lecturer as the mainstay of your program you know he will be there, you know he will stand up, you know he will say something, you know he will sit down when his time is up. The form and structure are safe. You feel at ease, or at least you do as soon as the speaker arrives.

In discussion, whether a panel or the whole group, you cannot tell what will happen. Maybe no one will talk. There may be that terrible ghastly silence. Maybe people's contributions will be off the beam. What if one person does all the talking? Suppose an argument starts? You feel all creepy as you contemplate the chairman's job. Simply to introduce a speaker looks much more inviting.

You can learn some techniques for chairing discussions. They do not work perfectly, and they never cover every situation that comes up. But if you know a few simple things to do, you need not face a discussion (whether a panel or with everyone taking part) with a great load of doubts and worries.

Your first job is to remind the audience of the purpose of a discussion. *The meeting tonight is to bring points out in the open, not to reach a final decision.* Assure them that every meeting need not have definite proposals with motions and seconds and action put down in the record. People may go away from a discussion with an empty feeling unless you start them off correctly.

Your second job is to state the problem. You want to say it so the group can understand clearly the topic for discussion. State it several different ways, but don't make a big speech.

Sometimes, because the chairmanship looks so forbidding, groups invite a famous name to fill the spot. And then the famous person cannot keep quiet. He states the problem, he gives his answers, he tells some jokes, and he gives his answers again. But discussion means that the panel talks, or that the whole audience does, if you have an all-group discussion. All the chairman has to do is to set the stage.

Having done that, *you shut up.* And that is the hardest lesson to learn.

We are all afraid of silences. Maybe only five seconds go by but they seem like eternity. You think you can hear the clock ticking on the wall. Your heartbeats say to you: Say something, say something . . . and you speak too soon.

Don't forget that people need time to word their ideas. They need time to put their finger on what they want most to say. It takes time for them to find the little courage they need to speak up.

Out of nervousness some chairmen feel they have to tell a story or make a joke, but this breaks the spell. You have stated the problem; now you want people to be thoughtful.

Other chairman get jittery. They tease the audience about not talking, or they call on someone to break the ice. The call comes as a surprise and creates a tense atmosphere. Everyone worries: "Maybe he will call on me next," and this chills the spontaneity that you want.

The only trick lies in not being impatient. Don't rush things. Don't hurry people along. Open up the question for discussion and then be quiet. Let a minute go by, if you have to. It does not take more than that. And a group can stand a minute's quiet without falling apart at the seams.

This quiet role continues. Once the discussion is started, your job is to stay on the sidelines. You do not argue with people, nor do you agree or disagree. You are the chairman — not the panel or the participants.

Many times, particularly if the question is a real one, you will have trouble getting a word in. Don't let that worry you. That is how it should be. People are talking as though in a conversation; the ideas are flowing thick and fast. You need not butt in; the meeting is moving along.

When you do take part, simply do the kindly thing. Let people know that their participation is welcome. This is hardly technique, not something you learn. It is just you, being a decent person, doing what any friendly soul would do: *You accept what people say.*

You do it with a nod of the head sometimes.

Or your interested look gets the idea over.

Or you say a good word: "That's an interesting point." "That's a good statement." Or you may just "Uh-huh."

These convey the idea that participation is appreciated. You create an atmosphere of friendliness that lets people feel safe about taking part.

From time to time you are more active. A chairman's job includes marking out the progress that has been made: noting the areas discussed, nailing down any agreements reached, reminding people of opposing points of view that have been stated but not reconciled. When there is much give-and-take, people do not always realize how much ground they have covered. Unless you help them to appreciate all they have done, a group often goes away feeling: "Oh, we just beat around the bush and didn't get anywhere." A brief summary at way-stations gives members the sense of accomplishment to which they are entitled and charts the path ahead.

The chairman's final job is to bring the meeting to a good close. It is wise at the end to restate the purpose that you made clear at the start: "We wanted to see how different people felt about this. That was our goal, and the discussion has done that for us." Then, just as you did at mid-point summaries, state again any agreements, any questions that are still open, any points not yet covered that remain for future meetings.

Some chairmen wisely turn to buzz sessions to help them with their job. Buzz sessions can assist you in giving direction to a meeting, for example. As chairman you want to be sure that the meeting serves the people who have come to it. Sometimes it is helpful to say: "Let's take a break here. Turn around and talk with those near you. We have thirty minutes left. As you see this problem, what do you most want to talk about in the remaining time?" The reports from the buzz sessions often indicate that more ideas are left than can be discussed. People are willing to come back for another meeting when their own thinking has made the need so evident.

Buzz sessions can also help you when it is time for a summary. "Let's stop at this point for a few minutes. We have not finished, but let's see where we are. In your groups, talk over what we have agreed on. What points have become more clear? What are some of the big ideas that stand out thus far?"

Using buzz sessions does not relieve you of the responsibility for thinking. From your vantage point you may pick up ideas that the groups miss. But with everyone reacting, everyone feeling responsible, important ideas stand less chance of being lost. If you are not sure of yourself as a leader of adults, it is a good feeling to have the whole group working along with you.

Of course, it is easy to say what a chairman *should* do: Clarify the purpose of discussion, state the problem, then shut up; accept what people say, point out agreements, then summarize. These jobs are not really hard, but it is easier to read about them than to do them. The reason why is People — those who talk too much and those who do not talk enough; those who talk too forcibly and those who wander up hill and down dale.

It takes art to deal with individuals. No tricks of the trade always apply. But some guides can help you over the occasional rough spots.

Take the fellow who talks at great length, interrupts others, and keeps on talking a blue streak. Sometimes you can say: "You've helped us a lot so far. Let's hear from some of the others now." The little praise satisfies, and he may be quiet for a while.

Another member wanders away from the topic. Often you can keep the discussion on the track by saying: "That's a good point, but let's save it until later."

If feelings run too high you may be afraid that, instead of being helpful, the discussion will hurt. To avert this, try saying: "Well, we seem to disagree here. One point of view is this. . . . Some of the rest of you are saying this. . . . Let's agree to disagree, for the present, and go ahead to the next question."

A chairman, like a good teacher, has to keep an eye on those who talk too little. These quieter members may have good ideas that the group needs to hear. You seldom do any good by calling on them directly. This shoots a note of fear into the meeting and tightens everyone up. You can call on the group in general however: "We need everyone's help. All of you feel free to take part." This open hand will encourage a few. Or you can be more specific: "Many of you have talked so far. Let's give everyone a chance. If you have already spoken, wait a while. Let's hear now from those who haven't taken part yet." Often the people up front talk the most. You can say: "You in the front have been a real help, but we want to hear from the back rows, too."

Whatever you do, don't nag. Don't make an issue of participation by trying too hard. Don't make people self-conscious. If they don't contribute to this meeting, there will be another. Watch people's eyes and mouths and their expressions so that you can give each person a chance to speak when he is ready. But if you press too hard, people will take longer to feel at ease.

USING AN OBSERVER

In some groups — particularly study groups which stay together through several meetings — an *observer* can be helpful. This is the name given to one person officially charged with keeping tab on the flow of the discussion. The observer may volunteer for the job, or be chosen by the group. He becomes a right-hand man to the chairman but, more important, he acts for the group. He does for the group what it would do for itself if the members could stand on the sidelines and watch their own performance. The observer is a means of insuring the maximum and most helpful participation. With this understanding he can speak freely, and no one is offended. He is telling the group what it wants to know.

There is no special technique for getting the observer's reports. Sometimes he breaks into the discussion when he feels that his records give him something important to say. More often the chairman calls on him for a brief report when there is a lull.

The observer usually tries to record how many people are participating. He may report, for example: "Forty of us are here, but my records show that only eight have talked so far." This factual analysis is both a tip to the chairman and encouragement to others to take part.

The observer also tries to keep track of *who* is contributing. He may show, for example: "There has been a lot of participation, but almost all of it has come from the old-timers. No mothers who are new to the group this year have spoken up yet. Only one of the fathers present has taken part." When many people are talking it is easy to confuse participation with widespread representation. If the many voices all speak out of the same background, the group loses ideas.

An observer can also be helpful by watching the nature of the discussion. There may be a lot of talk but, when you analyze it, you see that much of it is in the form of a question from the audience, an answer from the chairman. The pooling of everyone's experience is missing.

The technique of having an observer has been used in many professional meetings and in some parent groups. It does not fit every situation. Some groups become self-conscious if they know they are being watched; people who have not had much discussion experience are very apt to feel this way. Some groups are so small that an observer piles on too much structure and formality. When it is right to have an observer, however, one pair of eyes and ears charged with following carefully how the meeting proceeds can be a real help to a chairman and to a group.

You can practice playing the role of observer in a college class if you are a student, or in faculty meetings if you are a

*teacher. Doing it yourself will show you how it works; it will
also sharpen your insight into a chairman's job.*

PUTTING THE AUDIENCE AT EASE

One suggestion applies to all meetings, to those within the
classroom and to the PTA, to Fact Meetings and to discussions:
Make people feel at home.

In your room meetings, introductions may not be necessary.
People are more apt to know each other; that is one reason why
your meetings can be so good. In larger gatherings — groupings
such as an Upper Elementary Parents Meeting or a Primary
Meeting or the PTA — many may not know their neighbors.

Even within the classroom meeting, however, you cannot
be sure that everyone is known. Our increasingly urban and
suburban and mobile modern society keeps people strangers.
The teacher can make a useful contribution by always keeping
in mind that there may be newcomers.

Most often meetings are called to order with no attempt
made to introduce people. We do our business and go home.
Occasionally each individual is asked to stand up and introduce
himself. Formal self-introductions have two disadvantages:
They are time consuming and not well suited to large gatherings; they make many in a group uncomfortable. People usually
do not enjoy talking publicly about themselves; they slur over
their names and try to creep back into their shells as quickly as
they can. When they sit down their hearts are beating faster
than they like.

A better alternative is for each person to introduce the
neighbor sitting on his right. The chairman provides a few
minutes at the start of the meeting for these people to get
acquainted. He urges each one to pry good-naturedly into the
other's life and to come up with a few highlights that will make
the person stand out when the introduction is made. This can

be good fun. It is easier to talk about the other fellow than oneself. The introductions can be done with a real flourish that lends a note of humor and informality.

This method is also time consuming. And it may not achieve its full purpose if old friends sit together. It also puts some pressure on people who do not enjoy talking in public. Some say: "This is a good experience for them," but it is doubtful whether much helpful learning comes out of unnecessary and man-imposed suffering.

The buzz session can be used as a third and very helpful alternative. In five minutes or so people feel at home with those immediately around them. Morale springs into being. At later meetings the circle of acquaintance can always widen.

"THE MINUTES OF THE LAST MEETING"

The written word has certain uses in connection with meetings. Particularly in large gatherings so much time is consumed with the minutes of the last meeting, the treasurer's report, the reports of the various standing committees, and announcements by the principal. The history or routine news may be important, but listening to it puts everyone to sleep.

Much of this information could be in printed form, and placed on the chairs for the audience to read as they come in. People can look over such material while they are waiting for the meeting to start; they can take it home with them to read in the bathtub. Save precious meeting time for the more human touch.

After every meeting, too, there is always the wail: "If only the people who need it most had been here!" Why not mimeograph a summary of the meeting's highlights and mail it to the absentees? Why not mail the summary to everybody, those who were present and those who had to be away? We all know that so much of what is said goes in one ear and out the other, even when we are interested. A written record can be a great help.

In group meetings we must guard against expecting the ear alone to carry the full load of understanding. If you are telling a group of parents about the daily schedule in your class, mimeograph it. Then everyone can have a copy in front of him and a copy to take home. If you are discussing why one book was chosen and not another, mimeograph the advantages and disadvantages; then people can have the facts right in their hand.

If we are going to meet, we must take meetings seriously. If we are going to use time and energy, we ought to feel a responsibility for getting a return *in action* from the expenditure. The strategic use of the written word can nail down agreements, point up findings, clear the record on what was said, and hit once again at the important ideas.

WORK AND PLAY MEETINGS

Not all meetings have to deal directly with ideas or rely on words as their major technique. Many teachers have found real value in purely social meetings. Often these are supper meetings, a potluck with each family bringing some part of the menu, such as spaghetti, a salad, or some other easily prepared dish. When the weather is right, a classroom picnic outdoors can be the answer.

A party meeting is primarily for fun. Parents get a chance to know each other better. They see you as the teacher as well as each other in an informal, friendly, easy-going setting. The simple conversation, the good humor, the sharing of food, can lay a foundation on which later working relationships can be built. Many teachers regularly schedule such social meetings early in each year for this very reason.

Yet these fun meetings are more than preparatory. The

teacher is free to circulate, to chat with one parent and then another. Much of the talking is about the food, the weather, and the events right at hand. Often, serious conversations about children, school, and home and community life start up. These meetings switch back and forth from sociality to serious ideas as the conversation flows.

You can turn to work sessions, instead of to food, to bring parents together. Parents are invited, in the evening or on a Saturday, to come to school to do a job: to repair books or toys or equipment; to paint the locker room or the classroom; to landscape the grounds or to make curtains for the windows. But more than manual work gets done. The informality of the atmosphere makes it easy to do a lot of off-the-cuff talking about children, too.

These seemingly nonintellectual gatherings carry their fair share of intellectual content. In an offhand manner, many a good idea gets under a parent's skin. Many a key fact penetrates a teacher's mind, even though it comes by way of a joke or a passing pleasantry. Sometimes a great deal happens, even though very little may seem to be planned.

Good as both these types of meetings are in general, they must be used sensitively. Families fatigued by the hard job of earning a living may not need a work session. Parents plagued by the high cost of living may not appreciate being asked to contribute to a potluck supper. Mothers and fathers with full social calendars may not welcome a get-together that has no fixed agenda.

Some teachers combine the two ideas of work and fun by inviting parents to a meeting where the adults will have some of the same experiences that their children have in school. Parents of younger children finger-paint, for example. They build with blocks. They work at the easels or at the carpentry bench. Parents of older children sit at the desks, while the teacher teaches them a lesson as if the parents were the children.

Many of the same values — fun, good fellowship, building relationships — come through this type of meeting. Because this is an artificial setting, and because a child's response to problems and materials is different from an adult's, most teachers who use this technique are sure to provide ample chance for discussion, for reaction, for questions. Doing as the children do serves as a springboard for discussion, rather than as an end in itself.

6. Face-to-Face Relationships

Group meetings have long been the standby in home-school relations. The recent trend of supplementing the all-school PTA with many smaller room meetings is one step toward greater individualization and more personal relations between parents and teachers. Countless schools are taking the next logical step: They provide opportunities for individual teachers and parents to talk together face to face.

There are, of course, many kinds of such conferences. They range from a very fleeting conversation to the fixed-time, let's-sit-down-and-talk meeting either at home or at school.

The more on-the-run conferences, the easier the full-dress meetings are to manage. Parents and teacher have practice in talking together; they iron out many minor difficulties as these come up. A mutual trust is established.

To lay this groundwork, many schools open their classrooms a half-hour or so in the evening before the general PTA meetings. Parents who can, come early. They see their children's work in the desk and on the wall. The teacher is available for a brief how-do-you-do, and whatever that might lead to.

Usually the time is short. Other parents are around. The general meeting will start at eight. This is not the time for a rounded discussion of an individual child. These brief chats strengthen a relationship, however, and give some indication

131

of parents' interests and concerns. Areas are opened up that
can be explored when the setting is right.

Wise teachers seek out such opportunities at the PTA meetings. They do not sit in a row at the back but mingle with
parents. They do not busy themselves with administrative
doodads — the lighting, the curtains, the refreshments — but
are out where mothers and fathers can see them and talk with
them.

Some schools end their meetings with a "sit-down" cup of
coffee and a doughnut. This is not the polite drink-some-punch-
and-run — an awkward milling around in the hall with everyone
anxious to go. It is a planned time, arranged so that teachers
can relax with parents and talk with them.

When many such relationships prepare the soil, a Conference
labeled with a capital C and a Report labeled with a capital R
alarm no one.

THE HOME VISIT

One fast-growing practice is for teachers to visit the homes
of all of their children. In some schools, home visiting has
already become crystallized into a regulation: "You must visit
every home at least once." "You must visit every home within
the first month."

Home visiting is not a new idea. Countless teachers, particularly those working with young children, have long done it.
Raised to the level of a regulation home visits have a new and,
to some, a frightening sound. "How do you do it?" "What are
you supposed to look for?" "Suppose they won't let you in?"

So far as the technique of initiating a home visit is concerned,
no teacher need worry. In the first place, all that we have said
about the love parents feel for their children comes to bear
here. Worries about cold receptions, hostile looks, getting a
foot in the door, and so forth, are groundless. There always
will be individual exceptions, of course, but the simple fact that

you are the child's teacher and interested in him will assure you of a royal welcome in almost every home. Parents are delighted with the chance to talk with their child's teacher. They are pleased that you take the time to come to see them. They are emotionally moved, sometimes outwardly, that you care enough about their child to come.

Equally reassuring to those who worry: Every teacher already knows all the technique needed to arrange a visit. You did not learn this in the course of your professional training. Your whole life has taught it to you.

Nothing in making a home visit differs in any way from the countless other visits you have made in all the years of your past: visits to new neighbors, to church members, to fellow alumni of your college, to new colleagues. There are no special things to beware of, no special things to be sure to do, other than those "common-sensical," decent, and polite things which all of your living has already taught you to do.

Obviously, you do not drop in on people whom you do not know well without some advance warning. You telephone ahead, or perhaps write a note. You say the simple words that are self-explanatory: "This is Mary Jones calling. I am Johnny's teacher this year. I would like to drop in just to say Hello and to get acquainted." No further explanation is needed; this is more than sufficient to assure you of a ready welcome.

Obviously, you do not set the time yourself, with no regard for the other fellow's plans, any more than for any other visit. Obviously, you do not give a half-hour's notice, as if you and your visit were the only event in the parents' life. You ask, as you would under any circumstances: "What would be a convenient time for you?"

Obviously, you do not stay after easy conversation has ended. You do not stay if the baby is screaming upstairs, or if the supper is boiling over on the stove, or if your hostess is fidgeting to get dressed to go out. Your sensitivity, developed through years of visiting, tells you when to go.

Nor need you be any more tongue-tied than you ever are. Talk about whatever you and your hostess mutually enjoy: crops, the weather, the flowers and trees, politics, baseball, the news. Start with the natural things to say that would come to anyone's mind as they walk into a new home: the lawn, the path, the coolness of the house, the attractiveness of the drapes, the good-looking lines of the house—the kind of friendly opening move you have made a thousand times in the past.

You know, from your work with children as well as from other visiting you have done, that parents vary. Some will be talkative, more than you are. Some will be quiet, more than you are. Some will be completely at ease, some a little tense. No effort is required to chat with some; your first remarks or theirs will immediately ring a bell, and the two of you are off. With others, you may need to explore a bit before you find the area of conversation that interests the two of you.

No teacher should worry about home visits, but it is no surprise if, the first time, many parents wonder: *Why is she here? What does she want? Is anything wrong?* Home visits are as new to parents as they are to most teachers. Your initial explanation—"I just want to say *Hello* and to get acquainted"— and your easy friendly manner will soon break the ice. You have met reserve and suspicion before. The right way to act and the right words to say will come easily to you.

Obviously, more time will be needed—it may take two visits or three—with those parents whom life has taught to be suspicious: perhaps the lower-income families to whom a knock on the door has always meant trouble; perhaps those families whose own past school experiences were harsh; perhaps those with older children who have been in continuous trouble with the school. But if life has made certain families less sure in their human relations, you can count that these are the families who eventually will be most warm in their relationships. When they discover that you have no axe to grind, no bad news to bring, that you are simply a friend coming as a friend, their relaxation will be particularly gratifying.

THE REASON FOR HOME VISITS

You come as a friend, but you come to know the family better and, through them, to know the child as an individual. You do have a hidden motive. Your first goal is simply to say *Hello* so that two members of a team, parent and teacher, can be acquainted with each other. But the ultimate reason for this acquaintance is to know the child in his full color, shape, and form as a person.

Some schools have lost sight of this purpose. A few insist on home visits because they are "the thing to do." A few insist on home visits because they make some contribution toward "selling" the school; it is good (but vague) public relations if citizens have a chance to see teachers face to face. But home visits basically make sense only if a school's curriculum necessitates that teachers know individual children.

The big thing a home visit can do for you is to make a child come alive. It can give you the information you need to tailor-fit your program to every single child—his interests, his strengths, his needs.

Home visits are the necessary support to a modern program of education, whether you call it the activity program, the core curriculum, a child-centered program, a life adjustment program, or by any other name. Each of these means that the school is continuously geared to its present children.

In a book-centered program, in a standard and fixed curriculum, in a program with set grade standards, home visits can tell you little that you can use and put to work. In such programs the individual, no matter what he is like, must adjust to the school, or be failed. The school has no give; the individual must fit in. Under such conditions home visits can only result in the accumulation of useless information. They can lead to full files, but they cannot lead to action. Then home visits seem to teachers like an added chore and a waste of time. Parents' doubts do continue: "Why *is* she here?" It is hard to find things to talk about.

What do you need to know about a child in a modern school? Everything! What are you trying to find out about a child in a home visit? Everything! You want to know his personal past and his private present and his own very special future. Parents are the people who can best reveal this. Home visits are one area of home-school relations where clearly the parent has a great deal to give. He is the one person who knows the child and knows him well.

HOW TO COLLECT INFORMATION

Nursery schools were the first to make home visits. Teachers of very young children needed to know as much as they could about each child. As a result, they originally developed long and detailed questionnaire forms. Sometimes the teacher filled these out at the time of the first home visit; sometimes the form was left with the parent at the time of the visit to be filled out later.

Many public schools, feeling their way in this area, have followed this early nursery school practice. They have developed long questionnaires, which serve as the agenda for the home visit. In so doing schools face two pitfalls.

The first trap lies in collecting more information than can ever be put to work. Beware of developing something long, just because it seems the "modern" thing to do. Too many forms have been painstakingly filled out—and filed.

The second trap is more serious. Much as you may need information, beware of collecting it all in one fell swoop at the very start of a relationship. Too many questions can take a parent's breath away. The parent does not yet know the school well. Who are they anyhow to be asking all these questions? The parent does not yet have a close feeling toward the school. "It took me hours to fill out that darn form, and just when I was head over heels in shopping for school clothes." The parent

does not yet know the school program and why full information
is needed. "I cannot see that this is any of their business."

*Write to a group of schools for a copy of their entrance
questionnaire. As you examine those that are long, keep asking
yourself: "It this question necessary . . . now?" Put yourself in
the position of the parent filling out the form. How do you
think a parent might feel?*

In the long run you will need information that goes back to
the child's very early life:
When did he get his first teeth?
When did he say his first word?
At what age did he sit up . . . stand alone . . . walk?
These questions, and others like them, getting at a youngster's early development are important. The answers can give
very valuable clues to a child's rate of development. They can
give many leads into how early or how late a youngster is apt
to be ready to read, to work well with others in a group, to follow school routines, and so forth.
You will need information that makes parents plumb the
depths of their memories:
Has he had measles . . . mumps . . . chicken pox . . . whooping
cough . . . and, if so, when?
Has he had inoculations against typhoid . . . diphtheria . . .
whooping cough . . . tetanus? If so, when? And on what dates
did he have his booster shots?
All this, too, is important for a school to know. And there
are still more questions designed to get at the youngster's
susceptibility to colds, his food likes and dislikes, allergies, his
sleeping patterns, his amount of activity, and so on.
You will have questions that are hard to give a definite
answer to: What are his special interests? Does he make

friends easily? What toys particularly appeal to him? What fears does he have?

Other questions take a long time to write the answers to: father's name . . . father's education . . . father's business . . . and address . . . and phone number. Physician's name, address, and phone number. Other adults living at home. Other children at home . . . their birthdays. Other children in school . . . their present grade.

Sometimes the questions pry into personal affairs or sore points with some families: Was the child breast-fed or bottle-fed . . . and for how long? Does his father spend much time playing with him? Do mother and father agree on ways of discipline? What is the favorite method of discipline at home? Do you spank your child?

No doubt a good school needs all this information. No doubt it takes a long detailed form to record the complete picture of a child's growing up. There is real doubt, however, whether the information has to be collected all at once, whether it has to be collected at the first interview, and whether parents have to be the ones to fill out the lengthy form.

A good new practice is for teachers to fill out the form, *adding information gradually as they come upon it in their many relationships with parents.* Your first home visit gives you the answers to many questions that are on most forms. You do not snoop, but walls and rooms talk. The path up to the house has something to say. The basketball standard in the backyard shouts at you, and so does the big tree in the front with the swing hanging down. You learn through all you see more than you ever could through your questions, and then later you write down what you have learned on the form yourself.

You do not have to ask a parent: "What is your educational level?" You want to know because the answer will help you make more sense out of Billy. But, without asking the question, you hear the mother speak grammatically with an easy flow of words. You see books in the bookcase, pictures on the wall, a phonograph, the pile of magazines on the coffee table by your side.

You do not have to ask: "Tell me what goes on at home?" On the wall over the mantel is a picture made by Billy. The baby cries in its bedroom; grandmother walks in and is introduced; the dog barks in the backyard. You are struck by the absence of brittle, breakable bric-a-brac. This house says *livability* to you.

You visit the small house that bulges with people; the old house in a solid section of town (and grandmother lives right down the street); the not-so-old house where the neighborhood is going down. You see workshops in the basement, pup tents in the backyard, trucks roaring down some streets; a '47 Ford in one driveway and a station wagon in the other; the Madonna on one mantelpiece and the cubist painting over another.

All behavior tells you something. All responses. All choices and decisions. Everything comes with its overload: a comment, *plus* the person who words the comment in that particular way.

You walk in and talk first about the weather. Mrs. Jones says: "Hasn't it been cold and dreary . . . !" and you wonder: Is this her approach to life? A little downcast, perhaps a little on the sour side, life always hard to take . . .? You may be completely wrong, but you have a hunch.

Mrs. Brown has not even noticed the weather: "I've been so busy doing so many things. There is always so much to do. I seem to be on the go every minute." You hear the words and your puzzling begins again: A hectic person, perhaps, hanging on by her fingernails? A person who has to be busy—*Look at me, I'm important*—perhaps? A healthy, vigorous, efficient somebody, perhaps? Your hunch will depend on the tone, on what has gone before, on facial expression.

Mrs. Franklin says: "I hate the dampness because of Georgie's sinus." Is this overconcern and a tendency to (s)mother?

Mrs. Clark tells you: "The leaves have made our place a

mess. I've had to rake every day, and it still looks so awful."
Is she a perfectionist who likes every leaf in its place . . . and
every child straight and tidy?

You do not get conclusions or facts salted down. These are
guesses, hunches, impressions. You feel them; people do not
spell them out for you. If you take them as definite at this
point, you go beyond what you have; you read into them more
than you know. Keep all this in the realm of hunch. You will
hear more later, see more later, puzzle more later. You may
toss aside your first idea. Or, having listened, you may find
it confirmed.

A great deal of information comes at you. Some is clear-cut,
concrete, and factual; much is just the vague start of a story to
be picked up later. Your emphasis on the first home visit is
not on information, however; you are trying to build a relationship. You know that this visit is not your only crack at parents.
If you both feel at ease you will see a lot more of each other in
the future. There is time ahead. A long stretch of time.

You may need to ask a few direct questions about the child.
The nursery school, for example, must know: "What word does
he use when he has to go to the toilet?" First grades usually
want to know: "Whom should we call in case of an emergency?"
These one or two or three specific questions can be asked. No
one is floored by them. But it is good to keep the number down
at the start.

If anything is really important, you can be confident it will
arise in conversation. James may be very allergic to milk.
You certainly have to know that; but a parent, even more certainly, will volunteer the information. Mary's activities may
be severely limited by her doctor's orders. You need to know
this but a parent, from a stronger compulsion, has to tell it.

When you stress the straight collecting of information you
make the parent more reserved. Put your emphasis on building
a relationship. This encourages people to open up. Through
the years parents who are at ease will tell you even more about
their youngsters than you would ever think of asking.

*Chapter 3, "Seeing the Child as a Member of the Family,"
in* Helping Teachers Understand Children *(Washington, D. C.:
American Council on Education, 1945) gives a very good
and specific account of this gradual way of building up a
picture of a child.*

MAKING HOME VISITS POSSIBLE

Some schools want all the good they can wring out of home-
school relations. They will take whatever benefits come along,
but they do not want them enough to make any major readjustments. They are glad to talk about working with parents.
When it comes to the doing, they want the easy way out.

A school cannot take on a new concern for parents and still
go along in all its old ways. The words "home visits" can be
said as quick as a flash, but does the teacher use his own car
and gasoline to make these visits? And how many flashes does
it take in consolidated school districts for the teacher to drive
ten miles to where the parent lives? Even in close, compact
neighborhoods the question of transportation is a troublesome
one.

It is easy to write that the teacher who visits homes comes
back laden with information—facts and leads pop out at you
at every turn. But does the information stay in your mind, or
what does happen to it? The more you know the more you
need time to write it all down, the more you need a desk to
write it at, the more you need a file to keep it in, the more you
need secretarial help so the writing does not become a greater
chore than it is worth.

Hard as these problems are, the whole question of time is
even more difficult. In the past, those teachers who have
visited homes have found the visits so rewarding—so satisfying
to parents, so productive of support for themselves, so con-
ducive to making a joint plan for a child—that they have been
willing to make time for the visits after school, evenings, and

weekends. Obviously this is extra work. Occasionally such teachers are teased by their colleagues: "What an eager beaver! . . ." "Are you trying to be a principal? . . ." "Relax. You are making life hard for the rest of us."

These teachers make visits because they feel that their work is lightened in the long run. Even if you have to work out all the mechanics yourself this is true: When you know your families, life goes smoother; when parents know that you care, they will respond with warming support.

More and more schools, however, want the benefits so much that they are willing to make administrative adjustments. Some schools hire their teachers for more months of the year so that home visits can be made before work with children actually begins. Some have half-days of school at the start of the year; mornings are used for work with children, afternoons are available for home visits. In the course of the year, a few schools close down completely for a day or two. The children do not come to school, but their parents get an education. Occasionally, the school day is cut short to give an hour or a half-hour at the end of the day for adults to talk together.

Some few schools think home visits are important enough to warrant paying substitutes so that the regular teacher can have the time for leisurely visits. Once in a blue moon the principal sees here a real contribution that he can make to home-school relations. He takes over the classroom while the regular teacher makes her visits. If there is a high degree of parent participation in the classroom program, a teacher can turn over her group to some parents while she scoots out to get acquainted with others.

REPORTING TO PARENTS

Some schools never make home visits. They do not want their parents to observe. They will not let them participate. They have hardly any meetings of any kind. They think they do nothing which could be called parent education. They always use one tool, however: the report card.

Some schools have never thought of writing leaflets or bulletins or newsletters or notes. They use one form of written communication with parents, however: the report card.

The report card is routine business to these schools. They use it in an offhand way. They send home a *B—*, a *Satisfactory*, or an *Improving*. They write in red pencil on a theme. They give a *76* on a spelling test. Rating children, grading them, comparing them, and describing them is run-of-the-mill stuff. They do not think of it in the same breath as "parent education," "teachers and parents working together," "a community that supports its schools," and all of our other fine phrases in home-school relations.

A good booklet on this whole area is Reporting to Parents *by Ruth Strang (New York: Teachers College Bureau of Publications, 1947). The Association for Childhood Education International has an older but still useful pamphlet,* Records and Reports *(1942).*

Other schools see reporting as one of the crucial activities in working with parents. More and more of these schools are turning to face-to-face conferences with parents as their report card. The individual parent-teacher conference is the most promising step in a whole series of changes in ways of reporting that schools have made. In understanding this particular kind of conference it helps to know the intermediate steps that have led to it.

The initiative for change in schools' ways of reporting on children has usually come from educators. Sometimes their urge to tinker stems from a superficial cause. A school simply wants to do something different. The report card is a visible material *thing;* it is right out in the open . . . sitting . . . waiting for someone to come along and fool with it.

The strongest pressures, however, come from the deeper knowledge of today's teachers. Our growing understanding of children and of this changing world creates the need for revision. We want a report that makes more sense today than the old letter grade—*A,B,C,D,E;* or the numeral—*90,80,69;* or the generality—*Satisfactory, Improving, Progressing.*

For one thing, the modern school's concerns have broadened. The three *R*'s stay important, but there are so many other *R*'s: Reliability, Responsibility, Reasoning, Rhythm . . . There are *A*'s for Appreciation, Adjustment, Aptitude . . . *B*'s for Balance, Bladder Control, Bounteousness, Bravery, Buoyancy . . . *C*'s for Cooperation, and so on through the whole alphabet. A child cannot survive if he is prepared only in three areas of living. The sheer weight of the number of the school's objectives breaks down any single grade concept.

The nature of many of these new objectives also outmodes any simple flat score. It is impossible to translate many of the new goals into a *B* (plus or minus), into an 83 or a 79 or a 62. Conceivably, some day in the far future there may be objective tests of behavior that will produce scores like these in intangible items. At this point in our knowledge, flat scores are an absurdity.

We have also become increasingly aware of individuals. The old report card was better geared to rate a youngster in comparison with the achievement of his group or with some norm for his age level. This comparison is important for both school and parent to make. But children differ in native intelligence, in rate of growth, in past experience, in areas of strength and interest, in countless ways. Simple fairness demands that we also compare a child with himself, with his potentialities, and with his past. You cannot do this merely by writing "B" and letting it go at that.

As we have learned more about individual children's patterns of growing we have also become aware of the silliness of monthly reports. Youngsters do not grow in monthly increments. Some boys and girls stay on plateaus for long periods of time; some go on a jag of growing in one area where interest is all-consuming, only to spurt ahead later to catch up on other things. This is their normal way of progressing. Other children have a more even step-by-step pattern of growing but still not necessarily one tied into the calendar.

This knowledge has led schools to want to cut down on the frequency of their reports. Whatever they send home does not go every month as the old-time cards did. Some schools report every six weeks; some only once a term, some three times a year and others four.

DESCRIPTIVE REPORTS—THE PROS AND CONS

Considerations such as these have led many schools to substitute a descriptive report for the old letter grade or numeral. The description may be no more than a short sentence instead of the *B*: "George is taking more responsibility." "He is liked by the other children." "He is not sure of himself in arithmetic." These fifteen-word telegrams are often squeezed into spaces on a card or sheet that looks like the other report card, only bigger. If a teacher has thirty-five children in her class and a dozen or so items of behavior to cover, the trick is to find short adjectives she can write quickly.

Other schools send fuller reports. Their lengthier comments are usually letter-style. The teacher attempts to give the parents a word picture of their youngster in school. These lengthier letters, and even the short-sentence style, take time to write. Teachers do not grind them out every four weeks, and probably would have little new to say if they did.

The descriptive report makes good sense to school people. As we write words like "He is progressing . . .," we call up in our mind a great many specifics about Johnny that lead us to make this generalization. As the parent reads the words "He is progressing . . .," he reads them without benefit of the specific situations. The parent is left with a sentence that is longer but vaguer than that right-on-the-button 72.9%.

Our code words also complicate understanding. Education, like every profession and trade, has its jargon. Our words are short cuts; we use them to save us time. We know the situations, events, forces, and factors that they stand for. But words like *security, enrichment, adjustment, stable, mature, individual, curriculum, personality, integration, complex,* are mysteries to many parents.

If parents talk about their business they use a lingo they know: *therm, RBI, RPM, HP, amps, antibiotics.* Every group has its secret language. But educators face a special job of communication. It is not enough for us to talk; we must be understood. It is not enough for us to say something; the other fellow must listen and make sense out of what we say.

Another objection to descriptive reports bothers teachers as well as parents. The descriptive report allows little give-and-take. The report goes home; the parent reads it; the report is filed or thrown away. The one certain thing the parent can do is to wait until the next letter comes.

Today educators expect tests, and the scores they give us, to show the next step. We want to use them for action. We want some guidance from them to indicate where we go from here. We are coming to realize a very simple fact: There is not much point in amassing scores or adjectives or bits of behavior just for the fun of it. We ought to do something with them. They ought to have a meaning for us.

PARENT CONFERENCES

Wanting to put ideas to work is the final pressure leading many teachers to use the face-to-face parent conference as their official report card. Parents and teacher sit down together to talk over what Johnny has done and to make a joint plan for the future.

Many schools schedule these reporting conferences in the classroom. This is often the efficient thing to do. The teacher stays put, the parents come in for half-hour appointments. Schools frequently feel they have to do this when classes are large and time is short.

Some schools like conferences this way for another reason. The teacher can sit in back of her desk; she is on her home ground. The parent is the visitor, and will behave as such. There is less danger of conflict and argument. The school can keep the upper hand. Obviously, this feeling, even when deep down in someone's breast, can never create a helpful atmosphere for a conference.

Other things being equal, it is better for the teacher to go to the home to talk with the parents. While not desirable or possible in every case, the home is a more favorable truce site— the parent will feel comfortable.

When you visit the home for your conference you kill two birds with one stone. You and the parent talk about the child; at the same time, you add to your continually growing knowledge of the child's background. You build on to your accumulation of hunches, impressions, and facts about home life that make the child more vivid to you. Use this go-easy, drop-by-drop way of coming to know a child in his setting whenever you can.

No way of reporting is the wonder way. The parent who really cares about his youngster wants all kinds of reports coming at him in all kinds of ways. But this face-to-face conference has many virtues. It makes possible the time needed to interpret the child's development in many areas of growth;

it is best adapted to detailing the progress of each individual; it allows parents to participate in making a plan for the future.

One reference stands out above all others: Katherine D'Evelyn's Individual Parent-Teacher Conferences *(New York: Teachers College Bureau of Publications, 1945.) This book gives word-by-word accounts of many kinds of conferences, each with a very thought-provoking analysis.*

Individual person-to-person conferences reduce the chance for misunderstanding, too. "Gobbledygook" can be straightened out. Even more important, feelings can be clarified as you talk to people.

Most parents are a mixture of hot and cold about reports on their children. They do want the score. At the same time, they are afraid to hear it.

Getting a report on your child is like looking at a photograph of yourself. You are dying to see the picture, but you know ahead of time that the photo will not do you justice. Or like hearing your voice on a phonograph record. You want to hear it, but when you do you say: "Why, that doesn't sound like me at all!"

The parent's eagerness to find out, and his worry about what he will find out, are not surprising. Theoretically, the report is about the child. Actually, it is just as much the parents' report card, too. The report will tell how well the youngster has done, but it will also tell how the parent is doing. A child's report is not a bowling score or a golf score or the outcome of last night's canasta game—anyone can take those in his stride, win or lose. This report gives a life score; it touches on more than you know. You need to be on hand to see how the other fellow takes what you say, to soften the blow sometimes, to comfort after it lands, to clarify it, to let him find a release by exploding.

THE PARENT'S READINESS TO LEARN

The purpose of these acts is not simply kindheartedness or gentleness, although these are always desirable in human relations. You do these things as an essential to making a plan. So long as the parent is upset or bothered or unhappy, no clear thinking can go on about the child.

Your observation of a youngster in the classroom may give you many bright ideas for these conferences. You want the father to encourage John more or to tighten up on him; to favor this child less or another one more; to be less strict or to hold the line. You have the problem and the solution all worked out in your mind. They are on the tip of your tongue. This is your chance to say them, but you cannot blurt them out.

The parent wants to hear the good things first. He wants the praise, the compliments, the achievements, the success.

He does not want you to make them up. He does not want untruths, soft-soap, or flattery that is false. He wants that part of the picture where his youngster is strong, that part of the honest story where things are going well. That is where you begin.

Your ideas for reform, your suggestions for improvement, the way you would change the world all can come later. You both have to see a youngster in his strong suit first.

This kind of patience is hard to have. Teachers are apt to take a child's good points for granted. They want to dive in to the sore spots and clean them up. But the parent wants to hear good news. He needs the reassurance so that he can face up to the rest. If you have a half-hour conference it hurts you to see valuable minutes go by.

A few teachers scoff: "You have to butter them up, and then you can tell them off." This cheapens a basic principle into a trashy technique. At stake here is a fundamental understanding about people, not a trick you use to get along with parents.

With children we call it readiness to learn. We know it is a waste of time to try to teach reading to a two-year-old or algebra to a fifth-grader. Even the dog books say: "Wait until the puppy is six months old before you try to teach him to heel." Certainly in adult human relations this basic idea that the person must be ready is no less real.

You have to bide your time even after you have helped a parent see the child in his strengths and successes. You cannot yet flatly say: "Do this, and do it now." Until there is readiness, all the good ideas in the world, all the most perfect suggestions go by the board. They are not heard. Or if they are heard, they are not picked up. Or if they are picked up, they are not acted upon. Or if they are acted upon, they do not work.

You are not trying to pull the wool over someone's eyes. But how much you tell this time and how much you postpone until later, how detailed you are in telling the problem or how much you say in general, how positive you are in making the difficulty stand out or how you fit it into a total picture, depends on the parent.

One thing is clear: If a troublesome matter must be discussed, you open it up. From there on, the expression on the parent's face, the questions he raises or the tangents he brings in, his pursuit of the trouble or of side issues give you your leads.

Teachers are very smart about waiting for cues when telling children about sex. There we let the child set the pace, and we call that good education. Maybe we can be sensitive in sex education because we worry about telling too much. But this way of working must be carried over to parent conferences, even though you may be impatient to say a lot. Let the learner give you the signs on how much he can take.

You can go slowly if you remind yourself that there is always a next time. When you are confident that there is a future, this patient, gentle, and feeling way does not seem wasteful. It is the way you build up readiness. Readiness does not develop overnight, but, in time, the parent himself will sense the problem. Then he will talk. Then he will be in a position to listen, to learn, and to have ideas of his own.

Only when you think the world will end tomorrow do you feel that you have to say everything at once and get all troubles cleared up once and for all. This seeming speed is deceptive, however. If you push faster than the person is able to go, you push him away. Stay close to where the person is, and the person and you will have a chance to make headway later.

> *Virginia Axline's* Play Therapy *(Boston: Houghton Mifflin Co., 1947) makes very clear a way of working with troubled children that is similar to this. You ought to read in particular her Chapter 17, "Application to Parent-Teacher Relationships," in which she carries over her philosophy to the field of home-school relations.*

THE TEACHER ADJUSTS TO INDIVIDUAL PARENTS

One thing you must be sure to do: However you report, apply what you know about individual differences in parents.

Some people have a great faith in their youngsters; they know their children will make out. They see them often enough playing with their friends on the street. They have time to talk with their children about school work. They are not plagued by driving hopes of their own or by persistent worries about the children.

Other parents are anxious. They want the facts down to the last dotted *i*. Maybe this is their personality; in all they do—their job, their housework, social relations—they like things neat and clear and definite. Maybe this pattern is one they have with their child; in other matters they can be free and easy, but where the youngster is concerned they want minute details. They may be this particular with one child—a youngster who for some reason they worry about; with the rest of their family they know that everything will go along.

Some parents come to the classroom, attend all the meetings, talk with you a hundred times a term. Other parents get very few facts through these avenues. Maybe they work all day, or have younger children at home, or extensive church or family or community responsibilities. The first group is able to find out a great deal for themselves. The second group theoretically has the same opportunities but cannot take advantage of them.

You have to adjust to all these differences. You must make sure that each person finds out what he wants to know. There is no "good amount" in general for you to tell. You are dealing with people and not with a formula. What is enough for one may leave another person wondering and puzzled and unsatisfied.

You may feel: "Well, that ought to hold them." That is as much as you have written or told to anybody. If the Hortons had good sense about their child they would not want to know more . . . If they did not push him so . . . If they were not so overconcerned . . . But they are. Don't think now in terms of "oughts" and "shoulds" and "might have beens." Take each family as it is.

Some people want to know the exact score on an achievement test. They want to know exactly what an achievement test is and how much the score really means. Some want an exact comparison of their child with the rest of the group; telling them how he stacks up against himself is not enough. Some want your scores on tests: "Did he get an *80* or *85*?" It does not satisfy them when you say: "He is doing very satisfactory work."

You will have your long-time goals for these people. Over a long period you may want to help them to relax, look more at the sweep of development, focus less on the little points, have more confidence, and stop chewing their finger nails. But don't hit them over the head. Gradually you can lead them to a different outlook. The first step is to take them as you find them. If they want facts now, be as specific and as detailed and as exact as you know how to be.

You have learned with childen the basic reason for this. If

you satisfy a need, the child can grow. If you leave him empty, he harks back to the past and cannot look ahead. Apply this same reasoning to parents—it is true of people, not youngsters alone. All your dealings with parents can tell you the kind of treatment that will be right for each of them. Accept people as they are, satisfy needs, and you open up the door to improvement.

LESS FREQUENT REPORTING—AND MORE

One final trend in reporting to parents must be noted: Good schools today, and good teachers, are reporting *less often* but are doing *more* reporting. This paradox is not as crazy as it sounds. Teachers are sending home something officially labeled *Report Card* less often than the schools of yesterday did. But today's teachers are finding many more ways of letting parents know what is actually going on and how their youngsters are faring.

Almost all of home-school relations is a "report card." The parent who observes in the classroom is getting a report every minute that she is there. Her own eyes are telling her; she sees for herself what her youngster is doing. The parent who participates in the classroom program has the same firsthand opportunity to know the score.

Parents who take part in effective and sensible meetings have still another opportunity to keep their finger on the pulse of their child's school life. Often they get the information they want from the meeting itself. More often, the before-meeting and after-meeting informal conversations with the teacher give them a briefing on their child and his activities at school.

All this is rounded out by what might be called the *Group Report Card*—the classroom newsletter discussed later—and by the teacher's little notes she sends home about a child's special progress or achievement.

The parent finds so much that is informative flowing in to

him from every angle that the special day—Report Card Day—
now is not so significant. It will confirm what he already
knows; the different language may make problems and progress
somewhat clearer; the report may add more recent developments. But there is no brand-new note. The parent in a good
classroom has been kept in touch; he does not have to wait for
a special channel to give him the facts.

When schools make all these many avenues a report card,
parents get one satisfaction they seek: *They know*. They do
not have to grope or wonder or puzzle or put pieces together.
These many avenues do for the teacher what the teacher wants,
too. With enough communication you can give the rounded
picture of development that you consider important. You can
focus on the individual and his particular ways. You can do
the job of interpreting shades and angles and shadows that such
intangibles as *maturity* and *appreciation* and *leadership* require.
A seeming contradiction—fewer Reports (capital R), more reporting—works so that both parents and teachers feel satisfied.

PARENT PARTICIPATION IN REPORT
   CARD CHANGES

Reporting to parents is one of the sensitive nerve endings in a
school. When you touch it the patient howls. Changing the
method of reporting is the surest way to get a community up in
arms and to bring the roof tumbling down on the school's head.
Yet when the change comes because you add observation and
participation, meetings and conversations, notes and newsletters, no one screams.

*This strategy — "Don't take anything away; add new things
on" — applies to any area where parents are accustomed to one
set practice. Using this strategy can end some of the needless
anxiety parents feel about improvements in the teaching of
reading, for example. To move primary classes overnight from*

an exclusive reliance on workbooks and primers to the sounder base of experience can be very upsetting to parents. Insecurity heckles people when the old familiar way is gone. If you keep on with the old for a while, but, in addition and at the same time, feed in the new, parents are not bothered. They can take this gradual change because what they know is still a part of the picture. If the New is really good — whether it is a different approach to the teaching of reading, the start of the core curriculum or of social studies, or a new way of reporting — the New becomes more and more what parents care about. Because the Old no longer matters, they stop turning to it. When you finally drop it people are apt to say: "Oh! I hadn't noticed. . . ."

Parents come to rely more and more on these added methods of finding out about children. After this reliance has been built, when parents are no longer leaning on the monthly card, then the old report can disappear. The impression is not that you have taken it away; people do not like that. It *withered* away. No one was using it or counting on it any more. The old report card faded out, and no one cared.

Even more consciously, parents can choose the method of reporting they prefer. When they have experienced all the possible ways of getting information, they can sit down with school people to study the pros and cons of each method. The school has given them the base for an intelligent decision. When this happens, the first choice of parents will not be different from the one educators would make.

Mothers and fathers have a deep stake in knowing how their child is faring. Understandably, parents are bothered if the first they know of a change is when the superintendent announces a new procedure at a PTA meeting. Such arbitrary action hits at the bond between parent and child and shows a lack of respect for the ability of informed parents to participate in plan-making.

7. Observation and Participation

The most logical ending to a home visit—you might call it simply the polite thing to do—is to say to the parent: "Won't you come to school to visit me sometime?" Such an invitation leads into one of the little-used but potentially most valuable tools in home-school relations: *parent observation in the classroom.*

When a disagreement arises in a community about a school—it may be a wild tale or an honest difference of opinion—parents ought to be the ones who will rise up to say: "Hold on. That is not true. We know."

No way can achieve this better than having parents in the classroom and in the school as an everyday affair. People must see with their own eyes—not the show, not the exhibit, not the Sunday-best—but the day-by-day every minute life actually going on. This is the final proof. Parents on the spot, in the school, present when learning is going on, become knowing parents. They are not in the dark.

Some schools cannot wait for the parents to get out: "Just as soon as they go we can get some work done." Many others are glad to have parents come—at *party* time!

"We are having our Christmas celebration in each classroom. Won't you join us?"

"On the last day before vacation we always have a party for the children. Come and eat ice cream and cake with us."

"Friday is Johnny Smith's birthday. He is having his party at school. If you can drop in at 2:30 P.M. we should be glad to see you."

Halloween, Thanksgiving, Eastertime, May Day — some schools find many excuses for the parents to visit and, to an extent, this is all to the good. But parties are high times; the youngsters are excited. Parties are play time, and no academic work goes on. Parties are the exception; they give a false picture of the workaday world.

Youngsters love to celebrate with their families, and they are delighted whenever mother or father comes. Food is a good mixer; relationships come a little closer whenever people eat and play together. But if you want parents to know a school—if you want them to back it because they can tell anyone what really goes on—party-time visiting is not enough.

Nor is it enough for parents to come only at show-off time, when everything is all tinseled and bright.

"On December 13th the upper-grade chorus will sing carols in the auditorium. Can you be with us at 9:30 A.M.?"

"The second grade is putting on a little play in the classroom at 10:30 on Thursday morning. We would like all the mothers and any fathers who can to be on hand."

"Our doors are open to parents during American Education Week."

"The Fourth Grade has been working on puppets. We are putting on a show at 2 o'clock on Friday. Come and see what we have made."

The finished product has a place: the team on the field, the band in their uniforms, the painting on the wall, the choral group on the stage, the actors in their costumes. People ought to see all of these.

Attractive displays and performances play a part in winning good will. People apply the old idea that where there is smoke there must be some fire. A school that puts on a good show must have something underneath.

But the finished product does not reveal education in the

round. The heart of the matter is what goes on in the process. Education is the *how*. It is the problem and the problem-solving that precede the final performance. It is the day-by-day guidance and leadership and a give-and-take that build up to something you can finally see. It is the paper in the scrap basket; the question asked; the tool once held the wrong way (but now the youngster knows how).

Seeing the finished product helps most after people know the process that has gone into it, after they have had some chance to see the developmental steps that were involved. When the show comes last, then people can appreciate it, be thrilled by it, and feel a closer identification because of it. But when, as so often happens, the show is the only thing, good will is built on an unstable base. People may like the show, they may enjoy it, but they do not know the *why* or the *how*. Their favorable reaction is without firm roots, subject therefore to any chilling breeze that comes along.

PARENTS AS OBSERVERS

You have a strong base only when parents are in and out of school at any time. The prospect of their sitting in the room, watching, is not an inviting one to many teachers. Teaching is an isolated business. We do it alone behind closed doors, and a lot of us like it that way. We get the jitters when the supervisor or administrator or a visitor steps into the classroom. We are so used to working in privacy that we suspect visitors of looking only for mistakes. This talk of parents observing sounds like bringing in critics who will look down their noses.

Of course, we are not suspicious of people we know well. They can see us on the job, and we do not care. We know that if something goes wrong our friends won't hold it against us. We can count on their overlooking, and on their support and understanding.

You have to break the ice so that you feel this comfortable

way about parents. So long as you keep them out they are not your friends, and you suspect them and want to keep them out some more. A vicious circle is built up. Yet, as many teachers have found, when parents do come into the classroom and become familiar people, these mothers and fathers turn out to be amazingly human. And likeable. And appreciative of the opportunity.

SOME COMMON DOUBTS ABOUT
PARENT OBSERVATION

If parents have never observed in your room, the idea sounds strange at first. Many teachers ask: "What do they do? Just sit?" And the answer is *Yes*. Some of us remember our own college days when we had to observe in classrooms a certain number of hours and fill out forms. Our eyes got glazed, and our seats got tired. We find it hard to believe that anyone voluntarily would put himself in the observer's position. But remember: The parent is watching his own child. For a parent, this is a fascinating show.

Other teachers wonder about the disturbance that visitors may make in a classroom. Some teachers long for the one-way vision screens of the university nursery school. With parents sitting out in the open, in the more usual classroom, they cannot see how parent observation will work.

The screens of the nursery school do aid in one way. Parents are freer to come and go. They need stay no longer than they want to. They are not trapped but can leave when they have had their fill. But once you open your room to visitors, observation can run almost as smoothly. Parents sit, watch, and then, when they feel they must, leave without fuss or bother.

The parent may be a novelty for the first or second time. The youngsters may crowd around, or a young child may want mother to sit by him. You can look on this as a great disruption that should not be tolerated. Or you can feel good that this day your classroom gave a parent and a child an experience of oneness in school. Some teachers would say: "That's a side issue." Others place this in the core of educational concerns.

But even this kind of "disturbance" stops soon enough. The youngsters, like yourself, come to take the presence of parents for granted. They are pleased, but visitors are no longer a special novelty. The children are free to go ahead with their other interests.

Ninety-nine per cent of your parents will be grateful and so quiet you won't even know they are there. On the basis of experience with the one per cent, some teachers dread having any parents in the room "because they interfere."

A rare few will do things you do not want them to. Most of them act out of good intentions but they misunderstand. Visiting a classroom is new to them. They want to do the right thing, but the only background they can bring to bear is their general social experience as a hostess or a guest when they talk, act, and move around. They imagine that it is not polite just to sit and watch.

You can smooth this little wrinkle by a simple sheet of instructions. Make it clear that all an observer is expected to do is to sit and enjoy himself. Don't be bossy; write your notice in a friendly way.

"If your youngster comes up to you, be yourself. Don't push him off. He will get used to having you with us. You don't have to prolong your conversation with him, but don't shut it off.

"If you see something that the teacher does not see, do whatever you think is right to protect health and safety. But come to watch and relax. The teacher can never see all that goes on, but many little difficulties iron themselves out. An adult does not have to step into every situation.

"You know that our teachers are really friendly and that they want to talk with you whenever you have something on your mind. There may be some time during your visit when

the two of you can get together. If there is, the teacher will
let you know. Usually during the day the teacher has to give
her full attention to the youngsters. Please save your reactions
until later. We really want them then, when the children are
not around."

A simple brief sheet containing this kind of information is
enough for most people. It sets them at ease. They know the
score. Their own common sense suffices to tell them the rest.

A fraction of the one per cent who may cause trouble could
read a book about school visiting and still interfere. Words
cannot easily reach them. Something down inside pushes them
into doing the wrong thing. Perhaps they want you to like
them so much that they have to chatter. Perhaps they have
so many fears about their child that they have to butt in.
Perhaps they are so unsure of themselves that they must control every situation.

If you get angry when children create a disturbance, you
will probably get angry when parents create a fuss. If you find
it easy to call children names — "You are selfish . . . mean . . .
fresh . . . bossy" — you will probably want to call these few
parents names, too. If your inclination with children is to say:
"Well! If that is the way you are going to behave, you cannot
play with us" (or "go to shop" or "go outdoors" or "be on the
committee"), then you will also want parents to *earn* their
privileges.

But more and more teachers know about disturbed children:
"These few are the ones who need my help. These few must
not be shut out. They act the way they do because life has shut
them out. The need is to boost them, not be down on them.
To include them, not punish them by isolation. To be patient,
not make life more complicated by more blame and anger."

The same understanding applies to parents. The less-than-
one per cent can cause a disturbance, but they are the ones
who most need schools and teachers. Your acceptance of them

goes a little way toward helping these adults get their feet back on the ground. Your friendly relationship will not do the whole trick; probably nothing will. But at the end of a difficult day you have every right to feel pleased. You have helped them more than the most expert lecture on child care could. Such people need satisfactions out of their living more than they need words of wisdom.

You will feel better, too, if you realize how much these people have helped you. You feel tired. You may think that you have accomplished nothing today. But while the parent is observing your classroom, you are observing the parent. What you see is bound to make you more understanding, more sympathetic, more gentle as you work with her youngster. Mrs. Franklin was in your classroom for only an hour. She has been in Sam's presence his whole lifetime. You gain information you can put to work for Sam's good.

To help a parent by accepting him *or* to help a child by now knowing his family background better is a day's work well done. Some arithmetic may have been skipped, a few minutes of reading passed by. But you have come closer to touching people's lives — and that is what a school is for.

A teacher, of course, has to stay on top of the pile in her classroom. There may be very occasional times when you have to say No to a parent, just as teachers must say No to children. Saying No is never pleasant, but it need not make an enemy. Your No can be a firm one; it can stick; but you can still say it in such a way that the other fellow sees the point and accepts it. Your basic friendly attitude indicates that you are not angry with him. You do this every day with children.

PARENTS GAIN UNDERSTANDING OF CHILDREN

Teachers have a real stake in helping parents to understand children better. To do this we are apt to turn to lectures, movies, books, and pamphlets. But right here, in observation, is the firsthand way of learning: The parent sees his own child in action and in comparison with other children.

So many parents, after observing, heave a sigh of relief: "Why he's not so bad. . . ."

So many are reassured: "I notice that they all seem to be so active. I thought probably Tommy was the only one. . . ."

Parents are overwilling today to believe that they have made mistakes and that their children are not up to standard. The peace of mind they gain from seeing their youngsters alongside of others is a great boon. It gives them confidence to go ahead, and, more faith that they are not doing such a bad job after all. Many people need such a lift much more than they need new techniques.

But even the techniques come, too. As parents sit, trains of thought are started. New hunches come. Resolutions are made. These are not always formulated into words but, from watching what you do, running over in their mind what has happened at home, putting all this together with ideas they have read or heard, new approaches do develop.

Parents sit and watch. They come when they want to, and they leave when they have to. Sometimes not a word is spoken. A smile or a nod or a wink or a friendly look may be all. But the process is not as passive as it seems. A buzzing can go on inside that will show, as time goes along, in new ways of acting and feeling.

You will see the change in parents' improved relations with their children. The change will have its impact on your classroom, too. For inevitably as parents grow in their understanding of children, they grow in their understanding of good education.

ARRANGING FOR OBSERVATION

Parent observation may develop as a result of a discussion in a group meeting. A question arises about the teaching of arithmetic: "Do the children get enough drill?" "Does cooking really teach them enough about numbers?" Or a question comes up about discipline: "Are they allowed to do whatever they want to, or do you have to make them?" The best way the parent can get an answer is to come and see.

When there are specific questions like these, some schools prepare an observation blank to guide the parent as he watches. The sheet focuses attention on the significant things to look for. It usually provides space for the parent to record some of the action he sees. These specific incidents are then used in the meeting or conference that follows the observation. Most schools prefer not to use an observation blank. Parents feel more at ease when they can watch whatever interests them.

Usually observation comes about simply because of a parent's general interest in his child's adjustment and in the classroom program. At the first PTA meeting and through the start-to-school booklet many schools today extend an invitation for this kind of visit. But you need something more specific if you really want parents to come.

General invitations are like the passing social remarks that are a routine part of conversation. Two acquaintances meet by chance. When they have exhausted all the old memories, they separate. Both say heartily: "We must get together again sometime," and that is a polite way of putting it off. Neighbors meet in the store. One says to the other: "Drop in whenever you are near, won't you?" and that means: "We will be so surprised to see you."

If you want people to come, you are specific.

"We want you to come to dinner on Friday at 6:30 P.M." "Come to tea this Wednesday afternoon at 4." "We are having a dessert party Monday evening at 7." The time and the place mean you really expect your guests.

You have to be this definite with parents if you really want them. You have to pin down the invitation. Some teachers do it by telephone, some through a note, some when they visit the parent's home, and some when they meet the parent on the street. But they make an actual date: "A number of the parents have been dropping in to the classroom just to sit and watch and see how part of a day goes. We would love to have you come. What about this Friday at 9?"

Not every parent wants to observe. Not everyone should. Not everyone can. There is no pressure. Gratifying as a visit to the classroom can be, for the parent and the child and for you, nothing is so good that everybody must do it. You hold out a free invitation, not a club rolled up in newspaper.

Some people will not have thought of observing; the idea needs a little time to sink in. They will not come this time, but they may the next. Some people would love to visit, but it means so much rearranging of their whole household schedule that it is more trouble than it is worth.

You don't want observation in your classroom to be a duty call, so you don't press and you don't nag and you don't make it the hallmark of a good mother: "You must come, or you are letting your child down." But you do extend an honest invitation, and you make it specific so that the parent knows that he is welcome.

CONFERENCES FOLLOWING OBSERVATION

Great good comes if you can talk with parents after they have observed. This gives you the chance to reinforce what they have seen and to draw out generalizations from some of the specifics. You answer questions and clear up misconceptions. A lot of ideas are absorbed by the parent during observation. You want, if you can, to know how he has organized all these impressions and what he makes of them.

If a parent observes only occasionally you can schedule a definite follow-up conference. If the parent comes back again and again you don't have the time for this. You don't need the time as much, however. The parent may not understand all he sees the first time, but clarification comes as he sees more and more. Gradually, through the seeing and the talking, through all else that you do to help a parent understand, a deeper feeling for good education grows in the parent and in you.

PARENTS AS PARTICIPANTS

Just as parent observation stems naturally out of home visits, so parent participation is the next logical step beyond observation. It is one thing when a parent knows what is going on at school. It is better still when the parent feels that he has helped make the school the way it is.

MONEY-RAISERS

Some schools are convinced that *the* right way for parents to participate is by raising money. They are all for letting the parents run a picnic or a bazaar, a square dance or a festival — anything that will uncover extra cash the school can use.

The pride and joy of parents who engage in this kind of activity is further proof of the point made earlier: Adults are hungry for a chance to be useful. In money-raising activities men (and sometimes women) work long hours; they beg and borrow materials; they pester their friends to buy tickets and chances; they promote the school's spaghetti dinner or circus night. Wherever they go, abundant creative energy is released for the school's benefit.

No doubt some children make immediate gains as a result of such activities. Their particular schools blossom with motion picture projectors, shades and curtains, playground equipment, lecterns, phonographs, books, and countless other supplies and equipment. These would not be available were it not for these energetic parent efforts.

When you go beneath the surface, however, you begin to wonder: Is this exclusive concern with money-raising a desirable kind of participation in the long run? So often these activities are carnivals, bazaars, and of the circus type. Despite all the time that parents give to them, participation in them does not help the parent to gain a deeper understanding of the school's program. Sometimes, in fact, the emphasis on rewards, chances, and the exploitation of special talents runs counter to the school's approach. The activities even complicate the job of building understanding.

Often the split between home and school may actually be widened by the exclusive emphasis on fund-raising: "We'll raise the cash; you do the educating." Once the job is done, parents turn the money over to the school: "Here it is. Do with it what you will." Money-raising does not imply any need to think through what these children need and what will help them most.

This split can even be carried into the family itself. The money-raising activities are frequently the fathers' job. The chairman is a man; the committees are men; the major hustle is masculine. It is as though we say: The hard practicalities of business are for men; leave the women alone to fuss with the kids.

A further objection to money-raising is that those schools with wealthier parents, with parents who have more time to give, and more materials to give, get all the best of it. Other schools in less privileged neighborhoods have to get along with the supplies tax money alone will buy. Better educated, more vocal, wealthier parents look at their schools, and are pleased. Less pressure is brought to bear on boards of education to supply needed materials and services for all schools. Money-raising benefits a few children; indirectly, it can harm many others whose school needs are not brought to light.

The benefits individual schools get from fund-raising are real. Parent-raised money has made school lunchrooms possible; has landscaped school lawns; has paid for art, music, and other special teachers; has supported health programs, recreation programs, and many extra-curricular activities. Schools cannot drop this aid overnight.

The very success of these money-raising activities indicates how much adults are willing to pitch in, if they are given a chance. This ought to make you wonder if more constructive ways can be found for parents to have a real part in their child's education. Would it not be better for these parents to put their energies into securing improved legislation? Then all schools, not only a favored few, could have needed supplies and materials. Would it not be better for these parents to spend their time working in the school? In that way their understanding (which is the basis of all long-term support) would grow.

Many teachers hesitate to experiment with more meaningful parent participation. The idea of parents working in the school seems special, different, strange. Teachers feel inexperienced and inadequate and worry over what they are getting into.

Actually parents' participation is based on principles school people know by heart. The fact is: *Parent participation is the same as student teaching.* Every single teacher experienced these principles himself when he was in college and involved in his own student teaching. Many teachers who have cadets in their classes today apply these principles skillfully to the student teachers but do not carry them over to parents.

PARENTS OBSERVE FIRST

The first principle of student teaching is that the student must observe before he begins work with youngsters. The apprentice is not thrown cold into a group and told to take over. He has a good chance to become familiar with the group first and to see what is going on before he takes his big plunge. This opportunity to observe first is important for parents, too.

Emergencies do arise, of course. They happen even in college. In a crisis anyone is brought in to hold the fort until life gets back to normal. But the weight of practice is certainly to give students a chance first to stand on the sidelines. In the freshman or sophomore year students may come every day to watch children, to see how they act, and to observe how the classroom goes through its day. At the very least, the first week or two of student teaching is given over to observing.

We deprive parents who participate of this initial observation. Their experience in living with youngsters at home makes it possible for them to short-cut part of the observation. But if you cut it out entirely, the parent — or the student or anyone — is lost. You make the person sink down to the level of not knowing, only doing. Many times all of us get in situations that are over our heads. We mutter: "What's it all about?" and we don't like it. Observation eliminates some of this confusion.

PARTICIPATION IS GEARED TO EACH PARENT

Every one of us knows that piling on too much responsibility at once is not the way to start off a student teacher. Even after an initial period of observing the next step is still only an introduction to work with a whole group of children.

Student teachers may go for a walk with one child. Others may read a story to a small group. Still others may work with one or two children on a problem. The art of the supervising teacher lies in finding for each student where he can succeed. Then the good supervisor builds success on success so that the confident young teacher, liking the job and anticipating it, finally comes to full responsibility for the whole group.

Almost from the beginning some students are ready to work with a large group. Others need much time mixing paints, scoring tests, dittoing work-sheets — easing into the business of working directly with the group. When gradual participation is well handled, each student teacher comes along. Each parent will, too, if the same wise and sensitive approach is made.

There is so much work to be done in a classroom. Only a person fresh from a day with children could detail every one of the different jobs. Some work is behind the scenes: repairing books, cataloging pictures, duplicating teaching material, preparing the clay or the paint or the wood, getting tools in order, handling messages, and so forth. This is the housekeeping and administrative side of teaching. If it goes smoothly, the work with children will go smoothly. Lumps and bumps mean that the program stumbles along. Parents would feel good about doing many of these jobs.

Some work has to be done outside the school: books investigated at the public library, the price of equipment looked up in a catalog, two items compared right at the store, a nail keg picked up from the lumber yard. If there are enough hands and feet to go around, the program for children becomes a richer, fuller one. Many parents would feel comfortable and useful helping with these tasks.

Obviously the greatest amount of work is directly with children. The teacher does not have the time herself to do it all. Mary badly needs some one person just to spend some time alone with her, talking and being a friend. Billy could learn to read if it were only possible to work with him alone; Frank loves to throw and catch a ball, but there never is time enough for him alone outdoors; George has such trouble with arithmetic; Mary Sue can not hold a hammer right.

The individual gets lost in the clutter, but parent participation can be a way out. Ten minutes of drill on a child's particular weakness is worth six twenty-minute periods of buckshot instruction, much of it landing where he needs no practice. But the problem has always been: How can a teacher give individual help in a classroom of thirty and thirty-five and forty pupils?

Parents can take over some of this individualized work, or parents can do some of the teacher's routine work, so that the trained person is relieved to give the special individual attention. In many seventh grades, the teacher reads spelling words out of a book, and the children write them down. Can only a teacher do this? Or could a parent read the words and free the teacher to work individually with a child who needs more skilled instruction?

In many third grades, the teacher gives arithmetic examples out of a book, and the children bring their papers up to her. Could a parent in this room free the teacher to work intensively for a half-hour with George, who needs it?

Parent help leads to individualization *and* enrichment. Think of the second-graders who are crayoning, waiting for their group's turn to read to the teacher. Could they be listening to music played by a mother? Think of the youngsters who sit indoors because a cold in the head keeps them from going out-doors with the group. Could a parent who knows science do experiments with these youngsters?

Sitting at home in every community are photographers, cabinet makers, tennis players, trumpeters and cellists, square dancing enthusiasts, story-telling experts. These people go under the name of *mother, father, grandparent*. Some way must be found to bring this richness of skill, training, and pos-session into the classroom. The *community* must educate its children; the teacher should not be alone in this responsibility.

In addition to parents, two other groups of people can be turned into participants. Both need a chance to contribute to a community enterprise, although they have no children in school. The first group is constituted of those many young married women, childless at this stage of their married life, who gave up a job when they married, and are now at home. The second group is composed of older people, retired but still healthy and vigorous, no longer working for pay but still eager for work.

For a long time to come schools are going to be confronted with hordes of children. Not for many years will we have the school buildings and the trained staff to enable every grade to reach the standard of twenty-five youngsters that has so long been set. Today, without realizing what they are saying, teachers report: "Oh, I'm lucky this year. I have only thirty-five!" When you have been hit over the head with a hammer it feels good just to have your toes stepped on for a while.

We can bemoan our large class size. We can keep on talking hopefully about "next year" and that new building, which will be overcrowded the minute it opens it doors. Or we can face the fact that these millions of children are here now, that this is their only ninth year or sixth or twelfth, and do something creative about the problem of large class size.

The creative stroke — the practical stroke — is to use parents. Youngsters will get a better break than they are now getting. You, the teacher, will feel good about the program in your classroom, even though you have large numbers. Parents will have a satisfying sense of accomplishment.

A very aptly titled booklet, Fifty Teachers to a Classroom, *by the Metropolitan School Study Council (New York: Macmillan, 1950) gives page after page of ways parents can and have helped schools. See also the older but still helpful pamphlet,* The Community — a Laboratory, *by Jane Mayer and Miriam Sutherland, P.E.A. Service Center Pamphlet No. 1 (New York: Progressive Education Association, 1941).*

CONFERENCES BEFORE AND
AFTER PARTICIPATION

Some teachers object to parent participation on the grounds that "It's more trouble than it's worth." Parent help *is* trouble, but there can be real argument over how much it is worth.

Part of the extra load for the teacher arises because it is not enough for parents to come to see; not enough for them simply to take part in what goes on. You have to prepare your helpers for what they are to do and give them a chance afterwards to react to what occurred. This talking, before and after, puts participation in a setting. It is the guarantee that the values will be achieved.

Conferring is trouble, but it is not an unknown to the teaching profession. The conference with student teachers is an accepted and routine part of teacher training. Some supervising teachers meet their students every afternoon; others set a time aside once a week. But no college thinks of putting its apprentices on the job and then never finding out how they think or feel about their work. Parents need the same chance to react.

They need the opportunity even more than students do. Many parents, even though they have covered themselves with glory, are afflicted with doubts: "I probably did the wrong thing, but I had to do something. . . ." Parents have no course training to fall back on. Many lack confidence in dealing with their own children. Instead of gaining greater strength from participation, they carry home a load of misgivings.

The simple chance to talk over their participation, to raise a question, or to get some reassurance is often all they need to get the glow of satisfaction they deserve. Praise, a pat on the back, a good word from the teacher sets them up. Left to themselves, they puzzle and wonder and doubt.

Some parents question not their own activity but the way situations have been handled. They did what they thought they were supposed to do — either the teacher had told them or they followed her lead — but they did not approve. What they did was not comfortable for them; it did not seem right. They go home from participating, smoldering inside, dissatisfied, and disagreeing. If we can learn not to gloss over anything that might be unpleasant, these disagreements can be an excellent opportunity for teaching and learning.

Sometimes the parent is on the wrong track. As you more fully interpret a child or explain a setting or give the continuity, the parent begins to see your reasons and to give you respect. All the while his own understanding of childrens' needs goes deeper.

Just as often the parent has a good idea. It is so easy for teachers to get into a rut. We act in certain ways toward children or follow certain routines or handle situations simply because we started that way. A fresh eye comes along and sees another possibility. A fresh mind uncovers an approach that we have missed completely. Learning is never a one-way street.

These conferences also lead into useful discussions about individual children. The parent, naturally enough, through all of his participation is continuously interpreting his experiences in terms of his family and his own child. A general discussion about a parent's participation often turns into talk of John's feeling about school, his behavior at home and on the street. Ten minutes of discussion when the time is ripe can be worth more to a parent than an hour of listening to a lecture in a large group meeting.

It is, of course, not easy for parents and teachers to find the time to talk together. The parent who has been in the classroom for a tour of duty has her homework to catch up on. The teacher, too, has many other obligations. Often these conferences must be done "on the fly"—as the parent leaves the classroom; sandwiched in while the school work is going on; or, over the phone at the end of the day. These get-togethers are so important that time for them must somehow be found.

Parent participaton is a lot of work. You must:

Explain the general idea to parents . . .

Arrange a schedule so they can observe . . .

Discuss their observations with them . . .

Think out how each can help . . .

Prepare them for the specific job they will do . . .

Remind them of the time because busy people forget . . .

Talk it all over afterwards. . . .

Participation takes good organization. It involves you in many human relations. When you have been through all the steps you may need to count your blessings one by one. But they are real and are enough to buck you up.

You use time, but you save time: Mr. Gale picked up that roll of unprinted newspaper for you.

You use energy, but you save energy: Mrs. Hampton checked on the cost of autoharps at the music store.

You plan more, but you have more chance to sit back: Mr. Collins talked to your class today about salesmanship.

You use skill, but participation brings you skill: Mrs. Terry sang folk songs with the youngsters today.

You give, but you get: Mrs. Call's sense of humor pulled you up from the depths today; that mix-up would have been hard to take if you had been all alone.

Most rewarding of all: There is no better way to live and to teach than in an atmosphere of trust and approval, of understanding and support and agreement. Parent participation brings you this; the "trouble" is a small price to pay.

THE COOPERATIVE NURSERY SCHOOL

In many areas of home-school relations nursery education has shown the way. It has developed many ideas which apply equally well to other age levels. Parent participation is one of these.

The nursery school movement has been driven into parent participation. Particularly in the past decade many young parents found themselves caught in a lag. They knew a good nursery school would benefit their child, but they could not find one. Good schools are still few and far between. Where they exist they often have long waiting lists; and, because they are good, their operating costs are so high that many interested families are cut out.

This situation is similar to the public school situation today. At the nursery level many parents watch their child's only third year of life slip by, and they are unable to secure a school they know will be good for him. At the public school level parents watch their child's only eighth year turn into his ninth, and he still has forty-five in his class.

The one difference is: Some nursery school parents, instead of sighing, are creating *cooperative nursery schools*. The good cooperative nursery operates with at least one well-trained teacher. The parents do not go off on their own, any more than parent participation in the public school program means that the trained teacher takes a back seat. The professional worker is put in an even more key position than before.

Under this teacher's guidance the parents pitch in. Cash cannot buy its way into a cooperative nursery school, but services can. Some parents, those who like to and are good at it, work directly with the children as assistants to the trained teacher. One parent handles publicity. Still another, able in the field, is responsible for health inspections. Another takes over the financial details.

And so it goes. The key assumptions are that parents care for their children; that they are willing to work for children's well-being; that parents are a reservoir of the talents and strengths that youngsters need. Mrs. Brown plays the violin; Mrs. Grange is clever with her hands; Mrs. Thompson enjoys telling stories and does it very well; Mrs. Hanes has been a secretary, and is a whiz in the office.

In some cooperatives, mothers cook the noonday meal and wash the dishes. In all of them, there is a regular cleanup time. Parents scrub the floors. Parents wash windows. Parents paint walls. They pay some cash, too, just as school-age parents pay taxes. But these people want nursery education for their children, so they will also drive a nail, push a lawnmower, sand blocks, and spade dirt.

This capacity to give themselves to a cause lies dormant in most people. Somewhere along the line these cooperative nursery school parents have been helped to see what their children need for good growing, and to want it keenly enough to work for it. They have been helped to see how equipment and materials translate into good education, and to cherish this enough to work for it. They have been helped to see how little techniques and little incidents mean learning, and desire this enough to study and to talk and to discuss.

A cooperative is a working place. It is also a place where much talk goes on. Parents meet before the school gets under way to think through their goals, to analyze equipment, to study techniques. They meet regularly and often, after they are underway, to see how they are doing and how they can improve.

These add up to a lot of meetings, but the parents do not feel imposed upon. Few institutions call out a deeper loyalty and a keener devotion than the cooperative. This is the parents' school. These are their children. This is their work. These people give themselves to their school, and they will not hear a word against it.

The simple psychology operating here is one to which most public schools are blind: people putting themselves into something, making it their own, and loving it. These parents are grateful for the opportunity. Parent after parent spots a change inside of himself: "I feel good about our cooperative. It has done something for me." This good feeling carries over into relationships with children: "I work hard at the cooperative, but I don't feel so tired somehow. I don't see my youngster every minute the way I used to, but I am a much better person when I am around him. Raising children is exciting because we are all in it together."

This is not usually called *parent education*. Nobody is telling a mother what to do. But these feelings pay off in better parenthood, not only because of the gains from working directly with children (these are tremendous), but also because of the joys that come from doing a job, being treated as important, and being needed. You cannot be a good mother or father, no matter how many books you read, unless you get fun out of your own living.

Parents who are in cooperative nursery schools obviously become unusually good interpreters of what their school is doing and why. Public schools at all age levels need very much this kind of informed and devoted support.

> *If there is a cooperative nursery school near you, by all means visit it and talk with the parents. If this is not possible, read* Our Cooperative Nursery School *(Silver Springs, Md.: Silver Springs Nursery School, Inc., 1949) or send twenty cents to the Vanderbilt Cooperative Nursery School, Vanderbilt University, Nashville, Tenn., for their 16-page account,* Parents and Children Together, *by Olive B. McVickar.*

ROOM MOTHERS

Not many schools are yet geared for as much parent observation and participation and discussion as has been suggested. A growing number of schools, however, do have a Room Mother for each grade. This one person often is in the school to the extent that has been suggested here for all parents.

No rules govern the selection of Room Mothers. In some schools the PTA officers appoint them for each grade; in others, the parents of the grade elect the mother; elsewhere the teacher or the principal approaches an individual and asks her to carry the responsibility.

The underlying aim is to have some one person as the link between the teacher and the parent group. This liaison can be interpreted very mechanically. In some schools the major job of the Room Mother is to remind and nag the other mothers.

With this narrow concept it makes little difference how the Room Mother is chosen. The job is largely a secretarial one that does not affect the life of the classroom. Anyone who has the time can do it as well as anyone else.

In many schools room mothering is a dirty job. It takes in the telephoning and reminding described above, but it also includes whatever else the class or the teacher needs. The list of chores will vary from group to group. The important issue is not what the Room Mother does, so much as it is her relationship to the teacher. She is the handy man, the errand boy.

With a setup like this, it again matters little how the person is chosen. Her main virtues must be a willingness to take on any kind of job, and time on her hands to do it. Probably the parents in the group or the officers of the PTA know as well as anyone who can fill this bill. The teacher need not care who gets the job, so long as the proposed candidate is as strong as an ox.

The Room Mother, however, can have a very special relationship to the teacher. She can be the person who, more than others, is in the classroom watching and in the classroom helping, the one who has the special opportunity to be on the firing line of children's education. She can give a great deal to the teacher, not only of muscle and time but also of reaction and companionship and ideas.

If parents and teachers have this concept of the Room Mother, the teacher must have a real voice in deciding who the person will be. Someone picked at random, thrust upon a teacher, is not desirable. Ideally, Room Mother and teacher must like each other; they must talk the same language and really hit it off. Some element of a love match is essential in this Room Mother business.

In one school a nominating committee in each grade is appointed in the spring. This committee is made up of the retiring Room Mother, two other mothers well-acquainted with the group, and the grade's teacher for the coming year. The mother this committee agrees on is consulted before her name is presented to the other parents. She has ample opportunity to think about the job and to arrange her schedule so that she has the time to give the following year.

EXPLOITATION OF ROOM MOTHERS

The use of Room Mothers often illustrates some of the weaknesses in home-school relations. Only exceptional schools have managed to turn this promising position into one which gives joy and the release of creative energies. The secret is not a dark one: These schools treat Room Mothers with respect.

They help them get ready for the jobs they are to do. The work Room Mothers carry out is significant; mothers see why it is needed and how it fits in. And Room Mothers give their ideas as well as their poor aching backs. They are not the servant girls of the classroom, but adult equals.

Given this relationship, many possibilities open up. For one thing, the Room Mother can be a good companion to the teacher. Classroom teaching is lonely work. You are behind your doors all day long. Sometimes you like being on your own, but there are times when it is even more fun to share what goes on — to react to someone, to get his comments, to talk things over, to have a sounding board, or just to have company.

Strangely, many a mother at home works in a lonely way, too. When all the youngsters are in school, mothering is a particularly isolated job. After the frantic rush of breakfast, there are long hours of silence until 3 o'clock. During the war many of the women who worked for the first time said that they enjoyed the companionship of their fellow workers almost as much as they liked the pay check at the end of the week.

Men joke about how women gab on the telephone all morning long, gossip in the grocery store, buzz over the bridge table, or wallow in the soap operas. One explanation for all of this is the loneliness of social women left behind at home.

An effective Room Mother plan enables both the teacher and a parent to combat their isolation. These two people mutually support each other. Finer skills develop, at home and at school, from the relationship. More spirit comes into school life and home life from the increased human give-and-take. To be with other humans is a tonic for most people. We are not made to live alone and think alone and work alone all of the time.

Occasionally this beneficial relationship is broadened still more. Principals bring all the Room Mothers together for group meetings, tapping the impressions and ideas and re-actions of these key people.

The Board of Education is, of course, the body officially charged by law with determining the policies of the schools. Room Mothers meeting on a school-wide basis in no way compete with the school board. The supplement it. They widen the base of intelligence and experience and viewpoint on which the public schools rest.

From the Room Mothers' point of view such meetings are one more indication of the school's respect. The assumption is that the parent has been thinking while she has been doing her job.

In a few classrooms the Room Mother experience is so valuable to the parent and so helpful to the teacher that it is not confined to one person for the whole year. A rotation plan is followed whereby one Room Mother serves for a month or some such period, then another person has this special chance to know what is going on and to be a part of the classroom program. Some other schools, operating on the principle that doing things together is always more fun, change "Room Mother" to the plural. Two or three people who know each other well and who get along easily with the teacher hold this job at the same time. Occasionally a husband and wife constitute a "Room Mother" team.

Teachers who have a pool of school-experienced parents to draw on might think about organizing these people as a Room Council. You can turn to social agencies for an analogy here.

No public welfare agency ever thinks of operating without an effective and continuous relationship with a lay board. Even though only one activity is involved — the operation of a day care center for one age level, as an illustration — a group of citizens always knows the program, thinks about it, and gives guidance on over-all policies that relate to it.

The public schools operate on this same theory, but only for the school system as a whole. Too often a gap opens up between the Board of Education, overseeing all the schools, and Edgewood School down there on the corner and the seventh grade on the second floor. This gap thins out understanding of and support for an individual school's program; it cuts off the school from the many good ideas which a broader base of people could give; it deprives the parent population of the satisfactions that can come through contributing to their neighborhood school.

NOT EVERYONE CAN OBSERVE OR PARTICIPATE

One last word needs to be said. Not every parent has the time or the energy or the inclination to become an active Room Mother or busy observer or participant. And they need not. Promising as observation and participation are, they must be approached with the understanding that nothing, no matter how good, appeals to everybody.

Working parents, those with younger children, parents with large families, people with many other social or personal or community responsibilities, those who live far from the school — in each grade there always are some who cannot comfortably become involved in time-consuming arrangements. The minute a dull sense of duty becomes the base, the spirit is killed. These relationships must be voluntary.

Some teachers, for example, feel everyone must observe. They tell parents to come, or the word gets around: "You better do it." But people do not learn well under this pressure.

Parents are given to understand that everyone must take some part in the program: "She will call you sooner or later and it is wise to say *Yes*." The authoritarian note conveys the wrong idea even before the parent steps into the classroom.

Some teachers feel they must have a Room Mother. This compulsion dominates the opening parent meeting. This is the one business that must be accomplished. Whether people see why or know each other well enough to want to take the step makes little difference. They respond to outside insistence rather than to their own developed desires.

In home-school relations (to say nothing of the education of children) we must keep confident, almost with a happy-go-lucky air: If we don't get them now, we will get them later. . . . If we don't get them one way, we will get them another.

You can feel this relaxation if you are thoroughly persuaded that close home-school relations are satisfying to parents, helpful to teachers, and do mean better living for children. When something is that good, you can have confidence in it. You know that people cannot miss taking part, as long as you keep offering opportunities. You do not have to insist on any one thing. If parents do not come in the door you hold open now, they will climb in some window at a later time.

Since the prevailing basic idea in this chapter — that adults are naturally social, and eager to work with others — is a new idea for schools, you will do well to see the film Fitness Is a Family Affair *(twenty minutes, sound) from the Communication Materials Center (413 West 117 St., New York 27, N. Y.). Although this film oversimplifies the problem, as all films are apt to, it shows what happens to family and community life when people start working together. It makes clear how deeply adults want the satisfactions that come through cooperative endeavor. The film does not center on school life, but the implications for home-school relations are self-evident.*

8. The Written Word

Group meetings take a great deal of planning. Individual conferences demand time. Parent observation and participation mean adjustments in your classroom. One tool for working with parents offers a minimum of obstacles: *You can use the written word.*

Here is a technique that is simple to operate. You fit it into your time. You use it in your headquarters, your classroom office or your home. The technique is equipped with an eraser at the end of it. If you make any mistakes, you make them in private. You can wipe them out before the public sees them.

In one sense use of the written word is the oldest of all the ways of working with parents. Schools have always sent home a report card. But today, schools are realizing that pen and ink and paper have more and better uses than this.

NEWS NOTES OF GOOD CHEER

Some few schools have developed one good new idea because they know what bad reporters children are. Parents ask their youngsters: "What did you do in school?" One answer is almost sure to come from the young child: "Oh, play . . . ." Or sometimes the parent hears: "Work. That's all they give us — work!" But the parent has no idea what the play or the work is really like.

When parents ask older children: "Did you have a good day in school?" they are very apt to get the revealing answer: "It was all right." The parent is left to wonder: Now just what does that mean?

These schools, sensitive to how much parents care, have hit on a simple scheme—the teacher writes a very brief note home.

"Johnny made an excellent report today on butterflies. He certainly knows his hobby."

"Mary was upset right after you left, but she very soon got over it. Later she did some nice painting."

"George wrote an excellent paper in civics today. He organized his thoughts very well."

These notes take only a jiffy to write, but the reassurance they bring is tremendous. You are not writing a *magnum opus,* complete with a three-line salutation. Teachers dash the notes off—when there is a lull, after lunch, during rest time, or in a few minutes at the end of school. But parents read them and reread them because here is news they really care about.

This is an old trick with summer camps. They know how eager parents are for a word. Many of them put a postal card in a youngster's hand the minute he sets foot in camp: "Write a note home. Your parents want to hear." Parents are anxious for news even when their children are grown. They frequently write to their married sons and daughters: "Send us a postcard now and then. We just want to know that you are all right."

Some schools, knowing how much security brief notes can give parents and how much good will they win, make it even easier for their teachers by supplying note-size stationery with the school heading. But the form and style and beauty do not matter nearly as much as the clear message: Billy is doing fine! Those few words, saying that things are going well and are under control, could come on brown wrapping paper, and still be welcome.

There is, of course, no set time or set number of notes that should be sent, no set way to send them, no set facts to say. But these quick notes are for the good news, for the comforting news. If you cannot write to all your parents, be sure to keep in touch with those who most need a boost. If you do not like to write, phone!

This simple, decent, human thing to do can be squeezed into any teacher's schedule. A note is most welcome at the start of a school year, but a good word is always appreciated. It is welcome not only at the start of kindergarten or first grade. The note is as nice to get at the start of any grade . . . or even on a Wednesday in December.

NEWSLETTERS

An occasional school pushes this good idea even further. In addition to whatever spot-notes are sent, the teacher sends home a weekly or biweekly newsletter to inform the parents what is done each week—the stories the youngsters heard, the trips they took; the people who came into their classroom; the films the children saw; the problems they worked on, and so forth.

You lard all this with the names of the children who were involved, and with their words and the specific incidents in which they took part. You use good country newspaper style, not cold impersonal reporting. You write the tale of what happened through the names of the youngsters who made it happen. In that way you get vivid reading for parents.

Not every teacher can do this, of course. This technique comes easiest to the person who likes to write and who uses words with no trouble at all. Like so much of home-school relations, a teacher has to enjoy doing it. If the newsletter is a chore, you postpone it and feel guilty for not writing. Or you labor over the newsletter, your writing pains show through, and it is not much good to read.

But more teachers can compose this simple newsletter than know they can. This is a special kind of writing. Not a theme or an essay or a term paper, it is more like writing a letter. You don't have to dig down deep to puzzle: *What shall I say?* The story comes because you have lived through it. You write the chronicle of your days, of your children's days. The facts are at your finger tips, and the ideas flow.

Nursery schools, where parents call for their children, sometimes post their newsletter right at the door. Other schools are more likely to mimeograph it or ditto it—you can do it in a jiffy—and send it home through the mail.

Sometimes the principal writes the newsletter for each grade. Gathering the story gives him the excuse to be in classrooms instead of behind his desk. When the principal carries the ball, the newsletter cannot get out as often, but it is always welcome at home when it comes.

Here are the facts, down in black and white. This is what the youngsters are actually doing. This is the real meat. This tells the work that is going on. Parents who get this kind of report as the weeks go along are not at the mercy of wild rumors. They have a basis for supporting their school.

A growing number of camps have their counselors send this kind of newsletter home each week during the summer. Camps have a special need for doing this — the children are away from home. So far as camp administration is concerned, however, an equally important reason is that camps, privately operated and in a competitive market, depend on parents' approval. We in schools are apt to forget how much we, too, need exactly that. If you know any parents who have received newsletters from camps, secure a copy and analyze it.

START-TO-SCHOOL BOOKLETS

Many schools prepare start-to-school booklets for distribution to parents of youngsters coming to school for the first time.

The idea of a small factual booklet for beginning parents is a good one. Unfortunately, due to the manner in which many of these booklets are written at present, they fall short of the good they could do.

To appreciate the major error of many booklets, think back to the time when the starting first-grader was born. Every business firm in town saw the birth announcement in the paper or dug it up at City Hall. Greeting cards poured in from the diaper service, the milk company, the toy shop, the children's toggery, the furniture store.

The school should have been tremendously concerned. Here was a new youngster—and children are our business. But six years pass before we show we care. Students in school could easily create a school birthday card. It would be a worthwhile experience for them; new parents would be thrilled to receive it. Even such a simple way of showing that the school cares is overlooked.

The new baby comes home. Real problems arise, and his parents are truly concerned. Is he eating enough? Should he cry that much at night? Should they wake him up to change him? Why does he get so red in the face?

The Congressman is eager for the family's good will; he sends a government bulletin on infant care, and the parents are appreciative. The insurance company has a stake in this child; the agent sends a booklet, and the parents are grateful. The health department knows that these are anxious times for parents; it sends its leaflets, too. Many of the problems in these early years are problems of teaching: bowel and bladder control, eating habits, language patterns, social behavior. Education is our specialty, but the school may not even know that the child is alive![1]

The same not-knowing, not-caring occurs when a new family moves to town. The light company, the phone company, every milk company is aware that a new family has moved in. The

---

[1] See page 193 ff., "Birth-to-Six Materials for Parents" for a series of suggestions for reaching parents during these early years.

churches have no trouble learning the new address. Every movie house mails its circulars. The filling stations soon discover whether the family has a car. But the school does not care if the family comes complete with children.

No letter comes: "Welcome. We are glad you are here." No folder explains: "These are your schools. This is what they are like." The department stores urge the family to visit them. The school has a monopoly—it never says a word!

Check with families in your town who have a new baby. See how many cards, circulars, and folders from business firms they have received. This will give you a concrete idea of how widespread this practice is. It may help to start your ideas on what the school could do to build a relationship early with families.

The time finally comes. Now the child is five and a half. For better or worse, parents have worked out ways of living with him, they have managed to find solutions to the various problems that have come up. *Now schools care.*

They send their start-to-school booklet: "We are glad that your youngster is now of school age and that he will be with us this coming year . . . .

Be sure he knows his name and address.

Be sure he gets a good night's sleep.

Be sure you give him a nourishing breakfast.

Be sure he does not have a cold . . . ."

After a long dry spell of silence the school starts ordering parents around: *Don't* talk baby-talk to him. . . . *Mark* all his clothes with his name. . . . *Take* him to the doctor and the dentist . . . .

The advice is probably all good, but it comes at parents with a rush. The storm of *Do's* and *Don'ts,* from a group that has ignored parents before, sets a tone—a strident *you-listen-to-us-and-we-will-tell-you* tone.

But it may not be correct to say *sets* a tone. Maybe it *re-sets*

a tone. Maybe it recalls to parents those days when teachers
did not have to be close or friendly or useful—teachers talked
and children listened. Maybe it calls back old feelings still
floating around from the times when today's parents were children in school, and were being bossed.

The school has facts that parents need to know. Parents
will appreciate any booklet that informs them about such things
as entrance requirements, the dates of school holidays, the
length of the school day, arrangements for transportation, plans
for lunch at school. They will appreciate specific information
about the daily schedule of the classroom. They will be glad
for any background data about the school their child is about
to enter: the school's history, size, number of teachers, facilities,
and so forth. Such facts reassure; commands and unexpected
advice repel.

Parents will respond positively to a statement of the school's
philosophy: its goals for children, a description of its ways of
working with children. They will be pleased if the appearance
of the booklet conveys a flavor of friendly and creative living.
Your school story can whet parents' appetite for education; it
need not leave a bad taste in the mouth.

> *Write to a group of schools near you requesting copies of
> whatever booklets they send to their preschool parents.
> Examine the materials for their tone, their friendliness, their
> note of welcome, their attractiveness, their readability for
> parents.*

OTHER LEAFLETS PRODUCED BY THE SCHOOL

Many schools are expanding the idea that is basic to the start-
to-school booklets. They know that even if these are well-written and friendly such booklets only touch the surface.

Such schools ask themselves: Why not, instead of one booklet, no matter how good, a series of leaflets to parents, perhaps
one a month during the whole year before their child starts to
school?

"*Meet Our Staff*: This is the training we have had and the degrees we hold. . . . This is where we have taught before. . . . This is what we are like as people . . . ."

"*Visit Our Lunchroom*: These are the hours when the children eat. . . . This was the menu for October 7. . . . We have a new dishwasher. . . . We are planning to. . . ."

"*See Our Library*: These are the books children love the most. . . . This is the new collection we have added. . . . We need more books about. . . ."

Such schools also ask themselves: Instead of focusing on school-beginners alone, why not a start-to-school leaflet for every grade? Isn't each year a new year for parent and child?

"*This is Seventh Grade*: Children this age are interested in. . . . Their arithmetic will be like this. . . . They will be doing more of this . . . ."

"*This is Fourth Grade*: One change from last year. . . . A new area of work for this age is. . . . In deciding on text books. . . ."

Many schools are also exploring the possibility of leaflets to be used with parents before their children come to school or with parents of youngsters of any age on such questions as: Why We Take Trips; Why We Try to Know Children As Individuals; Why We Think Reading Is Important and What We Do about It; Why We Teach the Social Studies; Why the Arts Are Important. This is a list that could go on and on.

Business has discovered that workers have all kinds of misconceptions that hamper morale. When the workingman knows the straight story—about profits, management salaries, about competition, about the cost of materials—he is more willing to give everything he has to his job. Shut out from information and left to his own guesses, he is apt to have a chip on his shoulder.

The school story is the parent's business. How does the number of school children compare today with 1940? What is the cost of a school desk and of a blackboard and a map? Has the cost gone up or down in recent years? How long does a teacher study before she is certified? What has been the trend in teachers' salaries? What do teachers do during those long summer vacations?

You can find out what parents most want to know. Your ear to the ground for town gossip is one obvious way. Watching for references to schools in your local newspaper is another way: What do the "Letters to the Editor" say? Keep your eye on comments in national magazines, too. They often reflect what your local people are wondering about but are not yet saying out loud.

School people often sit on their dignity. We draw ourselves up—and away. The principal says: "Why don't they bring their complaints right to me? I'm approachable. Why do they have to do all this gossiping over bridge tables?" But you cannot be this passive, waiting in your ivory tower. Go out to the questions. Put your finger on them when they first arise, and no matter where they arise. Then you can do something about them.

It is better to be imaginative than over-dignified in thinking up ways to let the gripes come to the surface. Maybe a school Question Box will work for you. Business uses this idea to give people a chance to spill over anonymously. But however you get at them, the questions that need answering will range from the simple—"Why must schools close for teachers' meetings?"—to the complex—"What is the Board of Education? What does it do? Who is on it and how does it come into being and when and where does it meet?" Leaflets, teacher-written many of them, coming at parents at all places and times, are one way of setting the record straight.

Your school does not have to be a mystery house to parents: The child goes in September, and that is all they know. School can be a place the parent calls his own *if* he is informed on how it runs, what its problems are, what lies ahead on the horizon.

An important book to read in this connection is What People Think about Their Schools *by Harold C. Hand (Yonkers, N. Y.:*

World Book Co., 1948). Dr. Hand argues strongly against
guessing about parent dissatisfactions. He includes in the
book the "Illinois Inventory of Parent Opinion," a polling
device to reveal specific areas of satisfaction and dissatis-
faction.

All parents benefit by a steady flow of written information.
Certain groups of parents, however, may be particularly dependent on this avenue of communication. In families where
both parents work, for example, no one may have the time to
observe or to confer. In rural areas where distances are great,
parents may not be able to come to school to see for themselves
or to come to many group meetings. Sometimes lower-income
families do not feel comfortable at school meetings and shy
away from them. If you cannot send notes and newsletters and
leaflets to all your parents, pick out those who for any reason
are most out of touch. The written word is a particularly useful
technique for reaching them.

BIRTH-TO-SIX MATERIALS FOR PARENTS

The earliest that schools send printed materials to parents is
in the months just preceding the child's start to school. Yet
a youngster has already lived a long time by year six, and his
family has lived a long time with him. It is important for
schools to reach down into these early years.

Everyone knows that these early years are crucial years for
building attitudes in children. But we sometimes forget that
they are equally crucial for building attitudes in parents.
Right decisions in these years mean that the parent gets practice in applying some of the basic ideas about people that hold
true for all ages.

The parent who decides not to rush weaning is more apt
to decide later not to rush reading. The parent who decides
not to fret when the two-year-old is balky is getting practice

for taking adolescence in stride. Every one of the early little incidents has the double significance of being important for the young child's well-being *and* important in preparing parents for the future.

The parent who works out problems sensitively when his child is young is in an excellent position to be a good supporter of sound education as the child grows on in years.

We need to change our concept of who is a school child. We must come to see that a "school child" is the youngster who is in the school, or who was in school, or who will be in school—and that means *all* youngsters. Relatively few schools have public kindergartens. Hardly any have public nursery schools. But with a new concept of the school child we can find a way of extending a helpful hand to these young children and to their parents.

The importance of an early start has been clearly recognized in the series Pierre, the Pelican *by Loyd W. Rowland, a set of eight leaflets for the prenatal months and another set of twelve leaflets dealing with each month of the baby's first year. Prepared originally for the Louisiana Society for Mental Health, these are now available for one dollar per set from the New York State Society for Mental Health (105 East 22 St., New York 10, N. Y.). Some state departments of health and some mental health societies distribute them free to parents. You ought to read this series for its friendly tone, and to get the feel of the fundamental idea of beginning early. Could your school distribute this series? Or produce something like it?*

One suggestion has already been made: Schools can at least send a birthday card when a child is born, and on his every birthday until he comes to school. Equally as simple, something any school could do, is to send bibliographies of helpful materials to parents.

There are countless books and pamphlets that deal with all the age levels before the school-starting time. These range from free materials to ten-cent reprints, twenty-cent pamphlets, and three-dollar books. Many are as readable as a magazine story. Educators know about this rich lode. You got acquainted with these materials in your college training; advertisements for them appear in your professional journals; direct-mail notices cross your desk; they are displayed at professional meetings. They do not pop up, however, wherever a parent turns.

You could be the person who lets parents know that these materials exist!

A functional birthday card from a school, for example, could well go like this:

Happy Birthday!
Now Your Child Is One! Congratulations!
Do you know any of the following pamphlets? They are all about children the age of your own child. You may want to read some of them so that you can give your youngster the best second year of life anyone ever had! Why not send away for:

Your Child From One to Six. *It's only fifteen cents. You get it by writing to the Superintendent of Documents, Government Printing Office (Washington, D. C.).*

Avoiding Behavior Problems *by Benjamin Spock, M.D. Fifteen cents. Write to the New York State Society for Mental Health (105 East 22 St., New York 10, N. Y.).*

Enjoy Your Child: Ages 1, 2, 3. *The Public Affairs Committee (22 East 38 St., New York 16, N. Y.) sells this for twenty-five cents.*

When a youngster is two years old many a parent would be delighted to know that there is such a book as *Life and Ways of the Two Year Old* by Louise Woodcock (New York:

Basic Books Inc., 1952). At the next birthday your card could call parents' attention to *Three to Six: Your Child Starts to School* (Public Affairs Committee, 22 East 38 St., New York 16, N. Y.), twenty-five cents. Or you could let these parents know that fifteen cents sent to the New York State Society for Mental Health (105 East 22 St., New York 10, N. Y.) will bring them *What Nursery School Is Like* by Doris Campbell. Or that only five cents sent to the National Association for Nursery Education (Roosevelt College, Chicago, Ill.) will bring them *How to Distinguish a Good Nursery School.*

You can organize your suggestions for parents on an age-level basis or you can do it on a problem basis. Teachers know enough about child growth so that you can predict when different problems are apt to crop up in a home. You can save parents many a headache if you tell them about *Some Special Problems of Children Aged 2 to 5* by Nina Ridenour. This is an outstanding collection of eight short pamphlets on When A Child Hurts Others . . . Is Destructive . . . Uses Bad Language . . . Won't Share . . . Still Sucks His Thumb . . . Still Wets . . . Masturbates . . . Has Fears. The whole packet of eight costs only twenty-five cents from the New York State Society for Mental Health (105 East 22nd St., New York 10, N. Y.).

You may be a lifesaver if you tell parents about such pamphlets as *How to Tell Your Child about Sex* (Public Affairs Committee, 22 East 38th St., New York 16, N. Y.), twenty-five cents; *For Fathers Who Go to War* (Louisiana Society for Mental Health, 816 Hibernia Bldg., New Orleans, La.), twenty-five cents; *Making the Grade As Dad* (Public Affairs Committee), twenty-five cents. Your tips on these materials do not have to be sent only on a birthday. They can be sent midyear or at any time, and will always be welcome.

You might organize your suggestions in terms of young children's activities. Why wouldn't tips on children's books be a friendly gesture from a school? The Association for Childhood Education International (1200 15th St., N.W., Washington 5, D. C.) publishes *A Bibliography of Books for Children,* one

dollar, and *Children Books for Seventy-five Cents or Less,*
thirty-five cents; the Child Study Association of America (132
East 74th St., New York, N. Y.) publishes *Books of the Year
for Children,* twenty-five cents. Teachers know about these
and other sources; parents do not.

You use music all the time and know what is available. Reach
out to these young ages with a list of good records for young
children or songs that youngsters like to sing. You know Emma
Sheehy's good book *There's Music in Children* (New York:
Henry Holt, 1952, rev. ed.) from your college classes. Tell
parents about it and about her excellent record review column
in *Parents' Magazine.*

Art is another one of your fields. Why not produce a bulletin on art materials young children can use? The Nursery
Training School of Boston has done this. It has published
Formulas for Fun!, a booklet for parents on play materials all
of home-made ingredients (355 Marlborough St., Boston,
Mass.), fifty cents. Maybe your bulletin can tell where finger
paints, clay, and good children's paint brushes can be bought
in your town.

Parents are eager for help like this. We must see that it is
our job to give it. The gains children will make are self
evident. Think how fortunate a child is who is consistently
treated well from the time he is born until his schooling ends,
guided by one united (and informed) point of view. But we
shall gain, too. We shall have the good will and the support of
parents who are our friends—parents who know the school as
a useful place.

*In the bibliography you will find a list of some of the books
and pamphlets that are especially good for parents today. New
material is constantly being published, however. It is more
important for you to have some means of keeping in touch with
the field for the future than it is to know what has been published in the past. Drop a postcard to the following groups
and ask to be put on their mailing list:*

Association for Family Living, 28 E. Jackson Blvd., Chicago, Ill.

Child Study Association of America, 132 East 74 St., New York 21, N. Y.

Health Publications Institute, 216 N. Dawson St., Raleigh, N. C.

National Association for Mental Health, 1790 Broadway, New York, N. Y.

New York State Society for Mental Health, 105 East 22 St., New York 10, N. Y.

These groups not only produce their own material for parents but also distribute that which is produced by many other organizations.

It is one thing to send a list of suggestions to parents. But then, someone has to read the list. And if they read it, they still have to search to find the materials, or send away for them. Busy families often cannot operate this way.

Knowing families, you will try to cut out as many in-between steps as you can. Your goal will be to put good printed materials right into the hands of parents. Occasionally you will know of pamphlets that are free: from the Federal government or state departments; from commercial groups like insurance companies; from professional groups and nonprofit organizations.

Very often you yourself can reprint magazine articles, either from professional journals or popular magazines. You have to secure permission in advance from the publisher, of course. But then you can mimeograph the material and send it directly to homes with the compliments of the school.

You ought to start now to collect good magazine articles for parents, just the way you proably have a file of good pictures for children. You can reprint these as needed. Magazine articles are also useful on a bulletin board, if your parents call for their children. You will find, too, that you can give a parent an article to read when he might turn up his nose at a book.

Schools can also buy materials and send them directly to parents as a gift. Almost all of the parent pamphlets are available at reduced rates, if you buy them in bulk. This takes some cash, but the amount is just a drop in the bucket compared to the good it does.

Teachers can also create their own materials, written specifically for the parents of children in their school area. Not everyone likes to write, any more than everyone can be perfect at leading a group meeting or in talking easily with parents face-to-face. But each school has some teachers who enjoy working with words, and all of us have more skill and experience at writing than we realize. After all, we are the people who have written term papers by the dozens and who correct themes and essays with our left hands.

A principle is involved in all these steps that go beyond reading lists. Your follow-through demonstrates to parents a new kind of education. The old idea was that education was just words—people listened and read, but they did nothing. Education did not touch their lives directly. It was an academic thing, removed from action and from people's real worries.

You are trying with children to develop a classroom program in which education means changed behavior and better living. Parents must first see this new idea at work before they can understand and approve of it with children.

The more you go, beyond mere listing, to actually putting these materials into parents' hands, the more you show this new approach at work. You *teach* through what you *do*. In addition to bringing parents the good ideas in the pamphlets, you give them an experience in which education is not something abstract "over there"—school is not empty words and sounds. Your ideas come right into the living room and affect the way people live.

MATERIALS FOR PARENTS OF OLDER CHILDREN

Printed materials have a particular usefulness with parents of very young children whom the school does not serve through group programs. Do not be misled by this emphasis on the early years, however. Nothing about the written word limits it to parents of the under-six age.

The under-six years tend to be times when parents are particularly puzzled, but so too are the pre-adolescent years and those of adolescence. There never is a time in a parent's life when he is free from all cares about his child. There never is a time when a word of reassurance or of technique is not welcome.

Any parent of a ten-year-old, for example, will be relieved to read *Pre-Adolescents: What Makes Them Tick?* (New York: Child Study Association of America, 132 East 74th St., New York, N. Y.), twenty cents. The high school parent who has not read *This Is the Adolescent* (New York: National Association for Mental Health, 1790 Broadway, New York, N. Y.), twenty cents, will be delighted to learn of it. *Your Child and Radio, TV, Comics and Movies* (Chicago: Science Research

Associates, 57 W. Grand Ave., Chicago 10, Ill.), forty cents, will set many a school-age parent's mind at rest.

Be sure to turn to the bibliography at the end of the book and become familiar with the available materials on the age you teach. Keep your eye open, too, for good magazine articles. Parents of school-age children will be no less pleased than preschool parents to receive from the school a readable reprint that deals exactly with the problem that has been stumping them at home.

Nor are parents' questions only in the field of child development. In the area of school practices, for example, the teaching of reading is especially troublesome to parents. If schools could help parents know this story, more than half the battle in home-school relations would be won. The explanations you give your parents face-to-face are invaluable. The opportunities you provide for them to observe in your classroom are tremendously important. But to supplement these, turn to the very good published materials which explain the teaching of reading. These are written for parents and should be used more widely. Don't overlook: *Reading Is Fun* by Roma Gans (New York: Teachers College Bureau of Publications, 1949); *Helping Children Read Better* by Paul Witty (Chicago: Science Research Associates, 1950); *Ways You Can Help Your Child with Reading* by Sally L. Casey (Evanston, Ill.: Row, Peterson, 1950); *When Parents Ask about Reading* (Chicago: Scott, Foresman, 1949); and *If Your Child Has Reading Difficulties* by Ursula Cooke MacDougall (New York: The Dalton School, 1952).

9. Two Occasions for Vital Relationships

THE START OF SCHOOL

The time when a child first starts to school, whether to kindergarten or to first grade, is a significant time for home-school relations. The school has a golden opportunity to be a helper, not a nag or a boss; to be useful, not simply demanding and expecting; to be sensitive to what the parent is concerned about, not merely wrapped up in its own little "school world."

This is curtain-raising time. It can show parents that teachers are human and show teachers that parents do not have horns. What happens at this time and what does not—the tone underlying all that goes on—can affect a parent's feeling toward school in all the years that lie ahead.

Parents with children starting to school are the special concern of primary teachers. But the upper elementary teacher and the high school teacher get the dividend, or pay a price, for the commissions and omissions of these early days. The teacher of young children is not the only one who has to be concerned; everyone has a vested interest.

WHAT THIS TIME MEANS TO A PARENT

Attitudes formed, when parents first send a child to school, persist because these are no ordinary days. This is a crucial time in most homes.

Unless seventeen older children have taken the edge off, the first day at school is always a time of big excitement. We have no initiation ceremonies in our society. Starting to school, the first big step out into the wide world, marks the time to a child: Today I am a man!

Every parent wants this step to be a good one. He wants this to be a red letter day for his child: to like going, to like his teacher, to like his friends, to like the work. When the youngster comes home—the first day and for many days to follow—his posture, his exuberance, his facial expression, his step are carefully watched. Did school go well? He is not in tears, is he? He looks so happy!

Starting a child to school is a landmark for parents, too. It is the test of how well they have done their work up to now. Parents are embarrassed if the child clings to their hand and refuses to leave them. They are distressed if the child cries as they go away. They are bothered by his public screaming and by his less public but equally disturbing sudden shyness and clamming up.

If the youngster lets his parent down, the parent is angry with the child: "You're no baby; why do you act so silly!" . . . and with himself: "I wonder what I've done wrong?" Almost inevitably, some block is also thrown up between the parent and the teacher and school: "Why didn't they do something?" the annoyed parent wonders.

The teacher who is sensitive to what this step means and who does the little things that help it go well, earns friendliness and appreciation and deep respect. This is the youngster's *and the parents'* first major public performance. Make it a smooth performance, and the school wins a booster.

Starting a child to school has still another meaning for parents. The youngster senses: Today I am a man. The parent is also something today, but it is harder to predict what. Today I am . . . *old?* (All my youngsters are grown up now.) Today I am . . . *lonely?* (What will I do with myself with him in school all day?) Today I am . . . *free!* (The last one is off my hands.)

The feelings can run a wide range, but feelings are always there. This is not just another Monday. School-starting is a time for major readjustments in personal life, in family life, in routines, in ways of finding satisfactions. To many a teacher the children's faces and the parents' faces are simply more of the same; this opening day parade goes on every year. But it happens only once in a parent's life . . . or twice or three times or four. And each time it brings a different feeling.

Being blasé and being blind to the fact that something is going on inside the parent is not the way to win friends. You need the human touch that tells you: This is an important time. Even though you seem to do nothing special your sensitivity brings you closer to the person.

GOOD STARTS ARE NOT MADE IN HEAVEN

Some lucky youngsters take to kindergarten or first grade like ducks to water—perhaps those who have had many experiences in leaving their parents and in playing with others, perhaps those few who have unusual inner confidence. But many children falter, some only for a few uncomfortable moments while others stumble around for a longer time. A good start is not an automatic thing. It can happen *if* there is good planning.

The earlier you begin to plan the better. Starting to school is a very small step if there has been a lot of preparation; it seems like a huge one if it happens all of a sudden.

During the spring many good teachers visit the homes of all of the children they will have in their grade the following year.

Adults know how much a familiar face makes us feel at home. When we go to a large party we look feverishly until we find someone we know. We always try to sit next to our friends; it cuts down the tension. The teacher's visit to the home achieves this for the child.

The visit is rarely long enough to make a lasting friendship, but it is a start. The youngster has some fleeting notion, even months later, of what Miss So-and-So is like. She is his pal . . . she came to see him.

Teachers often follow up this visit with the invitation that flows logically from it: "Why don't the two of you drop into school some day? How about Friday at 2 P.M.?"

People look different in different settings. That *tall*, tall woman in the smock (so big, in contrast, with all of the six-year-olds around her) looks different from the nice lady who came to the house in a dress. If a youngster sees the teacher in her native habitat, there is an even better chance that he will feel like an old-timer when school finally gets underway.

He can see the teacher, the room, the lockers, the desks, the door. These no longer have to exist just in imagination. The child now has something real to which he can pin them all.

The commercial airlines realize how important this kind of preparation is for passengers making their first flight. They have very clear booklets that tell you what every motor sound

*means, all about emergency landing fields, the radio beams
the planes fly on, the different altitudes for travel in each
direction. The airlines want passengers to feel safe. That is
what we want for youngsters, and parents, coming to school
for the first time.*

With good planning, all the new children do not visit on
the same day: thirty first graders, thirty-five five-year-olds-
about-to-be-six, and thirty-five mothers milling around—noise
and confusion and excitement and crowds. The advance visit
is one new child and one new mother . . . a special date and a
special time. The visit may have to be after school when the
other children are gone. Many schools schedule it right in the
regular school day so that the youngster and the parent see
school life going on.

During these visits, either your home visit or the parent's
visit to school, you can tell mothers about (or give them) one
of the four inexpensive pamphlets that deal with starting
youngsters to school:

How a Child Feels about Entering a Nursery Center by
Doris Campbell. Fifteen cents and as good for six-year-olds
as Threes, despite the title. (New York State Society for Mental Health, 105 East 22 St., New York 10, N. Y.)

Preparing Your Child for School. Fifteen cents. (Superintendent of Documents, Washington, D. C.)

Three to Six: Your Child Starts to School. Twenty-five cents.
(Public Affairs Committee, 22 East 38 St., New York 16, N. Y.)
N. Y.)

Will Your Child Be Ready for School? by Olga Adams. Ten
cents. (New York State Society for Mental Health, 105 East
22 St., New York 10, N. Y.)

THE PRESCHOOL ROUNDUP

Most schools do not yet personalize their efforts to this extent. Their first relationship with parents and children is apt
to be at the preschool roundup. This is a fast developing practice frequently sponsored by the PTA. On one set day, or

several, usually in the late spring, parents are urged to bring their coming-of-school-age children to the school. A physical check-up and immunization, if needed, are apt to be the main order of business.

Much can be said in favor of this practice, particularly from a health standpoint. Once youngsters are past infancy they usually see a doctor only when they are sick. The start to school—and the start of each school year, in fact—is a good excuse for something very much needed, anyhow: a complete physical checkup.

The preschool roundup is questionable, however, when it is either the initial relationship of the family to the school or the sole preschool tie. Its emphasis on physical health does not do justice to the significance of school-starting nor to the total concerns of the school.

The roundup also has a tone that leaves much to be desired. This is examination time. It is a time for *doing* something to the child (and it hurts a little); it is a time for *telling* parents what they should do. The procedure is not well geared to making friends, either of the children or their parents. Old-timers who have a good relationship could take it; new people are apt to be a little pushed away.

Many schools, wisely, are trying to take the sharp edge off this introduction to school. One, for instance, has a display and sale of good inexpensive books for five- and six-year-olds at this time. Another school has a similar sale of the many inexpensive pamphlets for parents. These sales are simply organized, usually conducted at tables in the hall. They do indicate, however, that the school realizes that youngsters are whole and have many facets to their being. They give teachers a good chance to chat with parents, too.

EARLY GROUP MEETINGS

Many schools hold their first parent meeting around preschool roundup time. At their best, these meetings are not an occasion for *do-this* and *don't-do-that*. Nor do they pile on all of the factual information about the start of school. They provide a good chance for a friendly get-together and for parents to raise questions. Parents learn that school today does not mean: "They always tell you what to do." They discover that their ideas and reactions have a valued place today.

A filmstrip is available to use with parents whose children are entering kindergarten: Kindergarten and Your Child, *from the Audio-Visual Materials Consultation Bureau (Wayne University, Detroit 1, Mich.), $3.50. This is a possibility as a basis for discussion at the first parent meeting. It is more helpful, however, to focus on your own program — what you do with your children in your room. But see the filmstrip. It may give you ideas on how to do a still better job.*

A few schools hold not one meeting but a series. In the half-day kindergarten the teacher uses, as the spring comes along, some of her free afternoon time for "new parents." In schools which operate the full day, the starting grade is sometimes dismissed one afternoon a month so the teacher can meet with new parents as a group. Most often no special time is provided; the teacher must find time during the after-school or evening hours.

These meetings usually center on school life. The preschool parents hear talks by the teacher and by the principal; they see some of the materials the school is using. The meetings often result in parents coming to school to observe—to see for themselves what is going on. Before schooling begins is a prize time for parents to learn. Their own youngsters are not yet on the griddle. Ideas are easier to take and easier to give. A team sense begins to grow.

A few schools begin bringing parents together when the children are only in their second or third years of life. Occa-

sionally, the school simply suggests the idea of meeting together
and provides the space. The parents go ahead on their own,
but they have the school to thank for making the meetings
possible.

These very early meetings are apt to center on children's
behavior. Often the parents follow the study guides in such
magazines as *Child Study, The National Parent-Teacher,* and
Parents' Magazine. Parents do not always find clear-cut answers in these meetings. There is comfort, however, in learning that all two-year-olds and Threes and Fours act the same
way.

Some few schools have one person on their central staff who
is responsible for bringing preschool parents together. Usually
the starting grade teacher—kindergarten or first grade—takes
the initiative. There are many advantages if the teacher who
will have the youngsters for their first time in school is the
early bird. Relationships are established, and ways of working
together are found that carry over into the years ahead.

But principals can do this job and, in one school, the fifth
grade teacher organized a group of mothers of two-year-olds
and met regularly with them until the children entered school.
This illustrates the only essential consideration in deciding who
should be the leader: Whoever works with parents must want
to do it, must see the values, and feel they are worthwhile.

Only the exceptional school at present starts working with
parents this early in the game, yet much can be said for the
idea. Only the rare school problem can be solved the first
time it is tackled. Take the question of large class size. Two
big elements are involved in its solution: finding adequate
additional classroom space and hiring additional teachers.
Both of these are in turn dependent on the budget. In many
instances the budget is involved with the tax rate or a bond
issue; these, in turn, may hinge on who is on the Board of Education.

The parent whose six-year-old enters a first grade of forty-
eight children cannot do a thing. His child is caught. Within

that youngster's sixth year of life there simply is not time to
take all the lengthy steps that could eventually get him a decent
class size.

The parent is trapped, too. He may appreciate the difficulties that lie in the way of a solution. He may see that there
is no way out now. But because his eye is on his youngster,
the excuses are intellectual and carry very little emotional
appeal to him. The parent does not like the situation . . . or
the school or the teacher.

You hear parents verbalize their feelings: "They are working
on a traffic light for the corner. I just hope my child isn't killed
before they get it." "They want to soundproof the cafeteria,
but Billy will be an old man with indigestion before the job
ever gets done." "They are trying to get more playground
space, but Frank will be in high school by the time they get
anywhere." "They are talking about a special teacher in art.
A lot of good that will do Mary; she will be in college by the
time someone is hired."

If children could live their lives over and over again, you
would not hear these complaints. But a youngster is nine only
once, he is in first grade only once. A parent may be able to
see the obstacles, but that does not make him like them. Parents
are impatient for their children to have the best.

So many schools always find themselves behind in their
dealings with parents. They have two strikes on them before
they even come to the plate. So many problems that are real
to parents, problems parents would give their time and energy
and devotion to, have to be crossed off because they cannot be
solved at the moment. The parent feels: *What's the use?
What's the point?* He cannot do anything now—except get
angry.

An early start can lessen the anxieties parents feel about children in the preschool years and diminish the frustrations when
the child comes of school age. We must dip down into these
years before the child actually crosses our threshold. Unless
we show we care, we shall never fully command all the energy

and backing that parents could give to us. Nor will we be of the service to childhood that we potentially could be.

THAT OPENING DAY

The day that school finally starts can be a hectic time— wearying for teachers, over-stimulating for children, harrowing for parents. It need be none of these, however.

One very intelligent improvement is to stagger the entrance day for the beginning grade. A small number of children come at the regular opening time. After a day or so, when this group has their feet down, some more children join them. When these two groups know the ropes, a third group has its starting day, and so on until everyone is in. Opening day is spread over as much time as the children seem to need.

The advantages of this system for children are obvious. The youngster who is making his first step out from the smallness of his home does not have to meet a crowd. He does not feel lost or overwhelmed. The stage is set so that he can take this important step in his development with success. A school that says: "All forty of you come on September 5," puts up too high a hurdle for some children.

Those teachers who use this staggered start are delighted with it. It gives them the time to get youngsters placed, to iron out difficulties, to handle without flurry all the adminstrative details that arise. School begins in a peaceful way, and that is as it should be.

Parents, too, deeply appreciate the idea. They can see that their child is singled out and not swamped by numbers. They have a last chance to ask questions without feeling that they are in the way. The whole day is a smooth one and not a time for anxiety.

There are objections, of course. Many schools get their state aid on the basis of average daily attendance. A staggered start to school for the youngest children costs the community some pennies. Often not as much money is lost as one would think. Children who have unhappy, tense, and worried beginning days very frequently miss school later because of upset stomachs, colds, and other seemingly physical ills. The high initial attendance decreases as the confusion takes its toll.

Parents will object, too, if they are taken unawares. It is no help if the school sends a form letter home at the last minute: "Your child is to begin on September 9 and not September 5 as announced." The cold fact, the last minute, no explanation. Such a notice assumes that families have only *education* to think about—whatever the school works out will be all right.

But families are hardly ever upset if they know the reason for the plan: "This will help your child to get a good start. We can come to know him better and to help him get his feet on the ground."

They very seldom object if the arrangements are made sufficiently far ahead of time so that family plans can be adjusted, and so that children can be prepared.

Families are rarely bothered if their individual needs are not lost in some grand plan: "But I am beginning work on the 5th; I thought that was the day he would start to school." "But he has been counting on going with Frank; Frank is his closest friend, you know." "But we have a car pool and I am supposed to take the Frazier child to school." No plan is good if administered mechanically, with no feeling for the people involved.

PARENTS ARE WELCOME TO STAY

A staggered start to school makes possible one development about which teachers have very divided feelings: If only ten children come to school on opening day, as many of their parents can stay as need to. If all forty children come at once, their forty parents cannot stay — they would become an intolerable burden. A teacher could not cope with the numbers.

You have no choice but to shoo away the adults as quickly as possible.

Some teachers do not want parents to hang around. "They are just in the way." "I've noticed that the children cry more if their parents stay." "As soon as they go, the youngsters settle

down and we can get to work." Even though it becomes possible for parents to stay, they are not welcome.

Some start-to-school booklets make this very clear: "We have a well-trained staff, and our teachers are very sympathetic. On opening day bring your child to school, say goodbye to him, and then go. We will see that he adjusts."

Of course many youngsters (particularly those starting school at first grade) do adjust well. They have no need for their parents. Even a large number of five-year-olds want their parents to leave them as soon as possible. But through all the years from six down to two some children (more at the younger ages) want their parents close at hand at first. A few show their need by crying. The need is no less real with others even though they manage somehow to cover it up.

Teachers often say: "It's not the child, it's the mother! She just can't bear to part from him." They say this as though it were a powerful argument for getting that woman out of the room. Actually, the reverse is true. It makes no difference whether the parting is hard for the child or hard for the parent. The school's job is to make it easy and comfortable for both. When this first leave-taking goes well, all those to follow (camp, high school, college, job, marriage) are that much simpler to take. Too many "children" at the age of thirty-one still cannot bear to leave their parents; too many parents at the age of forty-one still cannot bear to have their children leave them.

The school's job is not to rip parents and children apart, callous to how they feel. The school's goal is to enable the parting to be a happy one so that it becomes a positive step in development. To achieve this it is important that some parents stay.

Not that they stay forever. Many youngsters only need to know that their mother is near at hand; a fleeting glimpse of her now and then is enough to buck them up. Some parents only need a little reassurance that everything is going along all right. Smart schools, sensing this, serve coffee and cake in the cafeteria for their parents on opening day. This gives many mothers all the comfort they need: the chance for a look-in at their child now and again. At the same time parents and the principal have a useful social hour together.

Some children (and some parents) need mother around for a longer time. In the good school there is no pressure to go. The child can stay by his mother's side. After all, he has twelve years of schooling ahead. He does not have to plunge into deep water on the first day.

The mother sometimes sits on the sidelines. (If you have a comfortable chair for her that is proof that parents are welcome.) Sometimes, after a while, the mother goes to work in the classroom. There are countless behind-the-scenes jobs a parent can do. She is near her child, and that is good for both of them.

After a while (a week for some, two weeks for others — the

time varies) the mother can go. Now both the child and she can take it. Usually the youngster gives the sign. Sometimes the teacher has to take the lead: "Mrs. Smith, I am sure you can leave now. Billy is feeling at home." The teacher can be this direct and yet cause no resentment. The parent has not been shoved out. She has seen Billy adjust with her own eyes; she has had a chance to build confidence. She can leave at this point because now she *knows* that her youngster is in good hands.

Based on their experiences with yesterday's school, parents think: "I will just be in the way if I stay in the classroom." Unless a school does something to break down this attitude, many parents will not dare to stay, even though they want to. Some teachers hide behind this feeling. By never saying anything explicit they side with the parent's assumption that she must get out as soon as possible.

Schools that stagger their start, schools that really welcome parents, must make their point of view clear: "Stay as long as you want to. We are glad to have you." If you do this, you obviously lay a good foundation for your later work with parents. You cannot say to a parent who wants to stay: "Go home," and then later, when *you* want something from her, expect her to come bouncing back.

The mother who learns from the very start that she is not in the way will feel much friendlier later. She will be more eager to work with the teacher and to take a full part in her child's education.[1]

PREADOLESCENTS AND HIGH SCHOOLERS

The younger the child, the greater the interest parents take in home-school activities. Nursery school and kindergarten mothers and fathers usually are buzzing with questions, eager

---

[1] Refer to the news notes suggested on page 184, and to the newsletters suggested on page 186. These have a particular value for parents of school-beginners, now that you have helped the child get off to a good start.

for conferences, glad to come to meetings. Primary school parents are faithful workers, appreciative of any chance to observe, steady participants in the PTA. But as the child becomes older, parent interest wanes.

This presents a very real problem to schools. Many accept this deterioration in home-school relations as natural and inevitable. They have an inactive high school PTA and are pleasantly surprised whenever upper elementary school parents attend meetings. Other schools puzzle over the question. Does the decline stem from our present ways of working? Are certain home-school activities particularly suited to parents of older children? Should a school gracefully bow to an inescapable situation, or are there creative ways to cope with it?

PARENTS' INTEREST IN OLDER CHILDREN

One positive fact seems clear: *Parents are interested in their older children.* The statement can even be put more strongly: Some parents are more concerned about preadolescence and adolescence than about any of the years since infancy.

Preadolescence and adolescence confront many parents with truly puzzling behavior. Their youngsters are much more self assertive than formerly. Issues of respect, of rudeness, of obstinacy arise with a sharpness the parent has not known since the child was a two-year-old. Often the boy or girl's behavior seems to regress. The careful child becomes casual about clothes and property; the compliant child becomes forgetful, resistant; the cooperative child has a million and one other things on his mind — he never gets around to doing chores he once was eager for.

Youngsters this age live their real lives in a world outside the home. Parents' own standards are no longer sufficient for deciding numberless questions: movies, bedtime hours, television viewing, dates, sororities and fraternities, dances. What the other fellows do, what other families allow, what the custom is, all intrude very importantly into family discussions.

New questions leap into the forefront. Sex education suddenly becomes desperately important. Lipstick, high heels,
allowances, smoking, use of the car, choice of friends — each
day brings some new problem which parents must thrash out
with an offspring less reasonable, more impatient than he once
was.

The years of preadolescence and adolescence are seldom
peaceful years for parents. Turbulent in themselves, they are
further darkened by the shadow of the future. The youngster
is approaching adulthood now. Will he go to college and, if
so, which one? What are his real interests? Is he doing his
school work and, even if he is, is the school giving him the
right work? Will he be prepared for a job? Is she going with
the right people? What effect will the draft have? Each event
in the lives of both boys and girls is seen, not only in its present
significance, but also in terms of some not-so-far-off but very
confused future.

If the existence of problems and concentrated thought about
children are basic conditions creating a need for home-school
relations, the years of preadolescence and adolescence ought to
be peak years of great activity. Questions about child development are both keen and numerous; questions about good education are many and much more pressing. The stage would seem
to be all set for the play to go on.

THE SCHOOL'S READINESS TO HELP

One obstacle stands in the way: *The average school is not
well geared to working with parents of older children.*

Customarily, the junior high school and the high school are
departmentalized. Each teacher teaches his specialty: English,
art, the social studies, science, mathematics. A few teachers
think only in terms of the content to be taught, the ground to
be covered, the facts to be mastered. A growing number try
to see the young student in relation to their special field of

competence. These teachers face two obstacles: They spend only a brief time each day with each student, *and* they touch many young people, sometimes more than one hundred, in the course of each day.

Teaching masses of learners and seeing them each for only spot periods of time, the departmentalized instructor is often trapped by the very organization of his school. Contrasted with the lower elementary teacher who stays with one group of thirty children all day, he is apt to be less aware of the individuality of his students and less able to use facts which could make each one stand out as a separate person.

These are the years of the home room teacher. In the usual secondary school this is the one person who most needs to know what each youngster is like and who could work with parents. Yet the same obstacles block this teacher that trouble all others on the staff. The home room period is a short period. Once that period is over, the teacher becomes a subject-matter specialist who deals with many other students. Guidance is only one of his many duties.

An increasing number of both junior and senior high schools are developing core programs. Such programs are a partial re-creation of the conditions of the lower elementary school. The students stay with one key teacher for a major part of the day; the students are active in their search for answers to questions; the curriculum centers more on problems in the students' living than on abstract subject matter. Under these conditions it pays to know young people as individuals. There is time to come to know them. Some one person can be identified as having the responsibility to know them.

It is hard to see how the usual subject-centered junior or senior high school can either carry out many significant activities in home-school relations or benefit themselves or parents by carrying them out. Perhaps the disinterest of parents arises in large part because parents sense the impasse. They see no handle on which to grab hold, no one to reach out to them, no existence of effective activity.

Given a certain set of conditions, perhaps the decline in parent interest is inevitable. Perhaps it must simply be lived with and accepted as the "natural" order of things. Given a *new* set of conditions — the core curriculum is one example — perhaps parents' constant puzzling and high interest in their children can be turned into a resource. Perhaps these years can become more peaceful for parents. Perhaps these years can become less stormy and more fruitful for young people.

CHANGES IN THE EDUCATION
OF OLDER CHILDREN

Junior and senior high schools are caught in a "chicken-and-egg" dilemma, trapped in the old question of which comes first. Parents are not apt to work closely with these schools until the schools reorganize their curriculum. Yet parents who are not intimately a part of the schools are apt to misunderstand and fight any reorganization.

The slowly developing trend toward a core curriculum is only one of many changes long overdue in the education of older children. The lower elementary school has its self-contained classrooms, its activity program, its awareness of individuals. The program for young children has been modified in many ways on the basis of research and experimentation. The revolution at the upper levels is still "coming 'round the mountain." Many factors — the war, inertia, entrenched interests — have dammed up change. But the pressure of new social conditions and of new psychological information is strong, and the dam must break sooner or later.

Courses in sex education are one illustration. It is apparent that sexual development is one of the outstanding characteristics of the adolescent. It is equally apparent that the sexual behavior of adolescents is one of the outstanding social problems of our times. Traditionally, junior and senior high schools have taken little or no account of the need for sex education. As the needs have intensified a few schools have ventured into this important area, some eventually with parent support, many with parent opposition, almost all with a sense of newness in the business of working with parents.

Work programs for adolescents seem sure to come sometime. Summer programs for adolescents seem a necessity. Larger blocks of working time, more first-hand experiences, a more community-centered curriculum, more attention to the personal and social needs of this age — these are merely a few of the developments most needed in the upper schools.

Somehow junior and senior high schools must begin to find ways of working with parents *now,* even before the schools are truly geared for this relationship. Unless parents can be brought in now, unless they can find now an effective relationship, needed changes seem headed for rough sledding.

THE NATURE OF YOUNG PEOPLE

The organization of the present junior and senior high school is not the only reason why parents slowly but surely show less interest in home-school relations. The nature of the preadolescent and adolescent is another very important factor.

The young child is a dependent child. He accepts his parents' interest and presence; he wants them, and he welcomes them. The first-grader is thrilled when his parent visits his classroom. The second-grader is excited when his parent stays to have lunch at school. The third-grader is "pleased as punch" when his teacher visits his home. The fourth-grader thinks it natural and even a good sign when his teacher and his parent sit down to talk about him. All these and other home-school activities are proof to the child that the adults in his world think about him and plan for him and care for him.

At some point in development, however, the child is no longer a child. His surety no longer comes when adults take the responsibility for him. He feels safer, stronger, better when he is a person on his own. No longer does he assume automatically that adults are on his side, working together for his benefit. He becomes more conscious of the fact that he is less dependent. Now the adults may be talking *about him*. He suspects that every plan is a plot.

The growing child has his new feelings of separateness and independence inside of himself. He very much has to reckon with the world around him, too. As a young child he could be publicly proud of his parents. Now their presence is a sign of the babyhood he is trying to leave behind. The child still wants and loves his parents, but he hopes they won't kiss him in public or sit near him in the movie or . . . come to school!

Obviously the child does not draw a sharp line between himself and his parents on some one birthday. The wall of proud sovereignty arises slowly, over a period of years. Parents see it being erected through such minor incidents as the giggling over the telephone, the closed door to the bathroom, the retreat to the bedroom, the club with its rules that are so all important, the fiercely close friendships with pals on whom the sun rises and sets. Sensitive to this development, a little baffled by it, the parent retreats in many areas. Home-school relations is only one field where many a parent feels that the role of wisdom is to stay in the background.

WRITTEN COMMUNICATIONS HELP

Three elements must be reconciled: (1) parents' great concern about child development and their fundamental interest in education during these years; (2) school's relative lack of readiness to work with parents; (3) young people's new and strong feelings of independence. What can be done where three such conflicting forces operate?

One approach seems very feasible: Junior and senior high school teachers can make extensive use of written materials. Both professional and popular magazines are continuously printing sound articles on the common behavior difficulties of these years. With permission from the publishers, teachers can mimeograph these articles and send them to each parent.

Organizations like the Association for Family Living (28 E. Jackson Blvd., Chicago 4, Ill.) sell many very inexpensive reprints and pamphlets dealing with these later years. You can let parents know that these materials are available, or, with a very small investment of your own money or the school's, you can put the best of these right in parents' hands. With a small amount of cash your room or your school can have a lending library of books and pamphlets for parents.

Reprints, pamphlets and books do not work wonders even when parents read them. Doubtless some materials will end up in the waste basket. But on the positive side they are an expression of interest on the part of the school. Parents appreciate them as such. Publications can give very practical help on some problems, and they always contribute toward the building of a friendly relationship. From the educator's standpoint — home room teacher, core teacher, guidance consultant, administrator — anyone can find materials, reproduce them, distribute them whenever time happens to be available. Done once for one group of parents, the major part of the task is finished, and the results can be used over and over again with successive groups. This is one home-school activity which can easily be fitted into even the tightest schedule.

In the same fashion, junior and senior high schools can do much more than they now do to encourage parents to read and think about secondary education. Professional journals are full of readable articles telling of different school's experimentation. Mimeographed reprints sent to parents can do much to build a background of information and to stimulate interest and thought. Not many books have been written for parents about secondary education, but the few that exist are full of vision. You can help many of your parents to know these materials.

Each junior and senior high school teacher can write his own materials, too. Nothing about adolescent development makes the news notes referred to on page 184 less welcome in the older child's home. A word of praise from the English teacher, the biology instructor, or the coach pleases parent and child of any age. Nor does anything about adolescent development rule out the newsletters suggested on page 186. The greater self-consciousness of teen-age boys and girls may indicate that, at the junior and senior high school levels, names of individuals should be used very sparingly, if at all. But the straightforward, factual story of what a group is doing—the books it has read, the discussions it has had, the people and places it has seen, the problems it has wrestled with—can be good and comforting reading to parents. It can also give them the base they need to do some constructive thinking about education.

TEACHERS ON THE SIDE OF YOUTH

The more personal approaches in home-school relations — parent observation, participation, conferences and reporting — all hold one potential threat. Instead of gaining strength and security as a result of them, the young person may feel that their impact is to keep him back in babyhood. This is not an insolvable difficulty, however. The answer lies in boys' and girls' feeling that teachers are on their side.

If a good relationship exists in the classroom; if students feel that the teacher is their friend; if they know you are with them and not against them, then the door is open to these closer and more meaningful parent-teacher relationships. The key is in how you and your students get along together.

If you are a good friend, the chances are that you will be welcome in the high schooler's home. If the atmosphere in your classroom is one of good fellowship, of easygoingness and of comradeship, the chances are that students will welcome parents in your room. What you can do in home-school relations is determined by what you do in teacher-student relations.

You have to treat these boys and girls as people. You have to look on them and think about them and feel about them as humans. You have to show to them the decency and consideration and regard that you would show to adults. Your feeling of respect puts you on the side of young people. It recognizes their most cherished goal — to be individuals.

In home-school relations you show respect to young people by making plans *with* them. You can talk over with them your desire to make home visits and agree on a time that suits them as well as their parents. The idea of parent observation in your classroom is something the group can discuss. You can afford to abide by their decision after they have thrashed out the pros and cons. If the vote is favorable, as it probably will be, the invitation can come from the group as well as from you. If you put it up to them, these young people can feel responsible for planning parent participation. They will have ideas here that will help you.

When you are planning individual conferences to report on school progress, and as the children become older, you have to think increasingly in terms of parent-*child*-teacher meetings. Much that must be covered now has to go to the young person as well as to his parents; the plans made must come from the young person as well as from you and the parents.

Your sensitivity will have to tell you what, at any age, is meant for adult ears and adult minds alone. For example, no useful purpose is served by including young people in discussions that center around adult plans for the guidance of children's behavior. This is especially true when the behavior stems from causes that the boy or girl cannot consciously control — a child's emotional needs, for example, or pressures in his environment. But a great amount of school performance and of social behavior is within the youngster's control. High values come from increasingly including the growing person as one of those responsible for his own behavior.

In the same way young people can help plan, with teachers and with parents, the group meetings that will take place. By being in on the planning and by participating in the meetings this age can gain from home-school relations what all ages need: strength, not threat . . . and a focusing on the problems that stand in the way of better living.

10. Evaluation

HAL DOREMUS

The proof of the pudding in home-school relations is whether or not youngsters' living is improved:

1. Do they have a richer, fuller, more nourishing life, in school and out, than would otherwise be open to them?

2. Do they have more consistent guidance in school and out, and, as a result, live more fully at the peak of their powers?

Final answers to these questions can come only through controlled experiments and through studies that examine children's living over long periods of time. Such studies are not now available, nor are they likely to be made. The length of time needed, the many variables involved, the difficulty of working with controlled groups of humans, all make this kind of evaluation unlikely.

Some tests can be made, however, which give an indirect measurement. Presumably youngsters will gain in proportion to the fullness with which a school carries on its home-school relations. Assuming that the techniques suggested are good, children's living should be improved as more and more of the ways of working with parents are used.

You or your school, therefore, can check a list of the various means of communication between parents and teachers as one measure of the extent to which you are probably helping youngsters to live more richly and with greater effectiveness. Here are twenty-five questions to ask yourself:

1. Do you have room meetings of the parents in your classroom in addition to the larger meetings of the PTA?
2. In your room and in your larger PTA gatherings, do you make use of all three types of meetings?
   (a) Fact Meetings.
   (b) Discussion Meetings.
   (c) Work and Play Meetings.
3. In your Fact Meetings, do you take advantage of the wide variety of techniques available?
   (a) Lectures.
   (b) Reading Panels.
   (c) Symposia.
   (d) Committee Reports.
4. In your Discussion Meetings, do you utilize the wide variety of available techniques?
   (a) Films.
   (b) Drama.
   (c) Role Playing.
   (d) Puppets.
   (e) The Funny Sheets.
   (f) Fiction.
   (g) Buzz Sessions.
   (h) Panels.
5. As you look over the content of your room meetings and of your PTA gatherings, are each of the four major concerns of parents adequately covered?
   (a) Child growth and development.
   (b) Your school's program.
   (c) Neighborhood agreements about children's behavior.
   (d) Community, state, national, and world affairs that affect children.

6. Do you and each other teacher hold at least one meeting at the start of each school year to explain the year's program to parents?
7. Does your school sponsor meetings for parents of children who are not yet of school age?
8. At your meetings (whether small groups or large) no matter what their goal, do you have exhibits for parents to examine?
9. At your meetings do you have for sale pamphlets, reprints, and books for parents?
10. Do you visit the homes of the children in your class?
11. Do you talk face-to-face with parents when you report on a child's progress in school?
12. Do you have many opportunities for informal chats with parents?
    (a) Before and after group meetings.
    (b) At Work and Play Meetings.
    (c) At incidental, unplanned occasions in the course of a year.
13. Do parents come to school to observe your classroom in its daily operation?
14. Do parents participate in your classroom program?
    (a) On special occasions, such as trips, parties, and so forth.
    (b) In the regular daily program of instruction.
15. Do you confer with parents about observation and participation?
    (a) Beforehand.
    (b) As a follow-up.
16. Do you have a Room Mother?
17. Do you send home frequent, brief, personal notes of praise about individual children?
18. Do you send parents a newsletter reporting on the activities of your group as a whole?
19. Do you help your parents to keep in touch with child development publications?

(*a*) By informing them of books and pamphlets available.

(*b*) Through a lending library in your room or school.

(*c*) By reprinting magazine articles and mailing them home.

(*d*) By buying and sending to parents inexpensive pamphlets available from many sources.

20. Do you help your parents to read about developments in education?

(*a*) By informing them of books and pamphlets available.

(*b*) Through a lending library in your room or school.

(*c*) By reprinting magazine articles and mailing them home.

21. Do your parents receive from you and your school leaflets the staff has prepared?

(*a*) To help a child make a good start to school.

(*b*) To prepare parents for the work that will be done in each grade of school.

(*c*) To clarify for parents the school's program in such fields as reading, the social studies, arithmetic, and so forth.

22. Does your school send written materials on child development and education to parents of children who are not yet of school age?

23. Does your school use a "staggered start" for its first-year children?

24. Are parents in your school free to stay with their school-beginning children until both the child and the parent feel comfortable about the youngster's adjustment?

25. Do older children in your school, preadolescents and adolescents, share in home-school relations in ways appropriate to their age?

(*a*) In planning for home visits.

(*b*) In planning for parent observation and participation.

(*c*) In conferences regarding their work and behavior.

(*d*) In group meetings.

MORE QUALITATIVE QUESTIONS

Note that each one of the twenty-five questions listed above is relatively mechanical. You could answer Yes to the entire list and still fall short of your goal of improving children's living. Parents observe, *yes* (but under compulsion). You use exhibits, *yes* (but no one looks at them). Your meetings employ a wide variety of techniques, *yes* (but people are bored). You need some way to get at the more qualitative aspects of what you do — how parents feel, how you feel, the emotional tone that characterizes these various means of communication.

If you can add to a high score on the quantitative questions a similar high score on more qualitative items, the chances are increased that your efforts in home-school relations will have the actual impact on children's lives that you desire.

The first twenty-five questions were simple to answer. You could read and answer immediately either Yes or No. Following are only five questions, but they are much more difficult. They call for more judgment on your part and for honesty in going beneath the surface to assess how you and others around you feel.

1. Is home-school relations in your school a two-way, give-and-take process?
   (*a*) Are your various efforts balanced so that parents have as much opportunity to influence your thinking and action as you have to influence their behavior?
   (*b*) Are you trying to sell parents some bill of goods: a way of living with children, your school's program, some facts you think they ought to know?
   (*c*) Are you using home-school relations as a technique to put over to parents some pet ideas you have up your sleeve about children or education?
2. Does your school truly regard working with parents as im-

portant, or are home-school relations an incidental concern tacked on for appearances' sake? Has your school recognized the importance of this new area, for example, through any of the following:

(*a*) Providing time for home visits?

(*b*) Providing comfortable adult chairs in classrooms for parents?

(*c*) Providing you with more secretarial services so you can keep a record of your work with parents?

(*d*) Providing a conference room where teachers and parents can talk together?

3. Do you and your colleagues enjoy parents? Do you like working with them and feel comfortable doing it? Are you sympathetic with parents?

(*a*) Do you confine your relationships to the more or less "official" times — your group meetings, conferences, and so forth — or do you call parents up on the telephone, look forward to seeing them unexpectedly, chat freely with them?

(*b*) Do you have approximately the same number of relationships with all your parents, or do you find it easier to get along with certain types — the wealthier parents, the better educated ones?

(*c*) Do many parents make you feel impatient? Do you want to squelch those who dominate meetings, or give those a good shove who won't change their ways, or turn a deaf ear to those who always have a complaint?

4. Does your work with parents square with what you know about all good education?

(*a*) Do you realize that there are causes that make parents act the way they do, just as there are causes that underlie the difficult behavior with which some children confront you?

(*b*) Are you aware that parents are learning through all that happens to them, just as you know that children are continuously being educated not only by what you say but by what you do?

(c) Do you try to search out for and begin with the problems parents most keenly feel, whether or not these check with your notions of a good program?

(d) Are you sensitive to individual differences in parents as much as you are to the spread of differences in children? Do you have variety in content and in ways of learning to take these differences into account?

(e) Are your various programs for parents planned so that parents can study their problems until they work their way through to satisfying solutions?

(f) Are your parents active in the solution of their own problems, or are pat answers handed to them on a silver platter?

5. Are you clear in your own mind that home-school relations ought to lead to continuously improving conditions for children, and not become a device whereby adults "gang up" on youngsters or a means for the preservation of the *status quo*?

(a) Can you spot instances where you have further individualized your program because of information that has come through your work with parents?

(b) Are you aware of ways in which your program has changed because parents have helped you to see new goals?

(c) Has your classroom program for children become richer, more varied, and more extensive as a result of your relationships with parents?

The assumption is that, if you can give good answers to this second set of questions, youngsters will be having the best that love and knowledge brought by a united team of parents and teachers can do for them. But even if, as is unlikely, all your answers are right, your task is not done. All of these suggestions are a beginning, rather than an end. Home-school relations is a new field. Very little research and experimentation are specific and peculiar and private to it alone. When you work in this field you need your imagination and creativity much more than you need your memory.

If the various practices from other schools work in your situation, do not be content with them. Use them as a springboard to your own better ideas. For that is the great need. Each teacher, each school, must generate its own bright, shiny, new ideas. The job is there for you to do — the thinking job, the job to ask and to keep asking: What would be better?

Are you pitching your ideals high enough? Are you daring to hope enough for man? Or are you accepting a lower level of behavior, thinking you must, but only because you do not dream?

These are the questions you must ever ask yourself as you work in this field. You must let war and prejudice, poverty, hate, greed, personal unhappiness, and social evil always make you puzzle: Do people have to be this way? Or can you educate, through your work directly with children and through home-school relations, to grow a better breed of man?

Bibliography

MATERIALS ON HOME-SCHOOL RELATIONS

Relatively few books and pamphlets have been written specifically in the field of home-school relations. Magazine articles which tell detailed stories of what individual schools and teachers are doing are therefore particularly valuable. Be sure also to keep in touch with the National Congress of Parents and Teachers (600 S. Michigan Boulevard, Chicago 5, Ill.) and the National Citizens' Commission on the Public Schools (2 West 45 St., New York 36, N.Y.); these two groups have already produced much helpful material, and will continue to publish more. Your state department of education, your state society for mental health, and the extension division of your state college of home economics are also excellent sources of material. Some of the publications of the Bureau of Child Development and Parent Education of the New York State Department of Education, which has long been a leader in this field, are included in the materials listed below to illustrate this point.

PAMPHLETS

Children Are Our Teachers by Marion L. Faegre. Children's Bureau Publication No. 333 (Washington: Superintendent of Documents, 1949. Fifteen cents).
  An outline and suggestions for group study to be used with that other excellent publication of the Children's Bureau, *Your Child from 6 to 12.*
Decision Through Discussion: a Manual for Group Leaders by William E. Utterback (New York: Rinehart & Co., Inc., 1950).
  A good example of the many specific materials available to help you learn the skills involved in discussion leading.
Discussion Aid for "A Healthy Personality for Your Child" by Marion L. Faegre and James L. Hymes, Jr. (Washington: Superintendent of Documents, 1952. Ten cents).

A valuable aid in all group discussions, as well as specific help for groups studying a Healthy Personality.

Discussion Guide for Parents (New York: New York State Society for Mental Health. Thirty-five cents).

A guide to group study at various age levels, based on the content in the following pamphlets: *Pierre, the Pelican; Enjoy Your Child: Ages 1, 2,3; Understand Your Child from 6 to 12;* and *Some Special Problems of Children Aged 2 to 5.*

Education for Responsible Parenthood by William G. Hollister, Eva F. Dodge, and S. T. Robbins (Raleigh: Health Publications Institute, 1950. Seventy-five cents).

A planned program to help lay people organize their own study groups, complete with background information and a discussion leader's manual.

Fifty Teachers to a Classroom by the Committee on Human Resources of the Metropolitan School Study Council (New York: Macmillan, 1950).

An outstanding booklet which gives thorough help on all phases of parent participation.

Guide for Child-Study Groups by Ethel Kawin (Chicago: Science Research Associates, 1952. Sixty-four cents).

A specific and comprehensive, inexpensive booklet growing out of wide experience with PTA study groups.

How to Use Puppets in Parent Discussion by Jean Schick Grossman (New York: Play Schools Association. Sixty cents).

A woman who has worked much of her life with parents in the lower income levels describes one technique she has found particularly useful.

Individual Parent-Teacher Conferences by Katherine E. D'Evelyn (New York: Teachers College Bureau of Publications, 1945).

The best material available in this important area: specific, down-to-earth, aimed at the classroom teacher.

It Starts in the Classroom: a Public Relations Handbook for Classroom Teachers (Washington: National School Public Relations Association, 1951. One dollar).

Although tinged with a touch of "selling the school," this has many specific suggestions which can be useful if carried out in a broader setting.

Making a Plan for Leading a Discussion Group (1946);
Points for Lay Leaders (1947);

Points for a Member of a Discussion Group in Parent Education
(1949);
Suggestions Concerning the Discussion Method (1949)
(Albany: Bureau of Child Development and Parent Education,
State Department of Education. Free).
Mimeographed materials which are samples of the excellent
publications this Bureau in New York has produced. Every
state should have such an office in its state department of
education.
Parent Education in the Nursery School by Edith Norton (Washington: Association for Childhood Education, 1949. Seventy-
five cents).
Do not be frightened away by the title. You can get many
good ideas from this pamphlet, no matter what age level you
teach.
Parent Participation by Jean Schick Grossman, ed. (New York: New
York Association of Day Nurseries, 1949. Twenty-five cents).
A brief summary giving the highlights of a workshop for
nursery directors; mimeographed and concerned with all
aspects of working with parents.
Parents and Teachers as Partners by Eva H. Grant (Chicago: Science Research Associates. Forty cents).
The editor of the *National Parent-Teacher Magazine* has
brought together many valuable insights and specific sugges-
tions.
Partners in Education by Muriel W. Brown (Washington: Associa-
tion for Childhood Education, 1950. Seventy-five cents).
This material grew out of the National Conference on Family
Life in Washington in 1948. Mixed in with many important
generalizations about schools and families are excellent descrip-
tions of school practice the country over.
Reporting to Parents by Ruth Strang (New York: Teachers College
Bureau of Publications, 1947).
One in a series sub-titled "Practical Suggestions for Teach-
ing," and living up to this description.
Study-Discussion Group Techniques for Parent Education Leaders
(Chicago: National Congress of Parents and Teachers, 1948).
Specific and practical and well worth your time.
Ways and Means of Reaching Parents by Jean Schick Grossman
(New York: Play Schools Association. Thirty cents).
This is 16 pages, but it develops a good point of view and
states briefly many suggestions.

Working with Parents by Hazel F. Gabbard. Bulletin 1948, No. 7,
  Federal Security Agency, Office of Education (Washington:
  Superintendent of Documents, 1949. Fifteen cents).
    This is the least expensive of the materials available, yet as
  sound and as complete and as practical as any.

BOOKS

Helping Teachers Understand Children by the Staff of the Division
  on Child Development and Teacher Personnel (Washington:
  American Council on Education, 1945).
    Although the book as a whole is valuable for its presentation
  of a way of studying children, Chapter III, "Seeing the Child
  as a Member of a Family," is particularly pertinent to this field.
Home and School Work Together for Children. Twenty-first Year-
  book, California Elementary School Administrators Association,
  1949. Order from Fred Zimmerman (3720 Penniman Ave.,
  Oakland 2, Calif.).
    A complete and sound statement, rich in examples from Cali-
  fornia schools, including good sections on the responsibilities
  of various members of the school team.
Home-School Relations: Philosophy and Practice by Sara E. Bald-
  win and Ernest G. Osborne (New York: Progressive Education
  Association, 1935).
    This 140-page book is out of print but well worth looking for
  in your library. It describes six schools' relationships with parents, analyzes the what and the why, and opens up many good
  questions.
Leading Parent Groups by Evelyn Duvall and Sylvanus Duvall
  (Nashville: Abingdon-Cokesbury Press, 1946).
    This brief book is geared more to church groups of parents
  than to school groups. It is comforting as well as instructive,
  however, to see how similar the needs and the procedures are.
Parents and Children Go to School by Dorothy Baruch (Chicago:
  Scott, Foresman and Co., 1939). Part II: "Parents at School,"
  pp. 29-170.
    Although centering on nursery education, this book contains
  a wealth of material on parent meetings, individual conferences,
  and parent participation. The general principles apply to all
  age levels.

Where Children Come First by Harry and Bonaro Overstreet (Chicago: National Congress of Parents and Teachers, 1949).

This is the story of the PTA, told perhaps too glowingly and too uncritically. You do get a feeling for the importance and inspiration of the idea, however, from knowing this history and sharing the authors' vision and enthusiasm.

Your Part in Your Child's Education by Bess B. Lane (New York: E. P. Dutton and Co., Inc., 1948).

This is a gold mine, if you are primarily concerned with group activities and group meetings for parents. Other possibilities in home-school relations are slighted, but this book is the best in what it tries to do.

MAGAZINE ARTICLES

New issues of journals come out every month, so no listing can pretend to be complete. The following, all from *Childhood Education,* are more to indicate the wealth of good material that is available through magazines. The titles give a sufficient indication of what the articles are about:

February 1945: "Parents Report to Teachers" by Hughes and Cox.

October 1945: "It Takes Both Home and School" by Taylor.
"Shop Nights" by Wittick.
"When Parents and Teachers Work Together" by Castle and Wiencke.

March 1946: "When Teachers Interpret Their Schools to the Public" by Wardner.

April 1946: "Parent Education on the Run" by Ward.

October 1946: "How to Find Out about Children" by D'Evelyn.

November 1947: "The Family: Bulwark of Democracy" by Wilson.
"A Teacher Visits Homes" by Rogers and Rice.
"It Takes a Lot of Doing: The Cooperative Nursery School" by Spitzenberger.

February 1948: "Planning for Child Growth Through Parent-Teacher Conferences" by Cutright.

March 1948: "What I Found Out about My Five-Year-Olds" by Redfield.

September 1949:   "Orienting the Three's and Four's" by Horwich.
                  "They Can Do It Themselves" by Mould.

January 1950:   "When Parents Learn with Children" by Lissim
                  and Silbert.

May 1951:   "I'm a Stranger Here Myself" by Lane.
                  "We Work Together . . .
                      "Throughout the School Year" by Bertermann;
                      "In School Planning" by Singsen;
                      "In Meetings and Discussions" by Hartrich.

October 1951:   "Citizen Groups in Action" by Larsen.
                  "Community Groups Add Strength" by Hayes.
                  "They All Did What They Could" by Rasmussen.

FILMS

You will probably get the best service on all films by renting them from your state or regional film library. If these centers do not have the film you want, try either of the following, both of which distribute on a national scale: Communication Materials Center (413 West 117 St., New York 27, N.Y.) or the New York University Film Library (26 Washington Place, New York 3, N.Y.). The films listed below have already been commented on at the place in the text where they can make their most effective contribution; the brief annotation here should be read in connection with the earlier description:

Family Circles (thirty minutes) (sound). See p. 32.
    This is intended primarily to awaken parents to the need for closer cooperation with the school. It is excellent for showing the changes that have taken place in family life; be critical as you look at the sections portraying home-school activities, however.

The Centre (twenty minutes) (sound). See p. 18.
    Although this is not, strictly speaking, a film on home-school relations, there is no better way to jog your imagination on what schools might do than to see this.

The Fight for Better Schools (twenty minutes) (sound). See p. 22.
    The grave weakness of this film is that it shows nothing at all

of the part teachers can and must play in building public understanding. It is well worth seeing for its other values, but ask
yourself: If you were planning a sequel, what would you show
teachers doing?

A PROFESSIONAL JOURNAL

No magazine exists at present which is concerned exclusively
with the professional aspects of working with parents. The journal initiated in May 1952, *Adult Leadership*, published monthly
by the Adult Education Association of the United States of
America (743 N. Wabash Ave., Chicago 11, Ill. Four dollars
a year) is exceptionally helpful however. It looks at all aspects
of adult education but its suggestions on group leadership, its
articles on techniques, and many of its tips on materials are
very applicable to work with parents. In addition, the format
and organization of the journal is outstanding — specifically
designed to prod the thinking of people working with groups.

MATERIALS INTERPRETING WHAT
SCHOOLS ARE DOING

In every parent group some members have the background
and the ability, as well as the time and interest, to read any of
the texts that are used in college education courses. The whole
range of our professional literature is open to these people. In
suggesting books to these few you can make your own choice
from those books that have made the most sense to you.

More people will enjoy reading an occasional article in our
professional journals. Tastes vary, but materials that are full
of specifics, giving the down-to-earth story of what goes on in
a classroom or school, are apt to be the most appealing. You
can follow the idea suggested on page 198. Mimeograph an
article you think is sound and readable, and send it directly
to parents. The Association for Childhood Education International has done something like this — bringing together good

articles from its journal — in the pamphlet *For Parents Particularly* (fifty cents). Valuable as this booklet is for parents, new, good, simple, clear descriptions of school practice are published every month. The best solution is for you to be your own reprinting company.

Several books and pamphlets have also been written specifically for parents. The best of these are listed below. Even these, however, have one limitation: Parents want most of all to know about *their* school, the one their child is in. While you make good use of textbooks, of reprints, and of the following books and pamphlets, be sure that you do not neglect to use newsletters, observation, and all of the other means you can so that parents know what is going on in *your* room.

BOOKS AND PAMPHLETS

A Good Day in School by Viola Theman (New York: Teachers College Bureau of Publications, 1950).
> This sixty-page pamphlet gives a concise, readable, and yet quite specific picture of many different kinds of school days . . . all of them good for children.

A Look at Our Schools by Paul R. Mort and William S. Vincent (New York: Cattell and Co., 1946).
> A brief book, simply written, which does much to clarify the psychology and philosophy underlying the modern school.

High Schools for Tomorrow by Dan Stiles (New York: Harper and Bros., 1946).
> This is a very moving story, written with fire, by a person who wants better secondary schools and makes clear the kinds of things he thinks such schools would do.

How Good Is Your School by Wilbur Yauch (New York: Harper and Bros., 1951).
> This is the newest book in the field and the best. Parents will enjoy its friendly style, its clear-cut writing, and its rich illustration from reality and imagination.

How to Distinguish a Good Nursery School (Chicago: National Association for Nursery Education, Roosevelt College. Five cents).
> This little leaflet is hardly on a par with the big books and

pamphlets listed here, but parents need help in choosing good nursery schools even more than they need help at older age levels. This folder is worth many times its cost.

How to Help Your Child in School by Mary and Lawrence K. Frank (New York: Viking Press, 1950).

A sound philosophy and a keen understanding of children shine through every page of this well-written book which answers many of the questions parents have.

Good Schools for Children (Atlanta: Southern Association of Colleges and Secondary Schools, 1951. Fifteen cents).

A series of thought-provoking questions for elementary school parents, designed to prod communities into action for better schools.

I Learn from Children by Caroline Pratt (New York: Simon and Schuster, 1948).

A personalized and readable story by one of the pioneers in modern education. The school described differs from most public schools, but the sensitivity and spirit of the book will appeal to many parents.

Little Red School House by Agnes DeLima (New York: The Macmillan Co., 1942).

This is the full-length story of one private school which pioneered in a direction that many public schools have since followed.

Look at Your School by Childhood Education Committee (New York: Public Education Association, 1951. Seventy-five cents).

This is an attractive, illustrated sixty-page booklet subtitled "A Handbook for Parents about Our New York City Schools." The practices and problems are not peculiar to one city alone, however.

My Country School Diary by Julia Weber (New York: Harper and Bros., 1946).

Another personal story which gains tremendously in readability because of this. Here is a live account that will help parents raise their sights.

Our Children and Our Schools by Lucy Sprague Mitchell (New York: Simon and Schuster, 1950).

This book was distributed by The Book Find Club, which put it in the hands of many parents the country over. It is a long book but only because it includes so many specific descriptions of classroom practices.

Parents Look at Modern Education by Winifred Bain (New York: D. Appleton-Century Co., 1935).

This is an older book, but because it was written specifically to help parents know what schools are doing it still has real usefulness today.

Progress to Freedom by Agnes Benedict (New York: G. P. Putnam's Son, 1942).

This is not about one school but about our whole public education movement. Some parents need help today in appreciating the significance of this unique democratic development.

Promising Practices in Elementary Schools (Atlanta: Southern Association of Colleges and Secondary Schools, 1952).

A picture book showing many excellent public schools in action.

Story of the Eight Year Study by Wilfred M. Aiken (New York: Harper and Bros., 1942).

A popular account of a significant experiment in which thirty high schools were freed from college entrance requirements to give their students the kind of education they needed just as high school boys and girls.

Were We Guinea Pigs? by the Class of 1938, University High School, Ohio State University (New York: Henry Holt, 1938).

This is a unique book, written by young people themselves as they take a long look back over their own high school education.

What Is Progressive Education? By Carleton Washburne (New York: John Day, 1952).

A leader long active in the field writes a simple and convincing explanation for parents.

What Nursery School Is Like by Doris Campbell (New York: New York State Society for Mental Health, 1949. Fifteen cents).

One of a set of three pamphlets designed to inform parents about nursery education so that they can make wise choices in selecting a school and aid in their child's adjustment.

Willingly to School by Claire Zyve (New York: Round Table Press, 1934).

This story, primarily about the early grades in school, is told almost entirely in pictures. All parents will enjoy thumbing through it, if you can still find a copy. Despite its publication date it still has a great deal to offer.

Your School, Your Children by Marie Syrkin (New York: L. B. Fisher, 1944).

Another book written primarily for parents, on the high school level, designed both to describe practices and to raise the level of wanting good schools on the part of parents.

FILMS AND FILM STRIPS

Observation and participation right in your class room are, of course, the most convincing ways of letting parents know what is going on in schools and of starting their thinking about what ought to go on. If you want to use a secondhand experience as the base for your discussion, the following are good possibilities:

A Child Went Forth (twenty minutes) (sound).

One of the most beautiful films about education ever made, this shows a group of three to eight-year-olds in a summer camp. Although primarily geared to younger children, the youngsters' enthusiastic responses to their firsthand experiences inevitably raise the question: Could not schools, for all ages, do something like this?

A Day in the Life of a Five Year Old (twenty minutes) (sound).

The commentary of this film gives a good statement of the goals of kindergarten education, and the film shows good activities in well-equipped rooms. Everyone behaves so perfectly that you get a somewhat false impression of life in school, but no film is perfect and even weaknesses can stimulate good discussion.

And So They Live (thirty minutes) (sound).
The Children Must Learn (twenty minutes) (sound).

These two films, which can be used independently or in consecutive showings, beautifully portray a meagre mountain life. In the moving way they raise the question: Can schools build better living? Some seeing the films say: "Oh, but our town isn't like that." If you can use these films as a jump-off into: "What are *our* needs? What should *our* schools be doing?" you will really have something.

Children in the Primary School — Ages Six, Seven, Eight Years. Filmstrip available from the Association for Childhood Education International (1200 15th St. N.W., Washington, D.C.).

An attractive and well-organized group of pictures of school activities related to the major needs of children in the primary grades.

Group Life for the Preschool Child. Filmstrip available from the New York University Film Library (26 Washington Place, New York 3, N.Y.).

This strip was edited by Eleanor Reich, long a teacher in the outstanding Harriet Johnson Nursery School. With a minimum of comment it shows how nursery activities meet the young child's needs.

Kindergarten and Your Child. Filmstrip available from the Audio-Visual Materials Consultation Bureau (Wayne University, Detroit, Mich.).

A filmstrip has one advantage over a film such as *A Day in the Life of a Five Year Old:* You can stop and discuss as the strip moves along. The disadvantage is that you miss the motion, activity, and the dramatic quality of a film.

Human Beginnings (twenty minutes) (sound).

Like *Human Growth,* which is described next, this film shows sex education evolving naturally as a part of classroom activities. This particular film focuses on five- and six-year-olds. The age of the children and their open discussion, which the film catches, bothers some parents. There is a great need for discussion following the film, and for a groundwork of good relationships preceding it.

Human Growth (twenty minutes) (sound).

Based on wide experience in Oregon this shows how schools can and have handled sex education with older children. The film is excellent and reassuring to many parents. Don't rush into this area, however. Be sure your parents know you and have confidence in your total program as the first step.

Living and Learning in a Rural School (twenty minutes) (sound).

The title here is self-explanatory. The film is an older one but good for stressing that sound education is not as dependent on "external pretties" as it is on teachers' and parents' concept of a program.

Living and Learning in the Garden City Schools. Ninety 2" x 2" Kodachrome slides available for rent or sale from Stanley Bowmar Co. (2037 Broadway, New York 23, N. Y.).

The story of how these slides were made to interpret the school's program to its parents is told in the article, "When Teachers Interpret Their Schools to the Public," referred to on page 237. Many other schools have also produced short movies and slides; if you can get hold of some in your locality these local films can also be useful as a basis for discussion.

Bibliography

Our Coming Generation (twenty minutes) (sound).

This intrepets the program of a day nursery through the activities of individual children from two through five years of age. Since programs for children under six so often are not supervised by the state, parents need all of the help they can get in building up their own standards. These, and not legislation at this time, are their safeguard.

Play Is Our Business (20 minutes) (sound).

This attractive film is valuable for two reasons: (1) It shows the activities in after-school, holiday, and weekend play schools — a new development which more and more communities must come to; (2) it demonstrates graphically how our changing ways of living affect children, and what schools ought to do as a result of the changes.

Pre-School Adventures (thirty minutes) (silent).

This older film portrays the program in the nursery school and kindergarten at the Iowa Child Welfare Research Station. This is still useful and does not suffer greatly from not having sound.

What Has the Nursery School to Offer? Filmstrip available from the Association for Childhood Education International (1200 15th St. N.W., Washington, D. C.).

Rose Alschuler, one of the leaders in nursery education, edited these pictures specifically for use with parents.

Who Will Teach Your Child? (twenty minutes) (sound).

Assignment Tomorrow (thirty minutes) (sound).

Both of these films are well done. They place the emphasis on the need for good teachers. Perhaps their greatest use is in large public gatherings where people may need a broad view as they consider large questions of community policy in relation to the schools. They go along in the same framework as *The Fight For Better Schools* (see page 238).

Wilson Dam School (twenty minutes) (sound).

There is no better film than this for showing the total program of a good, yet average, public elementary school. Incidentally, it includes some shots of parents observing in the classroom and of a teacher making a home visit.

MATERIALS INTERPRETING CHILD GROWTH
AND DEVELOPMENT

So much is being published about children for parents these days that your problem is more to weed and to sift, rather than to find. This is a real problem. Simply because words have been put between bookcovers does not mean that you can relax. Some of the words are not sound; more of them are understandable to a few people but not to large numbers of others.

You have to exercise your critical judgment. You cannot pass on to parents everything that comes along. You need a set of standards to guide you. One basis for these standards must be your knowledge of the people who will be the readers. The second basis can be certain general criteria such as the following:

1. *Is the material sound?* This is the first and most important question. Does it check with the best that is professionally known? To get an answer, you have to rely in large part on your own knowledge of children, on what you have learned in your studies, from the research, and in other books that you have read.

One indirect piece of evidence is the background of the author. Do you know him? Where does he do his professional work? How much part does he play in professional meetings and conferences? Free-lance writers frequently are responsible for newspaper columns and magazine articles on child care. Their articles always read well, and often, of course, they have been checked for accuracy before publication. But newspaper column, magazine story, pamphlet or book, you want to ask yourself: What evidence is there that this person knows what he is talking about? Is this sound information, or something simply written well enough to get into print?

2. *Is the material sufficiently reassuring?* Words take on a definiteness when they are set in type. They look so final, so authoritative. The author may mean them "in general," "on the whole," "usually," "with many children," and "often." When the words turn up on the printed page they begin to look like absolute standards and approved techniques.

The trouble is that parents seldom throw the book away.

Some are more inclined to throw the child away and start all over again.

Sometimes materials which meet the first standard perfectly — they are written by highly trained specialists — fail this second test. They sound so definitive that the parent feels: "The book knows so much and I know so little." "The book is so definite on this point and John is different." This authoritative note may be all right for students in training; for parents already perplexed it usually is not helpful. Ask yourself as you preview materials: Will this give the parent more faith in his powers? Will it help him, yes . . . but will it also encourage him to have more confidence in his own ideas?

3. *Is the material right for the parent you have in mind?* For most parents the following standards are apt to hold true:

Pamphlets are more acceptable than books;

Short materials are more appealing than five-hundred-page tomes;

Drawings and photographs and not too much type on a page help;

A sense of humor is a blessing;

Short sentences are better than those that go on for a whole paragraph;

Everyday words make more sense than special professional lingo;

Sentences with some *You's* in them are more fun to read than those that talk about "the parent," "the child," the great big beautiful abstraction.

But everyone has his own taste.

Some books, written originally as stiff college texts, are advertised as being good for parents. They are good . . . for a few parents. Some mothers and fathers will find exactly what they are looking for in the tightly-packed footnoted page. Not all parents will by any means, however, no matter what the advertisements may say.

4. *How much does the material cost?* Some people want a
bound book that has a cover and costs $3.50. Many more, how-
ever, will never read about children unless they can find what
they want in a twenty-five-cent edition. The chances are that
the lower the price of the material, the better chance you have
of getting it into parents' hands. In these days of rising costs,
this has become one very important criterion.

> *These criteria, incidentally, may help you when you try to
> write your own materials for your parents. The standards that
> helped me most in my own writing for parents came originally
> from* The Art of Plain Talk *by Rudolf Flesch (New York: Harper
> and Bros., 1946). I owe that small book a big debt of gratitude.*

MAGAZINES

Many of the major religious denominations publish their
own magazines on child and family life. One example is *The*
Christian Home, a monthly publication of the General Board
of Education of the Methodist Church. Since these publications
usually have audiences limited to their particular church, no
listing or commentary is made here beyond the general statement that the materials tend to be good, tend to reach large
numbers, tend to carry a weight of authority behind them, and
increasingly use professional people as contributors, regardless
of church affiliation. The interest of the churches in the child's
total well-being is most heartening.

The following are the magazines more generally available
to public subscription:

Child-Family Digest (5320 Danneel St., New Orleans 15, La.).
　　This is a new publication, made up of articles reprinted from
　　other, usually more technical, journals. The magazine is not
　　written for parents alone; occasionally its contents are more
　　technical than many parents can take. It should be in your
　　school library for parents, however.
Child Study (132 East 74th St., New York 21, N. Y.). Published
　　quarterly.
　　This is the journal of the Child Study Association of America,

now in its 28th year. It is always sound, although perhaps geared more to the better educated parent. By all means, however, you should know this journal and encourage your parents to know it. It might well lead to the establishment of a Child Study Association in your city; all our cities need one!

My Baby — and Young Years (53 East 34th St., New York 16, N. Y.). Published monthly, distributed free through many department stores.

This is primarily an advertising medium for local department stores who distribute it free to mothers. On the whole, however, its material is good.

National Parent-Teacher (600 S. Michigan Boulevard, Chicago 5, Ill.). Published monthly September through June.

By all odds this is the very best buy for parents. Its low price is deceptive and maybe even harmful, leading some to underestimate its consistently good material. You can have every confidence in urging parents to subscribe.

Parents' Magazine (52 Vanderbilt Avenue, New York 17, N. Y.). Published monthly.

This is the largest in size, most finished in make-up and appearance, most technically proficient of the journals for parents. Now in its 26th year and with good editorial direction, *Parents' Magazine* does an attractive and readable and sound job month after month from the cradle through adolescence.

The Child (U. S. Children's Bureau, Superintendent of Documents, Washington 25, D. C.). Published ten times a year.

Although not primarily for parents, the low price of this journal, its broad concern for childhood, and its excellent contributors strongly recommend it for your library for parents.

Understanding the Child (1790 Broadway, New York, N. Y.). Published quarterly.

This is the praiseworthy attempt of the National Association for Mental Health to get mental health concepts in magazine form for parents and teachers. Not illustrated, too brief, geared more to parents who read well, the Association gets an *A* for effort but a lower grade for performance. The basic idea is so good, however, that you ought to have this journal on hand and keep in touch with it. It is definitely on the right track.

Your Child's World (The Book House for Children, 360 N. Michigan Ave., Chicago 1, Ill.). Published monthly.

A small publication, usually 16 pages, but with a sound point of view. Not as good a buy as some of the others, but parents who have it will be helped by it.

PAMPHLETS AND BOOKS

Since new material is continuously appearing you are urged again to have your name on the mailing list of the various associations that distribute pamphlet material. The names of these associations are given below. Following each address you will find code letters. These same letters appear in the bibliographies that follow, after each pamphlet listed. By checking the code letter back to this page you can find the address from which the pamphlet can be obtained. More than one association may distribute a particular pamphlet but since the concern of all of the organizations is to help parents rather than to make a profit, only one code letter is used after each pamphlet.

Be sure that you get the publication list of the following groups:

Association for Family Living, 28 E. Jackson Blvd., Chicago, Ill. *A*
Child Study Association of America, 132 East 74 St., New York 21, N. Y. *Ch*
Health Publications Institute, 216 N. Dawson St., Raleigh, N. C. *H*
National Association for Mental Health, 1790 Broadway, New York 19, N. Y. *N*
New York State Society for Mental Health, 105 East 22 St., New York 10, N. Y. *Co*
Public Affairs Committee, 22 East 38 St., New York 16, N. Y. *P*
Science Research Associates, 57 W. Grand Avenue, Chicago 10, Ill. *SR*
Sixty-nine Bank Street Publications, 69 Bank St., New York 14, N. Y. *S*
Teachers College Bureau of Publications, 525 West 120 St., New York 27, N. Y. *T*
U. S. Office of Education, Superintendent of Documents, Washington, D. C. *USO*
U. S. Children's Bureau, Superintendent of Documents, Washington, D. C. *USC*

PAMPHLETS — ABOUT MANY AGES

A Healthy Personality for Your Child by James L. Hymes, Jr. Fifteen cents. *USC*

Answering Children's Questions by C. W. Hunnicutt. Sixty cents. *T*
Being a Good Parent by James L. Hymes, Jr. Sixty cents. *T*
Discipline by James L. Hymes, Jr. Sixty cents. *T*
Discipline Through Affection by Aline B. Auerbach. Fifteen cents. *Ch*
Do Cows Have Neuroses? by June Bingham. Twenty-five cents. *H*
Fears of Children by Helen Ross. Forty cents. *SR*
For Fathers Who Go to War by Lloyd W. Rowland. (New Orleans: Louisiana Society for Mental Health). Twenty-five cents.
Getting Along in the Family by Jane Mayer. Sixty cents. *T*
Helping Children Read Better by Paul Witty. Forty cents. *SR*
How to be a Good Mother-in-law and Grandmother by Edith Neisser. Twenty-five cents. *P*
How to Discipline Your Children by Dorothy Baruch. Twenty-five cents. *P*
How to Live with Children by Edith Neisser. Forty cents. *SR*
Jealousy and Rivalry in Children. Thirty-five cents. *Ch*
Making the Grade as Dad by Walter and Edith Neisser. Twenty-five cents. *P*
Mental Health is a Family Affair by Pratt and Neher. Twenty-five cents. *P*
Self-Understanding — a First Step to Understanding Children by W. C. Menninger, M. D. Forty cents. *SR*
These, Our Youngsters by Esther L. Middlewood. *H*
Understanding Children's Behavior by Fritz Redl. Sixty cents. *T*
What Makes Good Habits the Beginnings of Discipline. Twenty cents. *Ch*
What Makes a Good Home the Beginnings of Emotional Health. Twenty cents. *Ch*
Why Children Misbehave by Leonard and Flander. Forty cents. *SR*
When Children Ask about Sex. Thirty-five cents. *Ch*
You Don't Have to Be Perfect (Even If You Are a Parent) by Jean Schick Grossman. Twenty cents. *N*

BOOKS — ABOUT MANY AGES

Brothers and Sisters by Edith Neisser (New York: Harper, 1951).
Everybody's Business — Our Children by Mauree Applegate (Evanston, Ill.: Row, Peterson, 1952).
Father of the Man by W. Allison Davis and Robert J. Havighurst (Boston: Houghton Mifflin, 1947).

Life with Family by Jean Schick Grossman (New York: Appleton-Century-Crofts, 1948).
Living with Children by Gertrude Chittenden (New York: Macmillan, 1944).
New Ways in Discipline by Dorothy Baruch (New York: Whittlesey House, 1949).
Our Children Today by Sidonie Gruenberg, ed. (New York: Viking Press, 1952).
Parent and Child by Catherine Mackenzie (New York: W. Sloane Associates, 1949).
Understanding Your Child by James L. Hymes, Jr. (New York: Prentice-Hall, 1952).

PAMPHLETS — ABOUT CHILDREN UNDER SIX

Aggressiveness in Children by Edith Lesser Atkin. Thirty-five cents. *Ch*
Avoiding Behavior Problems by Benjamin Spock, M. D. Fifteen cents. *Co*
Do Babies Have Worries by June Bingham. Thirty-five cents. *H*
Discipline, What Is It? by Helen Steers Burgess. Thirty-five cents. *Ch*
Eating Problems of Children. Fifteen cents. *Co*
Enjoy Your Child: Ages 1, 2, 3 by James L. Hymes, Jr. Twenty-five cents. *P*
Formulas for Fun. Boston: Nursery Training School of Boston. Fifty cents.
Fundamental Needs of the Child by Lawrence K. Frank. Twenty-five cents. *Co*
How to Tell Your Child about Sex by James L. Hymes, Jr. Twenty-five cents. *P*
Packet for Parents: 13 articles carefully selected. $1.25. *S*
Pierre, the Pelican by Loyd D. Rowland. Two series. $1.00. *Co*
Some Special Problems of Children Aged 2 to 5 by Nina Ridenour. Twenty-five cents. *Co*
So You Want to Adopt a Baby by Ruth Carson. Twenty-five cents. *P*
Three to Six: Your Child Starts to School by James L. Hymes, Jr. Twenty-five cents. *P*
Understanding Young Children by Dorothy Baruch. Sixty cents. *T*
Your Child from One to Six. Fifteen cents. *USC*

BOOKS — ABOUT CHILDREN UNDER SIX

At Home with Children by Charlotte Garrison and Emma D. Sheehy
(New York: Henry Holt, 1943).
Babies Are Human Beings by C. A. and M. M. Aldrich (New York:
Macmillan, 1938).
Common Sense Book of Baby and Child Care by Benjamin Spock
(New York: Duell, Sloan and Pearce, 1946).
Infant and Child in the Culture of Today by Arnold Gesell and
Frances Ilg (New York: Harper, 1943).
Off to a Good Start by Irma Simonton Black (New York: Harcourt,
Brace, 1947).
Life and Ways of the Two-Year-Old by Louise P. Woodcock (New
York: Basic Books, Inc., 1952).
Your Child and Other People by Rhoda B. Bacmeister (Boston:
Little Brown & Co., 1950).

FILMS, FILMSTRIPS, AND PLAYS — ABOUT CHILDREN
UNDER SIX

A Long Time to Grow (thirty-five minutes) (sound). New York
University Film Library.
    A new film about two-and three-year-olds in a college nurs-
ery school, with the emphasis on what children are like while
they are learning and growing. Another excellent contribution
from Vassar.
And Then Ice Cream (ten minutes) (sound). New York University
Film Library.
    A film about that persistent problem, children's eating. It
shows two contrasting methods and presents the problem:
Which do you think is the better? Good for starting discussion.
David's Bad Day. Filmstrip available from Young America Films,
Inc. (18 East 41 St., New York 17, N. Y.).
    An interesting presentation of a five-year-old jealous of the
new baby. The strip pauses in the middle to ask: What would
you do? And then goes on to give its answers.
Helping the Child to Accept the Do's (ten minutes) (sound).
Helping the Child to Face the Don'ts (ten minutes) (sound).
    Two related films which show all that youngsters learn and
must learn through their daily living during the first few years.
The intent is to say to parents: Hold off; there is a lot of

learning going on anyhow. Some people read into the films: There is so much they must learn that we have to get started on it fast. But good discussion can avoid this misinterpretation.
Life with Baby (twenty minutes) (sound).

This gives an over-all view of the work of Dr. Arnold Gesell and makes very clear that there is a plan to the way youngsters grow. There are, incidentally, a number of other more specific films which look at each phase of growing during the early years. This one, however, can best be used to get at the important generalizations which underlie the whole process.
Preface to a Life (thirty minutes) (sound).

A very well done film in which you see the same youngster as he might develop under four differing parent relationships. Of all the films listed, this is the only one that might require special help from a psychological or psychiatric consultant during the discussion. Some parents in particular need reassurance after seeing it; it reminds them too much of "mistakes" they have made. But keeping this need in mind you can probably make good use of this unusual presentation.
Scattered Showers, a short dramatic sketch by Nora Stirling for the American Theatre Wing Community Plays. (New York: National Association for Mental Health). Producing packet, including four scripts and two Discussion Guides.

No scenery is required, and hardly any special dramatic skill and no major rehearsal time. Three mothers of young children meet while their children play in the park and get into difficulty. Discussion is very important following the play, but you can hardly miss having it.
When Should Grown-Ups Help? (thirteen minutes) (sound). New York University Film Library.

Four children, all preschool, are shown tackling the many problems this age meets every day. After raising the question of whether or not each child should have been helped by an adult, the film replays the same episodes. This is ideally geared for good discussion.

PAMPHLETS — ABOUT THE SCHOOL-AGE CHILD

Comics, Radio, Movie . . . and Children by Jozette Frank. Twenty-five cents. P
Fives to Eights and How They Grow by Barbara Biber. Fifteen cents. S

Pre-Adolescents : What Makes Them Tick? by Fritz Redl. Twenty cents. *Ch*

Parents as Teachers by the Committee on Emotional Stability of the Metropolitan School Study Council. *T*

Reading Is Fun by Roma Gans. Sixty cents. *T*

Teacher Listen! The Children Speak by James L. Hymes, Jr. Twenty-five cents. *Co*

Understand Your Child from 6 to 12 by Clara Lambert. Twenty-five cents. *P*

Your Child from Six to Twelve. Twenty cents. *USC*

Your Child and Radio, TV, Comics, and Movies by Paul Witty and Harry Bricker. Forty cents. *SR*

Your Children's Manners by Rhoda W. Bacmeister. Forty cents. *SR*

BOOKS — ABOUT THE SCHOOL-AGE CHILD

Growth and Development of the Preadolescent by Arthur Witt Blair and Wm. H. Burton (New York: Appleton-Century-Crofts, 1951).

How to Help Your Child in School by Mary and Lawrence K. Frank (New York: Viking Press, 1950).

The Child from Five to Ten by Arnold Gesell and Frances Ilg (New York: Harper & Bros., 1946).

These Are Your Children by Gladys G. Jenkins, Helen Shacter, and W. W. Bauer (Chicago: Scott, Foresman, 1949).

Your Children at School by Elizabeth Vernon Hubbard (New York: John Day, 1942).

FILMS, FILMSTRIPS, AND PLAYS — ABOUT THE SCHOOL-AGE CHILD

All Children Need Guidance, a series of two filmstrips available from the Popular Science Publishing Co., Audio-Visual Division (353 Fourth Ave., New York 10, N. Y.).

"Child Needs and Guidance" and "The Why and How of Guidance" both interpret guidance as meaning the everyday way in which parents and teachers treat children. Good emphasis is put on the need for parents and teachers to work together. A developmental picture is given, so that these strips could be used with parents of younger children, but the emphasis is on the school age.

Angry Boy (thirty minutes) (sound).

A very competent film which shows a boy from a "good" home who steals. The youngster gets help from a child guidance center; the film is in large part a plea for the establishment of such facilities. With good discussion, focusing on what the psychiatrist does, parents (and teachers) can come to see how youngsters can get some help while we are all working for the more specialized facilities that are so needed.

Guidance Problem for Home and School (twenty minutes) (sound).

Seven-year-old Danny is a problem to his parents, his teacher, and to himself. When the home and the school begin talking together, progress toward a happier adjustment begins.

Life with Junior (twenty minutes) (sound).

You see lively ten-year-olds in this picture, with all their activity and energy and foibles. It also demonstrates some of the services of the Child Study Association of America and argues for the establishment of groups like this in all communities. The part the school plays in these vigorous children's lives always seems to me a dismal role.

Meeting Emotional Needs in Childhood: The Groundwork of Democracy (thirty minutes) (sound).

One of the most satisfactory films available thus far. Although focusing most of all on the school-age years, this goes back to early childhood and forecasts ahead to the kind of adult we produce. It is delightful to see, reassuring while still very thought-provoking.

Palmour Street (thirty minutes) (sound).

A beautiful film about a Negro family — its children, family relationships, neighborhood problems. The youngsters range from infancy to adolescence, so the film has great usefulness for stimulating discussion among all parents.

Fresh Variable Winds, a short dramatic sketch by Nora Stirling for the American Theatre Wing Community Plays. (New York: National Association for Mental Health). Producing packet including six scripts and two discussion guides.

Tucky, a ten-year-old, disobeys the rules, lies, is rude. Helen, also ten, tells on him and thinks he ought to be punished. The adults differ on what you do when this age strikes out to be more on its own and gets caught between the demands of the child-world and those of the home-world. Be sure that you use the play for discussion, not simply as entertainment.

PAMPHLETS — ABOUT ADOLESCENTS

Guiding the Adolescent. Twenty cents. USC
Guiding the Adolescent by D. A. Thom. Twenty cents. Co
Helping Youth Choose Careers by J. Anthony Humphreys. *Forty*
cents. SR
Keeping Up with Teen-agers by Evelyn M. Duvall. Twenty-five
cents. P
Let's Listen to Youth by H. H. Remmers and C. G. Hackett. *Forty*
cents. SR
Living with Adolescents by Fritz Redl. Ten cents. A
So You Think It's Love by Ralph C. Eckert. Twenty-five cents. P
The Adolescent and the Family by Lawrence K. Frank. *Fifteen*
cents. Co
The Mental Health of Normal Adolescents by George E. Gardner.
Fifteen cents. N
This Is the Adolescent by Lawrence K. Frank. Twenty cents. N
When Children Start Dating by Edith G. Neisser. Forty cents. SR
When Fifteen and Fifty Disagree by Anna W. M. Wolf. Ten
cents. Ch

BOOKS — ABOUT ADOLESCENTS

Adolescent Development by Elizabeth B. Hurlock (New York:
McGraw-Hill, 1949).
Do Adolescents Need Parents? by Katherine W. Taylor (New York:
D. Appleton-Century, 1938).
The Adolescent by Marynia L. Farnham (New York: Harper &
Bros., 1951).

PLAYS — ABOUT ADOLESCENTS

High Pressure Area, a short dramatic sketch by Nora Stirling for the
American Theater Wing Community Plays. (New York: National Association for Mental Health). Producing packet including five scripts and two Discussion Guides.

Two adolescents cook up a scheme with one taking the lead
in what might be a high and bad adventure. The question of
how much parents should interfere at this age of fiery independence is graphically set up, and one solution is presented
for the audience to puzzle over.

Index

A

Active learners, 85–86
Adult Education Association, 239
Adult Leadership, 239
Agitation, parents and schools, 57–59
Alternates to the lecture, 98–101
American Education Under Fire,
    Melby, 57
American Home, 15
American Theatre Wing Community
    Plays, 106, 108
Aptitudes, teachers, 64–89
Association for Childhood Education
    International, 50, 196, 239
Association for Family Living, 198, 222
Attitudes, teachers, 64–89
Audience, putting at ease, group meet-
    ings, 126–127
Avoiding Behavior Problems, Spock,
    195

B

Better Homes and Gardens, 15
Bibliography of Books for Children,
    196
Birney, Alice, 36
Birthday card, 195
Birth-to-six materials for parents, 193–
    200
Booklets, start-to-school, 187–190
Buzz sessions, 115–117

C

Chairman, role of, group meetings,
    119–124

Child, the Family, the Community — A
    Classified Booklist, 113
Childhood Education, 237–238
Children:
    continuity of growth, 23
    love of parents for, 13–15
    materials interpreting growth and
        development of, 245–257
    older:
        changes in education of, 219–220
        materials for parents of, 200–201
        nature of, 220–221
        parents' interest in, 216–217
        teachers on side of, 223–224
        written communications help,
            221–223
    oneness of parents and, 15–17
    parents and, 11–34
    parents gain understanding of, 162–
        163
    wholeness of, 24
Children Are Our Teachers, 112, 115
Children Books for Seventy-five Cents
    or Less, 197
Children of the People, Leighton and
    Kluckhohn, 2
Child Study, 209
Child Study Association of America,
    197, 198, 200
Committee report, 100–101
Community, The — a Laboratory,
    Mayer and Sutherland, 172
Conferences:
    before and after participation, 172–
        175
    following observation, 165–166
    parent, 147–148

Cooperative nursery school, 175–178
Course of study, curriculum versus,
     79–82
Curriculum, course of study versus,
     79–82

D

Descriptive reports, 145–146
Developmental Tasks and Education,
     Havighurst, 20
Dewey, John, 48
Disagreement, parents and schools,
     57–59
Discussion Guide for Parents, 115
Discussion meetings, 103–104
Drama:
     for a take-off, 106–107
     spontaneous, 107–109

E

Education:
     changes in, of older children, 219–
          220
     people committed to, 35–36
     primitive, 1, 9
Education for Responsible Parenthood,
     85–86
Enjoy Your Child: Ages 1, 2, 3, 195
Evaluation, 225–232
Experience, teaching, as resource, 79

F

Face-to-face relationships, 131–155
Fact Finding Report: A Digest, 20
Fact meetings, 94–95
Family life:
     complexities, 5–6
     teachers out of touch with, 73–76
Farm Journal, 15
Fiction, group meetings, 112
Fifty Teachers to a Classroom, 172
Films, 104–106, 238–239
     Centre, The, 18
     *Experimental Studies in the Social
          Climate of Groups,* 73
     Family Circles, 32
     Fight for Better Schools, The, 22
     Fitness Is a Family Affair, 183
     Karba's First Years, 2
     Palmour Street, 70, 75–76

Films Interpreting Children and Youth,
     Hampel, Dale, and Quick, 105
Filmstrip, *Kindergarten and Your
     Child,* 208
Formulas for Fun! 197
Fresh Variable Winds, 106
Funny sheets, group meetings, 111–
     112

G

G.I. Bill of Rights, 36
Goals, home-school relations, 9
Good Schools Don't Just Happen, 59
Good Schools for Children, 59
Government Printing Office, U.S., 14
Grossman, Jean Shick, 110
Group meetings, 90–130
     alternates to the lecture, 98–101
     audience, putting at ease, 126–127
     bull sessions, 115–117
     chairman, role, 119–124
     committee report, 100–101
     discussion meetings, 103–104
     drama:
          for a take-off, 106–107
          spontaneous, 107–109
     early, start of school, 207–211
     expertness of opinion, 112–115
     fact meetings, 94–95
     fiction, 112
     films, 104–106
     funny sheets, 111–112
     "minutes of last meeting," 127–128
     objectives, 92–94
     observer, using, 124–126
     panel, 117–119
     play meetings, 128–130
     puppets, 110
     purposes, 90–92
     question period, 101–103
     reading panel, 98–99
     start of school year, 95–98
     symposium, 98–99
     work meetings, 128–130
Group Report Card, 153

H

Helping Children Read Better, Witty,
     201
High Pressure Area, 106

High schoolers, 215–224
Home-school relations:
  goals, 9
  materials on, 233–239
  no wonder drug, 2–3
  programs for children and, 3–4
  purpose, 1–2
  stay with the problem, 86–88
  treated too casually, 7–9
  two-way process, 8
Home visit, 132–135
  reason for, 135–136
How a Child Feels about Entering a Nursery Center, Campbell, 206
How Good Is Your School? Yauch, 59
How to Distinguish a Good Nursery School, 196
How to Tell Your Child about Sex, 196
How to Use Puppets in Parent Discussion, Grossman, 110

I

If Your Child Has Reading Difficulties, MacDougall, 201
Individual Parent-Teacher Conferences, D'Evelyn, 148
Infant Care, 14
Information, how to collect, 136–145
Ins and Outs, The, 106
Interest, importance of, 82–85

K

Key, Ted, 111

L

Ladies' Home Journal, 15
Leaflets produced by school, 187–190
Learns, active, 85–86
Lecture, alternates to, 98–101
Life and Ways of the Two Year Old, Woodcock, 195
Life with Family, Grossman, 110
Louisiana Society for Mental Health, 194, 196

M

Making the Grade As Dad, 196
McGavran, James Holt, *quoted,* 42

Meetings (*see* Group meetings)
"Minutes of last meeting," group meetings, 127–128
Money-raisers, participation, 166–168
Motion Pictures on Child Life, Lohr, 105

N

National Association for Mental Health, 106, 198, 200
National Association for Nursery Education, 196
National Citizens' Commission for the Public Schools, 37–38
National Congress of Parents and Teachers, 36–37, 233
National Parent-Teacher, 37, 209
Newsletter, 186–187
News notes, 184–186
New York State Department of Education, 233
New York State Society for Mental Health, 115, 194, 195, 196, 198, 206
Nursery school, cooperative, 175–178

O

Observation:
  arranging for, 163–165
  conferences following, 165–166
  not everyone can observe, 182–183
  parents as observers, 158–159
    doubts about, 159–162
  parents gain understanding of children, 162–163
Observers:
  group meetings, 124–126
  parents as, 158–159
    doubts about, 159–162
Older children:
  changes in education of, 219–220
  materials for parents of, 200–201
  nature of, 220–221
  parents' interest in, 216–217
  teachers on side of, 223–224
  written communications help, 221–223
On Being Human, Montagu, 19
Opening day, 211–212
  parents welcome to stay, 212–215

Organization of this book, 10
Our Cooperative Nursery School, 178
Overstreet, Harry and Bonaro, *quoted,*
    36

                          P

Panel, group meetings, 117–119
Parents:
    adults, 62–63
    attitudes change slowly, 6–7
    bad meetings discourage, 43–47
    behavior is caused, 27–29
    birth-to-six materials for, 193–200
    "burned" by today's school, 41–43
    children and, 11–34
    conferences with, 147–148
    gain understanding of children, 162–
        163
    have much to give, 22–24
    humanness of, 24–25
    individuals, 26–27
    interest in older children, 216–217
    love for their children, 13–15
    memories of school, unpleasant, 38–
        41
    observe before participation, 168–
        169
    observers, as, 158–159
        doubts about, 159–162
    older children, materials for, 200–
        201
    oneness of children and, 15–17
    opening day, 212–215
    participation by, 19–22, 166–178
    participation geared to each, 169–
        172
    patience needed, 29–31
    progress watched by, 17–19
    readiness to learn, 149–151
    reports to, 143–146
        less frequent – and more, 153–
            154
        participation in report card
            changes, 154–155
    services to, 77–78
    schools and, 35–63
    school suspected by, 47–51
    start of school, meaning to, 203–204
    study of, 11–12
    teacher adjusts to individual, 151–
        153

Parents *(contd.):*
    teachers and, can get together, 59–
        62
    understanding needed, 29–31
    unsure, 31–34
    working with today's schools, 36–38
Parents and Children Together,
    McVickar, 178
Parents' Magazine, 197, 209
Parent Teacher Association:
    bad meetings discourage parents,
        43–47
    parents have been "burned" by, 41–
        43
Participation:
    conferences before and after, 172–
        175
    cooperative nursery school, 175–178
    geared to each parent, 169–172
    money-raisers, 166–168
    not everyone can participate, 182–
        183
    parents as participants, 166–178
    parents observe first, 168–169
    Room Mothers, 178–180
        exploitation of, 180–182
Peckham Experiment, Pearse and
    Crocker, 18
Pierre, the Pelican, Rowland, 194
Play meetings, 128–130
Play Therapy, Axline, 151
Pocket Book of Infant and Child Care,
    Spock, 14–15, 34
Preadolescents, 215–224
*Pre-Adolescents: What Makes Them
    Tick?* 200
Preparing Your Child for School, 206
Preschool roundup, 206–207
Primitive education, 1, 9
Programs for children, home-school re-
    lations and, 3–4
*Promising Practices in Elementary
    Schools,* 59
Public attitudes, social conditions
    affect, 54–56
Puppets, group meetings, 110

                          Q

Questionnaire forms, information, 136–
    142
Question period, 101–103

R

Readiness to learn, parent's, 149–151
Reading Guide for Parents, 113
Reading Is Fun, Gans, 201
Reading panel, 98–99
Readings on the Psychological Development of Infants and Children, Solar and Senn, 113
Reality Practice As Education Method, Hendry, Lippitt, and Zander, 109
Relationships:
   face-to-face, 131–155
     descriptive reports, 145–146
     home visit, 132–135
      reason for, 135–136
     information, how to collect, 136–145
     parent conferences, 147–148
     parent's readiness to learn, 149–151
     teacher adjusts to parents, 151–153
   home-school (*see* Home-school relations)
   preadolescents and high schoolers, 215–224
   reporting to parents:
     less frequent — and more, 153–154
     parent participation in changes, 154–155
   start of school, 202–215
Reporting to Parents, Strang, 143
Reports to parents:
   descriptive, 145–146
   less frequent — and more, 153–154
   parent participation in report card changes, 154–155
   report cards, 143–145
Role playing, 108
Room Mothers, 178–180
   exploitation of, 180–182

S

Saturday Evening Post, 66 fn., 111
Scattered Showers, 106
School:
   changes in, difficulties in making, 51–54

School (*contd.*):
   disagreement and agitation, 57–59
   leaflets produced by, 187–190
   materials interpreting activities of, 239–245
   parents and, 35–63
   parents' unpleasant memories, 38–41
   practices that irritate, 76–77
   readiness to help, parents of older children, 217–219
   start of, relationships, 202–215
   suspected by parents, 47–51
Science Research Associates, 200–201
Services to parents, 77–78
Social conditions, public attitudes affected by, 54–56
Some Special Problems of Children Aged 2 to 5, Ridenour, 196
Spock, Benjamin, 14, 34, 195
Start of school, relationships, 202–215
   early group meetings, 207–211
   good starts not made in heaven, 204–206
   meaning to parents, 203–204
   opening day, 211–212
     parents welcome to stay, 212–215
   preschool roundup, 206–207
Start-to-school booklets, 187–190
Stop Sniping at Parents, Whitman, 33
Story of the Eight-year Study, Aikin, 52
Symposium, 99–100

T

Teachers:
   adjusts to individual parents, 151–153
   aptitudes, 64–89
   attitudes, 64–89
   experience as resource, 79
   family life, out of touch with, 73–76
   in retreat, 71–73
   lecture approach, 68–71
   on side of youth, 223–224
   parents and, can get together, 59–62
   superior position of, 67–68
That Men May Understand, Rugg, 58
There's Music in Children, Sheehy, 197
This Happened in Pasadena, Hulburd, 57
This Is the Adolescent, 200

Three to Six: Your Child Starts to School, 196, 206

U

Understanding Your Child, 28
Using Mental Hygiene Films, 105

V

Variety, need for, 88–89

W

Ways You Can Help Your Child with Reading, Casey, 201
What Nursery School Is Like, Campbell, 196
What People Think about Their Schools, Hand, 192–193
Where Children Come First, Overstreet, 37

Who's Trying to Ruin Our Schools? Morse, 58
Will Your Child Be Ready for School? Adams, 206
Work meetings, 128–130
Written word, 184–201
  birth-to-six materials for parents, 193–200
  leaflets produced by school, 190–193
  materials for parents of older children, 200–201
  newsletters, 186–187
  news notes, 184–186
  older children, 221–223
  start-to-school booklets, 187–190

Y

Your Child and Radio, TV, Comics and Movies, 200
Your Child from One to Six, 14, 195
Your Child from Six to Twelve, 115